Dr. Charles Louis Metz

and the

American Indian Archaeology

of the

Little Miami River Valley

Dr. Charles Louis Metz and the American Indian Archaeology of the Little Miami River Valley

by

Kenneth Barnett Tankersley
and
Robert Brand Newman

Little Miami Publishing Co.
Milford, Ohio
2016

Little Miami Publishing Co.
P.O. Box 588
Milford, Ohio 45150-0588
www.littlemiamibooks.com

Copyright © 2016 Kenneth Barnett Tankersley and Robert Band Newman. All rights reserved. No part of this book may be reproduced or transmitted in any form or by any means, electronic or mechanical, including photocopying, recording or by any information storage and retrieval system without written permission from the author, except for the inclusion of brief quotations in a review.

Michael Joseph Berger, Photographer

Printed in the United States of America on acid-free paper.

First Edition.

ISBN-13: 978-1-941083-07-9

Library of Congress Control Number: 2015958952

To the descendants of Charles Louis Metz and Amelia Berger Metz and the American Indians who have lived in the Little Miami River valley since time immemorial.

Contents

Preface **xv**
Acknowledgments **xvii**
Introduction **1**

Chapter 1 The Early Life and Times of Charles Louis Metz **11**
   The Metz family arrive in America **11**
   The Metz family in Cincinnati, Ohio **12**
   The Metz family in Highland County, Ohio **15**
   The Metz family in Plainville, Ohio **16**
   The Civil War **17**
   Medical school **22**
   Amelia (Molly) Berger **23**
   An aspiring archaeologist **24**
   Madisonville **27**

Chapter 2 The Literary and Scientific
         Society of Madisonville **31**
   Phebe Ferris **31**
   The intellectual community of Madisonville **33**
   Charles's medical practice **35**
   Centennial Exposition **36**

viii   *American Indian Archaeology of the Little Miami River Valley*

                The formation of the Literary and Scientific Society of Madisonville   **37**
                Initial meetings of the Literary and Scientific Society of Madisonville   **40**
                Archaeological excavations in the Little Miami River valley   **43**

Chapter 3   **Frederick Ward Putnam and the Peabody Museum**   **47**
                Peabody Museum of Archaeology and Ethnology at Harvard University   **47**
                Frederick Ward Putnam   **48**
                Theoretical opposition   **51**
                Publications of the Literary and Scientific Society of Madisonville   **52**
                A return to Florida   **53**
                Discontent and financial strain   **54**
                Putnam returns to Cincinnati   **56**
                1881 publications   **56**
                Putnam's protégé   **57**
                The Turner site   **58**

Chapter 4   **The Cost of Archaeology**   **63**
                The Little Miami River valley archaeological survey   **64**
                Buffalo Bill in Cincinnati   **64**
                Fieldwork resumes   **65**
                Eleventh Cincinnati Industrial Exposition   **67**
                Return to the Turner site   **67**
                Krakatoa, the flood, and panic of 1884   **69**
                Working with the Smithsonian Institution   **70**

Chapter 5   **AAAS and Beyond**   **75**
                American Association for the Advancement of Science (AAAS)   **75**
                Carl Schurz and the American Indian   **78**
                Pleasant distractions   **80**
                More family matters   **81**
                1884 Ferris Cemetery publication   **83**
                Determining antiquity   **85**
                Back to the Hahn Field site   **86**

Chapter 6	**Turning Back the Hands of Time**	**93**
	The Turpin Farm site	**93**
	Charles's health	**94**
	An American Paleolithic	**98**
	Pipe dreams	**100**
Chapter 7	**Revisiting the Turner Site**	**105**
	The Eighteenth Report of the Peabody Museum	**105**
	On Methods of Archaeological Research in America	**106**
	Long days of winter	**108**
	Fieldwork at the Turner site	**110**
	Thirty-fifth annual meeting of the AAAS	**113**
	Archaeological field camp	**114**
	Fort Ancient	**117**
	Competition	**119**
	Ice Age archaeology	**120**
	Completing the Turner Site excavations	**120**
	Looking ahead	**121**
Chapter 8	**The World's Columbian Exposition**	**123**
	Planning the World's Fair	**123**
	Working with Warren King Moorehead	**125**
	Conflicts with Moorehead	**128**
	Building the anthropology and archaeology exhibitions	**131**
	Opening day	**133**
	The exhibitions	**135**
	Buffalo Bill's Wild West and Congress of Rough Riders of the World	**137**
	Returning to the fair	**138**
	Closing tragedies	**139**
	Accolades	**141**
Chapter 9	**The Phebe Ferris Will**	**147**
	Indians on display	**147**
	Shawnee and the Ferris Cemetery	**149**
	The passing of Phebe Ferris	**151**
	Phebe's Last Will and Testament	**152**
	Contesting the will	**154**

Accusations of murder   155
Questions of Phebe's sanity   156
Sustaining Phebe's will   158
Affirmation   159

Chapter 10   The Twentieth Century   165
Resuming fieldwork   166
Algonquian connections   167
The Ferris Cemetery   169
World War I   171
Golden anniversary   176
Continuing work with the Peabody Museum   178
The professionalization of Ohio Valley archaeology   179
Founding of Mariemont   181

Chapter 11   And In The End   187
Charles's passing   188

Epilogue: The Legacy of Charles Louis Metz   193
James Bennett Griffin   194
New Deal archaeology   194
Radiocarbon dating   195
Post–World War II archaeology   196
National Historic Preservation Act   198
The National Environmental Policy Act   199
Archaeological and Historic Preservation Act 1974   200
American Indian Religious Freedom Act   200
Archaeological Resource Protection Act   201
Native American Graves Protection and Repatriation Act   202
Sacred Lands Act   202
John C. Court   203
Current threat   204
Looking into the future   205

Contents   xi

Appendix A   Family Letters   207
Appendix B   Archaeological Notes and Letters   215
Appendix C   Madisonville History   285
                     The History of Madisonville   285
                     The platting of the town of Madisonville   286
                     Pioneers   288
                     First built houses   288
                     Brick buildings   289
                     Distinguished men   290
                     James Whitcomb   291
                     Imprisonment from debts   291
                     Town amusements   292
                     Madisonville's early industries   292
                     Tavern   293
                     Summary   293
                     Snake story   294
                     The bee story   295

                     Notes   297
                     Index   315
                     About the Authors   335

List of Figures

Introduction

I.1, Dr. Charles Louis Metz.

Chapter 1

1.1, The Jealous Wife painting by Flemish master David Teniers the Younger, ca. 1650.
1.2, Drawing of Camp Dennison, Hamilton County, Ohio, June 15, 1861.
1.3, Minié ball from Confederate brigadier general John Hunt Morgan's raid on Camp Dennison, Hamilton County, Ohio, July 14, 1863.
1.4, Brass microscope used by Charles Louis Metz in medical school and in his medical practice, ca. 1865.
1.5, Charles Louis Metz, Plainville, Hamilton County, Ohio, ca. 1871.

Chapter 2.

2.1, Front of the Metz family home located between 6111 and 6113 Madison Road, Madisonville, Hamilton County, Ohio, ca. 1872.

2.2, Back of the Metz family home located between 6111 and 6113 Madison Road, Madisonville, Hamilton County, Ohio, ca. 1873.

2.3, An ancient Egyptian *ushabti* gifted to Charles Louis Metz from Literary and Scientific Society of Madisonville member Judge Hunt on November 26, 1878.

Chapter 3

3.1, An exotic, shell tempered, Mississippian vessel (beaker) excavated by Charles Louis Metz from the Madisonville site (Ferris Cemetery), ca. 800 to 1600 C.E.

3.2, Brass magnifying glass used by Charles Louis Metz to examine artifacts and read small print.

Chapter 4

4.1, Photograph of the Turner site, Hamilton County, Ohio illustrating the Elevated Circle, Mound 12, Graded Way, and the Great Enclosure, ca. 1883.

4.2, Photograph of the Turner site, Hamilton County, Ohio illustrating the Graded Way and Turner farmhouse, ca. 1883.

Chapter 5.

5.1, Chillicothe Fairground Mound, Ross County, Ohio (left to right, Mr. Douglas, Mr. Charles Low, Charles Louis Metz, Frederick Ward Putnam), ca.1884.

Chapter 6

6.1, Clovis spear-point preform similar to those found by Charles Louis Metz in Madisonville and Loveland, Hamilton County, Ohio, ca., 13,500 years old.

Chapter 7

7.1, Families of Charles Louis Metz and Frederick Ward Putnam at the Great Serpent Mound, Peebles, Adams County, Ohio, ca. 1887.

Chapter 8

8.1, Charles Louis Metz's map of archaeological sites in the lower Little Miami River valley, ca. 1891.

8.2, Charles Louis Metz's map of archaeological sites in the lower Little Miami River valley with a detailed illustration of the burial mounds and an earthen enclosure on the northwest side of the intersection of Plainville Road and U.S. 50, ca. 1891.

8.3, World's Columbian Exposition, Rain in the Face, ticket, ca. 1893.

8.4, Charles Louis Metz's Ohio Archaeology exhibition inside the Anthropology Building, World's Columbian Exposition, Chicago, Illinois, ca. 1893.

8.5, Front of Charles Louis Metz's World's Columbian Exposition Bronze Medal awarded in 1895.

8.6, Back of Charles Louis Metz's World's Columbian Exposition Bronze Medal awarded in 1895.

8.7, Front of the Metz family home and medical office, 6111 Madison Road, Madisonville, Hamilton County, Ohio.

Chapter 9

9.1, Lakota on the lawn of the Cincinnati Zoological Gardens, ca. 1896.

9.2, Lakota, Quick Bear, posing for a photo at the Cincinnati Zoological Gardens, ca. 1896.

9.3, Lakota family posing for a photo at the Cincinnati Zoological Gardens, ca. 1896.

9.4, Lakota family posing for a photo at the Cincinnati Zoological Gardens ca. 1896.

Chapter 10

10.1, Map illustrating the source areas of artifacts found at the Turner site, Hamilton County, Ohio

10.2 Amelia (Molly) and Charles Louis Metz

10.3, A butterfly and wing enclosed in a pendant, a gift to 21-year-old Ethel Helen Caroline Metz from Frederick Ward Putnam, December 25, 1907.

10.4, Charles Wilbur Metz, First Lieutenant, 148th Infantry, United States Marine Corps, ca. 1917.

Chapter 11

11.1, Office sign indicating Charles Louis Metz's his office hours, ca.1926.

11.2, Pad of calling cards—C. L. Metz, M.D., Madisonville, Ohio, with office hours, ca.1926.

Epilogue

E.1, Location of archaeological sites in the lower Little Miami River valley investigated by Charles Louis Metz.

Preface

This book examines the life, times, and archaeological contributions of Charles Louis Metz to the foundations of Ohio Valley archaeology and the history of American archaeology. Although he was nationally and internationally known at the time, Charles has entered the ranks of "forefathers of whom we have no memory."[1] Since archaeology became more self-conscious as a sub-discipline of anthropology, it has become more interested in its own history.[2]

In order to understand Charles's contributions to Ohio Valley archaeology and the history of American archaeology, it requires the reader to discover and reconstruct the intellectual climate and theoretical currents of the time.[3] A history of Ohio Valley archaeology up to the time of Charles's death in 1926 provides the reader with a historically oriented view of his position on some of the most important issues on American Indians during his time.

Charles was well aware of the fact that he led a unique and unusual life. He also knew that he had made significant archaeological and anthropological contributions. It had always been Charles's intention to write his autobiography, but there was always someone who needed his help and there was always something that needed to be done. After he passed, it was his children's intention to write their father's biography, but they, too, were consumed by a lifetime of public service and helping others.

In 1969 Frederick Wilbur Berger, Charles's grandson, helped his aunts Margaret and Marie Metz donate their father's professional archives and that of the Literary and Scientific Society of Madisonville (LSSM), which he founded, to the Cincinnati Historical Society Library (CHSL). It was their hope that one day their father's papers would be used to write his biography.

The CHSL collection, curated today in the Cincinnati Museum Center in Cincinnati, Ohio, includes Charles's archaeological correspondences, field notes, maps, and photographs. The archive also includes his personal letters, which provide a keen insight into the life of a son, a brother, a husband, a father, and a friend. In addition to the CHSL archive, Charles's family archive was passed down to his great-grandson Michael Joseph Berger. Together, these archives allowed us to bring Charles back to life as well as the times when he lived.[4]

Acknowledgments

Research for this book was made possible with support from the John C. Court Family Foundation, the Charles Phelps Taft Foundation, and the College of Arts and Sciences, University of Cincinnati. We greatly appreciate the assistance of the Cincinnati Preservation Association, the Cincinnati Museum Center, the Mariemont Preservation Foundation, and the living descendants of Charles Louis Metz. We are especially grateful to Helen Black, Catharine Chapman, Paula Christian, Kristi Corrado, Barry Isaac, Gary Hicks, Mary Newman, Dan Policastro, Joe Stelzer, Jenny Ruth Tankersley, Tony Woodward, Robert Genheimer, and the Ohio Valley anthropology and archaeology students of the University of Cincinnati who continue to follow in the footsteps of Charles Louis Metz. We also wish to thank David Connolly for his German-to-English translations of the handwritten letters of Dr. Charles Louis Metz. And thanks to Owen Davey for the cover work artistry, and Michael Berger for the photography. We are especially grateful to Barbara Gargiulo for her invaluable editing and dedicated perseverance, without which this book would have never been possible.

Introduction

Dr. Charles Louis Metz was one of the most accomplished American archaeologists of the late nineteenth and early twentieth centuries. Although he has not been acknowledged in the history of American archaeology, Charles was one of the first archaeologists to use the direct-historical approach. He excavated the Madisonville site in the Little Miami River valley of Ohio, historically occupied by the Shawnee, to establish their cultural continuity back into prehistory. Charles's theoretical approach and archaeological findings have been historically obfuscated, and in many cases, attributed to contemporary, upper class, well-connected archaeologists affiliated with East Coast institutions. Nevertheless, his life's work laid the crucial framework for all subsequent archaeological research in the Ohio Valley.

Like many German immigrants, the Metz family was passionate about American Indian culture and empathetic to their oppression and persecution. The Metz family arrived in the United States on the heels of the Indian Removal Act and witnessed firsthand the Miami being boarded at gunpoint onto steamboats in Cincinnati and bound for Kansas.

Charles grew up at a time when the United States neither recognized nor treated American Indians as persons. It was a time when American

Indians were thought to be recent inhabitants of the Western Hemisphere, and when the burial mounds and earthworks in the Ohio River valley were attributed to an earlier "white race." It became Charles's life mission to demonstrate that American Indians were, in fact, the true architects of the earthworks and mounds of the Ohio River valley and that they had lived in the region since the Ice Age.

As a child, Charles's first book was a McGuffey's Reader filled with fictional stories about American Indian life in the Northeast. Charles loved the book so much that he kept it throughout his life. As he got older, Charles keenly read the family copy of Squier and Davis's 1848 *Ancient Monuments of the Mississippi Valley: Comprising the Results of Extensive Original Surveys and Explorations.* It described and illustrated many of the earthworks and mounds that Charles saw while traveling on horseback with his father, a physician, as he made medical rounds in Hamilton, Clermont, Brown, Highland, and Adams counties, Ohio.

As a teenager, Charles developed a passion for civil rights. As a member of the Turner Society, Charles listened to Abraham Lincoln speak about people escaping from the oppression of slavery. During the Civil War, at the age of fourteen, he served as a drummer for the all-German speaking Ninth Ohio Volunteer Infantry known as *Die Neuner.* They trained at Camp Dennison. This was the largest military hospital in Ohio during the Civil War. It was located east of Cincinnati. Charles helped his father, Francis, who served as a surgeon at Camp Dennison. At the hospital, Charles saw Sisters of Charity caring for wounded soldiers regardless of the color of their uniform or skin. He also witnessed the cruelty of war when Morgan's Raiders attacked the hospital and fought convalescing Union soldiers.

Charles came from a long line of medical doctors—from his father, Francis, to his great-uncle, Johannes Michael Metz, a surgeon in Napoleon's army. Because of his medical training and experiences at Camp Dennison, Charles was able to enter medical school at the age of eighteen.

While in medical school, Charles read every anthropological, archaeological, and natural science book he could get his hands on. With each book, his passion for studying American Indian culture grew stronger. At the time, it was not politically correct to feel compassion for American

Indians. President Andrew Johnson and Congress were considering the cost, in terms of money and time, to exterminate them.

After graduating from medical school in 1871, Charles and his new wife, Molly, moved to Madisonville where Charles joined his father's family medical practice. One of his first patients was a wealthy heiress who would forever change his life. Phebe Ferris was a well-to-do spinster from one of the founding families of the area. She discovered an archaeological site on her family's estate, which she named "pottery field," for the bits of reddish-brown pottery that littered the ground.

Phebe gave Charles permission to excavate the site, provided that it was done professionally. Charles renamed it the "Ferris Cemetery" site. Today it is known as the Madisonville site, one of the most famous archaeological sites in Eastern North America.

Charles invited a group of his closest personal and professional friends to join him in the excavation of the Madisonville site—Judge Joseph Cox, whom he had known since the Civil War; fellow medical doctor, Frank Warren Langdon; and attorney, Charles Frank Low. They discovered that the Madisonville site was an extensive American Indian cemetery filled with exemplary pottery and utilitarian artifacts from the time of European contact. With Phebe's consent, they displayed artifacts recovered from the site at the annual Cincinnati Industrial Expositions and the Centennial Exposition in Philadelphia. Charles used their initial findings at the Madisonville site as the basis for his 1876 article "The Mound Builders" published in the *Harvest Home Magazine*.

Charles met weekly with his friends to present papers on archaeological and anthropological topics. By 1878 these weekly meetings grew into the Literary and Scientific Society of Madisonville (LSSM), a formal archaeological support group. The LSSM was quite productive, publishing a number of archaeological papers in professional journals. The first was Charles's 1878 "The Prehistoric Monuments of the Little Miami Valley" published in *The Journal of the Cincinnati Society of Natural History*. It was the first systematic and comprehensive archaeological survey of the region and attributed the earthworks and mounds to American Indians. His conclusion was diametrically opposed to the conventional theories of the day.

In 1879 the archaeological publications of the LSSM attracted the attention of Frederick Ward Putnam, then curator of Harvard's Peabody Museum of Archaeology and Ethnology at Harvard University. He came to Cincinnati to attend one of the weekly meetings of the LSSM and to examine artifacts from the Madisonville site. Charles found that Putnam shared his archaeological interests and anthropological view of American Indians. They quickly became trusted colleagues and lifetime friends.

Following the 1880 LSSM publication "Archaeological Explorations near Madisonville, Ohio," in the *Journal of the Cincinnati Society of Natural History*, Putnam returned to Cincinnati to visit Charles and inspect his archaeological excavation of the Madisonville site. Charles's findings convinced Putnam that it was, indeed, one of the most important sites in the Ohio Valley and it had gone unrecognized by previous archaeologists. Putnam offered funding from the Peabody Museum, on one condition—that all field notes, maps, photographs, artifacts, and human skeletal remains would be curated at Harvard University. Ultimately, this agreement meant that Charles would lose control of the artifacts and their interpretation.

In 1881 Putnam came back to Cincinnati to pick up his first installment of artifacts and documents from the Madisonville site. A month after his visit, the LSSM published "The Madisonville Pre-Historic Cemetery: Anthropological Notes" in the *Journal of the Cincinnati Society of Natural History*. Charles's "The Prehistoric Monuments of Anderson Township, Hamilton County, Ohio," also published in the *Journal of the Cincinnati Society of Natural History*, closely followed it. It was the culmination of his many years of fieldwork in the lower Little Miami River valley and served as a baseline for all archaeological research in the region. It included maps and locations for nationally significant archaeological sites including Hahn Field, Madisonville, the Mariemont Earthwork, Sand Ridge, Stites Earthworks, Turner, and Turpin.

By 1882 Charles had become Putnam's protégé. In addition to the LSSM, Charles's archaeological fieldwork in the Little Miami River valley was conducted under the prominent auspices of the Peabody Museum. With the financial backing of Harvard University, Charles was able to expand his excavations to the Turner site, a complex of geometric earthworks, mounds, and villages on the eastern side of a shallow crossing of the Little Miami River, about four miles upstream from the Madisonville site. Somehow, despite its enormous size, the Turner site was completely overlooked by Squier and Davis in their 1848 publication, *Ancient Monuments of the Mississippi Valley.*

The Turner site was not only remarkable because of the size, shape, and design of its geometric earthworks and mounds, but also because of the raw material composition of its artifacts. Charles discovered flaked-stone artifacts manufactured from cave minerals—copper, gold, meteoric iron, mica, obsidian (volcanic glass), and silver. Additionally, there was a plethora of artwork in bone, clay, shell, and stone depicting the material and spiritual lives of American Indians more than two thousand years ago.

Thanks to Harvard's funding, Charles was able to expand his fieldwork to other archaeological sites in the Little Miami River valley including the Hahn Field, Milford Earthworks, and Sand Ridge sites. However, the financial demands of Charles's prolonged archaeological surveys and multiple site excavations at so many sites exhausted his funding at a time when the country was falling into a prolonged recession. Because of his dire financial situation, Charles met with Cyrus Thomas, the director of Mound Exploration at the Smithsonian Institution. Charles agreed to provide Thomas with exemplary samples of pottery from the Little Miami River valley in exchange for funding his excavations.

Charles joined Putnam at the thirty-third annual meeting of the American Association for the Advancement of Science (AAAS) in Philadelphia and the thirty-fifth annual meeting of the AAAS in Buffalo, New York. Charles presented the results of his excavations in the Little Miami River valley in anthropology sessions, which included papers presented by Alexander Graham Bell and John Wesley Powell.

Charles's presentations at the AAAS meetings attracted the attention of William Henry Holmes, an assistant geologist for the U.S. Geological Survey working under John Wesley Powell. Holmes was also the curator of Aboriginal Ceramics at the Smithsonian's National Museum. Like Thomas, Holmes wanted to acquire quintessential examples of pottery from Charles's excavations for the Smithsonian. Following the AAAS meetings, Charles was hired as a full-time Ohio Valley archaeologist by Harvard's Peabody Museum and he was elected as a Fellow of the AAAS.

Charles recognized that archaeological sites in the Little Miami River valley contained sixteenth-, seventeenth-, and eighteenth-century Spanish and French trade goods. He assumed that archaeological sites, which lacked European trade goods, were more than four hundred years old. Charles realized that some archaeological sites contained pottery, some contained bowls carved from stone, and others had vessels made from freshwater and marine shells. He believed that these sites represented a sequence of thousands of years of American Indian prehistory.

Of the archaeological sites that did have pottery, Charles recognized that there were differences in the thickness and temper of ceramic vessels. The Turner site pottery was thick and tempered with crushed igneous and metamorphic rocks. The Sand Ridge site pottery was comparable in thickness, but tempered with crushed limestone. The Hahn Field and Turpin site pottery was thinner than that found at the Turner and Sand Ridge sites, but it was tempered with crushed mussel shell. The Madisonville site had the thinnest pottery and it was tempered with heat-altered mussel shell. Given that the Madisonville site also contained European trade goods, Charles believed that the differences in ceramic temper and thickness represented changes in the technological development of pottery, which spanned a long period of time, likely thousands of years.

Contrary to the conventional academic wisdom of the time, Charles was convinced that American Indians had been in the Little Miami River valley since the last Ice Age. In 1885 he discovered a tear-dropped shaped, flaked-stone artifact in the glacial gravels of Madisonville. Although it was not known at the time, Charles had discovered a 13,500-year-old Clovis spear point preform. In 1887 Charles discovered a second Clovis spear point preform in glacial gravels near Loveland, Ohio, at a depth of thirty feet below the surface and in close proximity to mastodon bones. The discoveries of Clovis artifacts in the Little Miami River valley were made almost fifty years before a Clovis spear point was found in unambiguous association with mammoth bones in New Mexico.

As the president of the World's Columbian Commission and the chief of the Department of Ethnology and Archaeology for the World's Columbian Exposition, Putnam asked Charles to serve as a "special assistant" in charge of the Ohio Valley archaeological exhibition at the World's Fair in Chicago.

On opening day, May 1, 1893, Charles was on stage along with President Grover Cleveland, Vice President Stevenson, Secretary of State Gresham, Secretary of the Treasury Carlisle, Secretary of the Navy Herbert, Secretary of the Interior Smith, Secretary of Agriculture Morton, Spanish notables, and direct lineal descendants of Christopher Columbus. Charles listened to the presidential address and watched President Cleveland turn on the fair's electrical lights and power.

In acknowledgment of Charles's outstanding contributions to the Columbian Exposition, Congress presented him with a bronze medal and vellum-impressed diploma. Charles's exhibition at the Columbian Exposition acted as a catalyst for interest in Ohio Valley archaeology and the professionalization of the discipline in academic institutions and museums.

Following the Columbian Exposition, Charles wanted more than ever to determine the cultural identity of the people who constructed the burial mounds and earthworks in the Little Miami River valley. He knew that the Madisonville site had been used by a Shawnee war party as recently as 1810. He had also recovered French and Spanish trade goods from the site including cut sheets of copper, a copper bell, iron axes and celts, iron pot fragments, glass beads, a lathe-turned bone flintlock awl and vent pick, and spent honey-colored pistol and rifle gunflints.

The copper, iron, and glass artifacts were unquestionably Spanish in origin and dated to the sixteenth century, the time of the conquistador, Hernando de Soto. The flintlock awl and vent pick and honey-colored gunflints, on the other hand, were French in origin and dated to the late eighteenth and early nineteenth century. They were likely discarded or lost at the site by the 1810 Shawnee war party.

The French artifacts may have originated as trade items from French fur traders who traveled through the Great Lakes and Midwest regions by canoe. Jesuit priests, or Black Robes as American Indians knew them, frequently traveled with traders. Charles recovered two Roman Catholic chalices manufactured from exemplary Madisonville shell-tempered pottery. They suggested that the Madisonville inhabitants had been in contact with at least one Jesuit priest. The diaries of Jesuits documented more than twenty Shawnee villages in the Ohio River valley during the seventeenth and eighteenth centuries. Unfortunately, they did not provide the exact locations of the villages.

At other archaeological sites in the Little Miami River valley, Charles discovered human figures carved in bone, clay, ground-stone, and shell, which illustrated the clothing, hairstyles, and material culture of the Shawnee. He also found zoomorphic images of patrilineal Shawnee clans engraved on bone and shell and carved in clay and ground-stone pipes including the bear, buzzard, deer, eagle, owl, panther, rabbit, raccoon, snake, turkey, turtle, and wolf.

In addition to Shawnee clan symbols, Charles discovered a large cache of copper tinkling cones at the Turner site. They were identical to those sewn onto the dresses of Algonquian women who perform the jingle dance. The Turner site also produced a human cranium incised with the figure of a *manitou*, the spiritual life force of Algonquian-speaking people. It was composed as a combination of anthropomorphic and zoomorphic symbols. Nearby, Charles found underwater panthers and horned serpents, Algonquian mythological spirits known as *mishipeshu* and *mishibijiw*, engraved on stone and carved from mica and red slate. Charles believed that the absence of European trade goods at the Turner site suggested that Algonquian-speaking people inhabited the valley for thousands of years.

While Charles did not live long enough to defend his discoveries or see his theories and interpretations about American Indians vindicated, his research paved the way for future typological classifications and archaeological syntheses of Ohio Valley prehistory. It also served as a vital foundation for historic preservation. The Work Projects Administration (WPA), the Civilian Conservation Corps (CCC), and the National Youth Administration (NYA) carefully reconstructed the Great Serpent Mound in Adams County, Fort Ancient in Warren County, and Fort Hill in Highland County, Ohio, using Charles's field notes and maps. Today, these internationally significant archaeological sites are managed as Ohio State Memorials.

Charles's research on American Indians inspired many future generations of philanthropists who helped establish Ohio Valley archaeology programs at the University of Cincinnati (UC), the Cincinnati Museum of Natural History, and the Cincinnati Preservation Association. Today, these institutions are educating and training undergraduate, graduate, K-12 students, and the public in Ohio Valley archaeology.

With the advent of radiocarbon dating, the age of the Hahn Field, Madisonville, Sand Ridge, Turpin, and Turner sites was shown to span more than two thousand years of prehistory. The artifacts and features, which Charles excavated at these sites, helped define the Middle Woodland (Hopewell), Late Woodland (Newtown), and Fort Ancient cultural periods. These sites are now listed on the National Register of Historic Places and form a long corridor of nature preserves, public parks, and rural land in the lower Little Miami River valley.

Because of Charles's work on the tribal affiliation of the American Indian inhabitants of the Little Miami River valley, Algonquian tribes such as the Shawnee can now seek the repatriation of human skeletal remains, grave goods, and items of cultural patrimony. Currently, they are buried in drawers in the storage rooms of the Peabody Museum of Archaeology and Ethnology at Harvard University. The recent Native American Graves Protection and Repatriation Act gives American Indians the rights to the return of grave goods and rebury the remains of their ancestors.

Charles knew that the archaeological sites and sacred cultural properties in the Little Miami River valley are nonrenewable. Once they are disturbed, they are gone forever. With academic, community, and public support, these sites will continue to be protected and preserved in perpetuity.

I.1. Dr. Charles Louis Metz

CHAPTER 1

The Early Life and Times of Charles Louis Metz

IN THE FIRST HALF OF THE NINETEENTH CENTURY, German families fell in love with American Indians because of the translated writings of American author James Fenimore Cooper. His early romanticized frontier novels such as *The Pioneers* (1823), the *Last of the Mohicans: A Narrative of 1757* (1826), *The Pathfinder* (1840), and the *Deerslayer: or The First Warpath* (1841), not only generated German empathy for American Indians, they portrayed America as the land of freedom and opportunity.[1]

The Metz family arrive in America

Nineteenth-century German Catholic families not only had to deal with religious and political oppression, but property was almost impossible to acquire by working-class families. Dr. Franz (Francis) Michael Metz and Maria Barbara (Babette) Metz (née Reichert) and their four children were seeking both the freedom and opportunities described by Cooper. They immigrated to New Orleans, Louisiana, in 1842 from the town of Jockgrim in Bavaria, Germany. The voyage across the Atlantic Ocean was long and hard. More Germans died in route than survived.

The Metz family loved fine art and music. They brought with them an English violin in a wooden coffin case made by a member of the London Furber family, and two framed oil paintings on wood, which had been handed down through generations of the Metz family. They were painted by David Teniers the Younger, a Flemish master who lived from 1610 to 1690. One of the paintings was a landscape and the other was called the *Jealous Wife*. It portrayed a wife watching her husband and his mistress. Francis's father, Johannes M. Metz, gave him the painting on the day of their wedding in March 1840 in the city of Metz, Germany. They also had a beautifully engraved French sword from the Napoleonic War.

As an experienced German medical doctor, Francis had no trouble establishing a family practice in New Orleans.[2] Numerous German families from the Rheinland-Pfalz were living New Orleans where they had turned the insect-filled coastal swampland into working farms, what became known as the German Coast, formerly Choctaw land.

By 1842 European immigration was encouraged to quickly populate the recently abandoned southeastern United States. The Indian Removal Act, passed by Congress on May 28, 1830, and signed into law by President Andrew Jackson, forced the removal of the "Five Civilized Tribes" to lands west of the Mississippi River, which not only included the Choctaw, but also the Cherokee, Chickasaw, Creek, and Seminole. In the Midwest, it also directly affected the Kickapoo, Lenape (Delaware), Miami, Shawnee, and Wyandot as they, too, were forced west.

Babette felt uncomfortable in the swamp-filled countryside. A firsthand encounter with an alligator during a picnic at Lac des Allemands (French for Lake of the Germans) was the last straw. Babette declared that she was "disgusted with life in the south" and demanded that the family move north. Francis agreed and the family made arrangements to move to Cincinnati, Ohio. It was the last stop on northbound steamboat-shipping routes from New Orleans. Cincinnati also had a thriving German-Catholic community.[3]

The Metz family in Cincinnati, Ohio

The Metz family arrived in Cincinnati, Ohio, in 1845. They chose to live on Mohawk, a street in the German "Over-the-Rhine" neighborhood named after a tribe frequently and prominently featured in Cooper's novels. While Cincinnati did not have swamps filled with alligators, venomous snakes, and quicksand, American Indians were still living in the Ohio River valley.[4]

Less than four years before the family moved to Cincinnati, a group of vigilantes with axes murdered and dismembered Wyandot families in Ohio, including Chief Summunduwat. On July 21, 1843, surviving members of the Wyandot tribe were forced from their homes in Upper Sandusky, Ohio, and transported to downtown Cincinnati where they were loaded up on steamboats bound for Westport, Missouri.[5]

By happenstance, Charles Dickens was in Ohio at the time and witnessed the removal of the Wyandot. As a champion of the working class his heart went out to the Wyandot. He wrote that they were "a fine people, but degraded and broken down." The Wyandot reminded him of the helpless and impoverished families living in the streets of London.[6]

On October 12, 1846, Babette was five months pregnant with Charles. She and Francis watched a platoon of sixty-four soldiers escort 350 Miami down Main Street and onto the *Colorado*, a steamboat on the Ohio River bound for the Marais des Cygnes River in Kansas. The Miami had been forcibly removed from their homes in Peru, Indiana. Although some of the Miami families found clever ways to escape the removal, most were not so lucky.[7]

While the last families openly living as American Indians were being forced from their homes, Edwin Davis and Ephraim Squier began their archaeological survey of the Ohio River valley and its tributaries. Since the arrival of Christopher Columbus, the origin and antiquity of American Indians in the Western Hemisphere had been questioned. The most popular theory of the day posed by nineteenth-century-American antiquarians was that the continent was originally inhabited by an ancient race of white people that greatly preceded the American Indian. Large burial mounds and complex geometric earthworks in Ohio were considered evidence in support of this theory.

It was clear from the outset that Squier and Davis supported the lost race theory. Davis, a medical doctor by training, had excavated burial mounds in the area of Chillicothe, Ohio, and was convinced that American Indians could not possibly have created them. Squier was a journalist and newspaper editor who appreciated amazing tales, which grabbed the attention of the reading public. He was also trained in civil engineering. Squier and Davis decided to conduct a large-scale civil engineering survey of burial mounds and earthworks in Ohio to prove that the technology used to construct them was beyond the capabilities of the American Indian.

The fieldwork of Squier and Davis was Eurocentrically biased from the outset. They assigned archaeological sites with perceived European functions—buildings, cemeteries, effigies, and forts. With this classification in hand, Squier and Davis mapped hundreds of archaeological sites with a "compass and chain" in southern Ohio including the Fort Ancient, Hopewell, Mound City, Newark, Seip, and Serpent Mound earthworks. They also added the maps and research notes of James McBride, John Locke, William Lytle, Constantine Rafinesque, and Charles Whittlesey.

Although Squier and Davis amassed an unprecedented amount of data, the precision of their maps was deliberately exaggerated to support their conclusion—the technology used to construct the earthworks of the Ohio River valley could only have been that of an ancient white race. Their report, *Ancient Monuments of the Mississippi Valley: Comprising the Results of Extensive Original Surveys and Explorations*, was published in 1848 by the Smithsonian Institution. It was widely read and reprinted again and again to meet the demand of American readership.

Copies of Squier and Davis's book made their way into American homes, including the Metz family household. As Davis was a medical doctor turned archaeologist, it was no wonder that the book would inspire Charles's career. He was born at the peak of Squier and Davis's archaeological survey on the morning of January 1, 1847. Charles was the fifth of ten children and baptized on February 28, 1847, by Father Wilhelm at Saint John the Baptist Catholic Church on the corner of Green and Bremen (now Republic) streets in Cincinnati.[8]

In 1848 during the Thanksgiving holiday, a delegation of Ojibwe including ten tribal leaders, two women, and a baby rode around the Metz home in full regalia playing the drum and singing. For the next week, the Ojibwa performed traditional songs and dances from the balcony of the

Masonic Hall on Third Street to raise money for their trip to Washington D.C. They planned to meet with then President James K. Polk to discuss the hardships of their forced removal to the West.[9]

At the age of three, Charles wandered away from home in search of his mother who had gone to the local market. An elderly woman who had no children seized the opportunity and kidnapped him. Francis acted quickly and was able to track down the old woman and locate her home. He found little Charles in a closet crying, but safe and unharmed. After this traumatic event, "his mother refused to remain any longer in the city."[10]

The Metz family in Highland County, Ohio

Nat Roush, a family friend from Allensburg, Ohio, suggested to Francis that he should move his family to Highland County to be closer to his patients in Hillsboro. The Metz family departed the very next day at the crack of dawn in a wagon containing all of their worldly possessions. They rode all day until they reached their new home near Hillsboro, just as the sun was setting. The Metz family lived in the farmhouse for five months until they were able to purchase a brick home from Roush in nearby Danville. Francis became the family doctor for Allensburg.[11]

After the kidnapping, Francis kept Charles close to him. They traveled together on medical rounds across the rural landscape of Highland and Adams counties. With his father, young Charles rode on horseback past some of the most significant archaeological sites in the Ohio River valley including Fort Hill, the Plum Run Mound, the Rocky Fork Mound Group, the Great Serpent Mound, and Workman Earthworks.[12]

Charles also traveled with his father's assistant, Dr. Fleck, to get medical supplies in Cincinnati. On one of these trips, Charles had his first face-to-face encounter with a locomotive at a train stop at Russell Station, Ohio. Dr. Fleck escorted young Charles to the railroad platform, held him tightly, and pointed to an oncoming train some three miles away. Fleck said to Charles, "there come the devil." The bellowing clouds of dense black smoke and the rumbling roar of the coal black locomotive exacerbated by the Doppler Effect, scared Charles to the point that he fainted.[13]

Charles was not only a sensitive boy he was deeply religious and a devout Roman Catholic. Believing that the devil was actually coming toward him was just too much for young Charles. A woman standing on the platform came to Charles's aide. She brought him back to consciousness by bathing his face in water. As Charles was being soothed, she berated the novice doctor for frightening the child.[14]

For American Indians, the train really was the devil that Dr. Fleck proclaimed to Charles. They played a key role in the attempted elimination and removal of the American Indian. Trains destroyed the bountiful ecosystems, which American Indians depended upon for their livelihood, food, and shelter. Trains brought soldiers, militias, and endless waves of immigrants who took their land and killed their families. Trains also transported American Indians to lands far from their ancestral homes and in many cases, to imprisonment and death.

When Charles was not traveling with his father he was in school in Danville, learning to read and write from a large brown wooden tablet, which had a small blackboard and a scroll on top with inscribed numbers, letters, and single syllable words. Charles loved to read. Francis bought him a McGuffey's Reader at the Danville general store. It was full of fictitious stories about a Mohawk warrior such as *The Lone Indian* and *Powontonamo*. Charles loved the stories so much that he kept the book with him for the rest of his life. He developed a real passion for reading about American Indians, archaeology, and related natural history subjects.[15]

The Metz family in Plainville, Ohio

In 1856 the Metz family moved to the corner of Walton Creek Road and Wooster Pike in Plainville, Ohio. One year later, Babette gave birth to her tenth and last child, a boy. Charles was ten years old and now one of four boys and two girls. The Metz's had four other children who died in their infancy including three boys and one girl.[16]

In 1856 Cincinnati newspapers were running stories about the "Battle of Seattle." European settlements in the Washington territory had overrun the Suquamish and Duwamish homeland in the central Puget Sound. They were attacked by rifle and artillery fire, which killed twenty-eight men and seriously wounded another eighty. Their leader, Chief Sealth (Seattle), surrendered.[17] While most Cincinnati readers perceived the news as a great victory for America and manifest destiny, it was disturbing news for empathetic German emigrants who thought of American Indians as kindred spirits.

Charles attended a local ungraded country school for the first three years that the Metz family lived in Plainville. His parents were deeply concerned that Charles was not getting a proper education and they believed it would adversely affect his future in the medical profession. In 1860 Charles's older sister Maria Anna was engaged to James Byland, who lived in Newport, Kentucky. Charles's parents arranged for him to live with James so he could attend the Ninth District School located between Vine and Race streets in Cincinnati as a "pay pupil."[18]

The Civil War

While living with James Byland, Charles joined the German Turner Society of Cincinnati. In addition to introducing him to gymnastics, the Turner Society gave him a broad perspective on the social, political, and cultural values associated with German-American citizenship. The Turner Society was also a strong supporter of Abraham Lincoln. At 8:00 p.m. on February 12, 1861, Charles attentively listened, along with other members of the Turner Society, as Lincoln spoke from the balcony of the Burnet House in Cincinnati. Lincoln told the German-American audience that he understood the Turners had escaped oppression in their homeland and he welcomed them to the United States. Members of the Turner Society were invited to serve as his bodyguards at the presidential inauguration on March 4, 1861.[19]

Politically, Lincoln's antipathy of human enslavement was well known. On the day of Lincoln's inauguration, seven southern states with slave-based economies seceded from the Union and formed the Confederate States of America. In a show of force on April 12, 1861, the Confederate military fired upon Fort Sumter, South Carolina. Lincoln immediately called for all of the states to provide Union troops to retake the fort.

Kentucky governor Beriah Magoffin refused Lincoln's order and instead called for Confederate forces to attack the city of Cincinnati. James

Byland responded to the news by enlisting in the Kentucky infantry of the Union army. This news not only deeply concerned the Metz family it also meant that Charles could no longer attend school in Cincinnati. The Civil War impacted the lives of all American citizens and the Metz family felt the pain perhaps more than others.[20]

William Dennison was the governor of Ohio and his home was in Cincinnati. He assured the city's government, business owners, and citizens that he would establish a military camp to protect the city. He chose approximately five hundred acres of farmland in New Germany, located just five miles east of the Metz family home as the location for the military installation. It was the homestead of Christian Waldschmidt, a veteran of the American Revolution, who founded the community of New Germany. His dilapidated homestead, barn, and surrounding property were named Camp Dennison in honor of the governor. The Waldschmidt home also served as a temporary headquarters for Union general Joshua Bates.[21]

Camp Dennison served sixty-nine Ohio, two Kentucky, and two Illinois volunteer infantry units, ten Ohio volunteer cavalry units, the Second Regiment Heavy Artillery unit, nine Indiana, one Ohio, and one Michigan battery light artillery units, three Indiana cavalry companies, two Indiana sharpshooter units, and the Camp Dennison Guards. It was also a safe haven for citizens from the Confederate state of Tennessee who supported Lincoln's vision and wanted to fight for the Union. Men from eastern Tennessee, such as Porter James Carmichael, from Piedmont, carefully made their way northward to Camp Dennison and formed the First Tennessee Cavalry.[22]

Between seventy-five thousand and one hundred thousand Union soldiers were mustered in and trained at Camp Dennison including the all-German speaking Ninth Ohio Volunteer Infantry known as Die Neuner. The Ninth Ohio was made up entirely of members of the German Turner Society of Cincinnati. They performed all of their drills and training in German. A Cincinnati newspaper reporter wrote, "In two respects the Germans take to life at Camp Dennison like ducks to water: lager beer and military drill. There is little of the first but the second abounds. Training incessantly, exploiting boundless tenacity, they have already achieved extraordinary precision and skill."[23]

Like most physicians in the area, Francis Metz volunteered his medical services at Camp Dennison. He enlisted on December 1, 1861. At age fourteen, Charles was too young to enlist in the military as a soldier, but as a member of the Turner Society, he was old enough to serve as a drummer for the Ninth Ohio Volunteer Infantry at Camp Dennison. Brig. Gen. Jacob D. Cox, Ohio District Commander, fondly remembered hearing Charles's drum at Camp Dennison, writing that it would "waken longings for home and all the sadder emotions."[24]

As the war progressed and the carnage grew, Cincinnati was flooded with injured Union soldiers and Confederate prisoners of war. Following the battle of Shiloh, April 6 and 7, 1862, Camp Dennison installed some twenty-three hundred hospital beds in pine barracks to accommodate the rapid increase in patients. It became one of the largest Civil War military hospitals in the United States. Dr. Alfred Buckingham was the acting assistant surgeon in charge of the hospital.[25]

The Camp Dennison hospital caseload grew rapidly. Doctors Buckingham, Metz, and other local surgeons eagerly welcomed six Sisters of Charity who served as their nurses. Following the battle of Shiloh, ten additional Sisters of Charity came to Camp Dennison including Sister Anthony O'Connell. She had exceptional medical skills. Sister Anthony earned the respect of the doctors in her ability to save soldiers from the bone saw. She became the Camp Dennison hospital administrator and a trusted nurse. Sister Anthony showed no prejudice in treating the wounded regardless of the side of their military service, ethnicity, or the color of their skin.[26]

Winters at Camp Dennison were raw and harsh. Many soldiers contracted pneumonia and there was a measles epidemic. As if epidemic illness and the cold and wet weather were not enough, the troops refused to use their latrines and instead defecated on the hillside directly above their only source of drinking water. The sewage-contaminated water gave them cholera, typhoid, and dysentery. Remarkably, however, only 340 Union soldiers and 31 Confederate prisoners of war died at Camp Dennison, a testament to the skills of the surgeons and the Sisters of Charity.[27]

While the conditions of Camp Dennison would have traumatized and discouraged most people away from the medical profession, they inspired and energized Charles to read medical books under his father's keen tutelage. In addition to medical books, Charles read, as did most of the literate troops stationed or convalescing at Camp Dennison, dime novels published by Beadle and Company. They were filled with stories of American Indians. They were especially popular at Camp Dennison because two of the novels were set in Cincinnati: *Joe Phenix's Double Deal* and *Deadwood Dick Jr. in Cincinnati*.[28]

Charles was sixteen years old on Sunday, July 12, 1863, when Lt. Col. George W. Neff received a telegraph warning him that Kentucky-born brigadier general John Hunt Morgan and his Confederate cavalry were on their way to attack Camp Dennison. The telegraph stated that Morgan commanded a seasoned and well-trained force of almost twenty-five hundred cavalrymen and six pieces of artillery.[29]

On Monday, July 13, Neff received a second telegraph message from Brigadier General Cox stating, "The Camp must be held!" Neff had only seven hundred armed men and another twelve hundred unarmed, which included the Forty-third Company of the Second Battalion, members of the "Corps of Invalids." Neff posted guards at all of the nearby railroad bridges. He also had fifty men dig rifle pits and fell trees across Morgan's anticipated path.[30]

At the break of dawn, Tuesday, July 14, Neff had an "Invalid Corps" under the command of Captain Van Doehm, which consisted of 350 convalescing soldiers and militia including veterans of the battle of Shiloh, ready and waiting for Morgan. His Confederate cavalry and howitzers appeared along the Little Miami River at 6:00 a.m. Morgan's first brigade, under the command of Confederate colonel Basil Duke crossed the river at Branch Hill just north of Camp Dennison at 7:30 a.m. Eight Union soldiers guarding the Madisonville-Obanion-Cambridge Turnpike Bridge near Camp Dennison were playing cards and caught off guard by Duke's cavalry. All but one of the guards, however, was able to escape the attack.[31]

Duke's brigade continued onto the railroad bridge at Miamiville and easily overran the Union guards. Meanwhile, Confederate lieutenant Elias D. Lawrence shelled the Union rifle line, barracks, and hospital wards of Camp Dennison with two howitzers. The Union soldiers at Camp Dennison returned a six-hundred-gun volley. Lawrence quickly realized that he was outgunned and retreated.[32]

Neff and about 150 members of the Invalid Corps quickly boarded the Little Miami River train, which had brought much-needed arms to Camp Dennison. Within minutes, they arrived at the Miamiville Bridge before Duke's men had a chance to burn it. The Union and Confederate troops rapidly exchanged rifle fire from opposite sides of the river. Neff then led the Invalid Corps in a bayonet charge across the bridge as his troops were loading their muskets on the run.[33]

The Invalid Corps was able to drive off Duke's brigade and save the Miamiville Bridge with the loss of only one soldier despite the fact they were greatly outnumbered and outgunned. More importantly, the skirmishes at Camp Dennison and Miamiville diverted Morgan's raiders away from their primary target in Ohio—the Miami Powder Company located near Xenia. It was a key source of black powder for the Union army. After the battle, Charles picked up a spent soft lead minié ball that was shot at him in the hospital. He kept it for the rest of his life as a reminder of the battle at Camp Dennison and a grim reminder of the cruelties of the Civil War.[34]

By 11:00 a.m, Morgan's troops had moved on to Camp Shady, the unmanned Camp Dennison supply depot just upstream. They stole horses, pillaged and burned fifty military wagons, and cut telegraph lines. Morgan's troops also used railroad ties to derail and set fire to a locomotive known as the "Kilgore" and three coaches carrying 115 new Union recruits. Before moving on, Morgan spared the young recruits and told them to walk the tracks to Camp Dennison.[35]

Morgan's efforts were in vain. The Civil War came to an end on April 9, 1865, when Confederate general Robert E. Lee surrendered at the McLean House, Appomattox Court House, Virginia. Incensed by the loss, John Wilkes Booth assassinated President Lincoln five days later. Members of the Turner Society served as guards as Lincoln's body rested in the rotunda of the White House. His body lay in state for forty-eight hours between April 19 and April 20, 1865. During that time, the Cincinnati German Turner Society flew the United States flag on York Street. They chose Charles to raise the flag. It was an honor, which touched him deeply and he never forgot it. Afterward, Lincoln's casket, and that of his third son

William "Willie", who died on Thursday, February 20, 1862, from typhoid, was placed on a funeral train that traveled approximately seventeen hundred miles to Springfield, Illinois.[36]

The funeral train was scheduled to travel the same path Lincoln took when he assumed the office of President of the United States in 1861. In Ohio a Cleveland-Columbus-Cincinnati Railroad engine known as the "Nashville" pulled the train. While on display in the Rotunda of the Columbus Statehouse, Lincoln's embalmed body unexpectedly began to decompose. It had become discolored and gave off putrefying odors. Lincoln's face had to be covered in chalk and his body packed in ice. Fearing that it would not survive the trip to Springfield, Illinois, the stop in Cincinnati was canceled. Charles and his fellow members of the Turner Society were extremely disappointed. They had hoped to pay their respects to a man they considered a saint.[37]

Following the end of the war, Union soldiers returned to Camp Dennison where they were mustered out of service. Camp Dennison was decommissioned in November 1865. Some of the more substantial barracks were converted to homes and others were dismantled and the wood used to build new houses. The Metz family resumed their daily life in Plainville, Ohio.[38]

Medical school

Because Charles had studied medicine with his father at Camp Dennison, he was able to enter the Miami Medical College in Oxford, Ohio, at the age of eighteen. Although Charles excelled in his medical classes, he could not get the war out of his mind. His 1865 and 1866 medical school lecture cards and notebooks are filled with military doodling and drawings of soldiers, forts, and American flags.[39]

Charles's professors were among America's foremost leaders in the medical profession including Doctors Clendenin, Mussey, and Williams. Today, Elkannon Williams is known as the father of ophthalmology. Charles learned medicine at a time when the profession was in a period of transition from the use of home remedies and a bit of quackery to a fact-based science. Although he was taught to use ether as a general anesthesia during surgery and belladonna to dilate the eye, Charles was also instructed in the use of leeches, bleeding, and strong purgatives as curatives.

While in medical school, Charles lived in downtown Cincinnati at 418 Vine Street. He remained in close communication with his new brother-in-law, James Byland, who married Charles's sister Anna and moved to New York. Anna was the editor of *Fortschritt*, the only German paper edited by a woman in the United States. Her husband, James, was the editor of the *New York Republican*. He also worked for an insurance company and Charles hoped to join them after completing his medical degree. Charles wanted to establish a practice in New York City and serve as a medical examiner for James's insurance company on the side.[40]

Although Charles was developing a keen business side, he remained deeply spiritual. On October 25, 1868, at the age of twenty-one, he composed "My Prayer."

> Heavenly Father, I kneel before Thee, humbly, submissively, imploring Thy mighty aid to assist me in my great undertaking, which without Thy Almighty power I cannot hope to succeed. Help me, Heavenly Father in my efforts to do right, to do my duty as a son and as a brother. Help me suppress, all vain feeling, all pride, all wantonness and lead me into the path of Honesty, Virtue, and Uprightness and Religion. Help me to forgive and forget my enemies. Lead me from temptation and sin and teach me to acquire purity of soul, purity of mind and purity of body and to suppress all evil passions that may tempt me. Give me success in my duties to mankind as Thy servant. Teach me to love my enemies, and all those who bear ill will against me. Protect all those that I love, and when Thou thinks fit, take this poor penitent sinner into Thy Kingdom. When the hour of Death is at hand, have mercy on my soul. Heavenly Father to Thee I commend my soul, my future life. Amen.[41]

Amelia (Molly) Berger

When Charles was not in class he continued to accompany his father on medical rounds to get practical experience in diagnosing. In 1869 Charles met Amelia (Molly) Berger in the home of one of his father's patients. Molly was a petite young woman, nineteen years old, under five feet tall, and "cute as a button." It was love at first sight and all of his dreams to move to New York City dissolved. Molly was two years younger than Charles, born on December 16, 1849, to Andrew and Julia Berger. They owned a substantial farm in Vera Cruz, Brown County, Ohio.[42]

Charles and Molly's courtship was brief. Father Bartholomew Lebowitz married them on May 4, 1870, in the Church of the Holy Ghost in Vera Cruz. The day before the wedding, he presented Molly with a small, inscribed German bible.

> To Wife Amelia Berger as a pious remembrance of her last hours of her Maiden life from her most affectionate friend.
>
> Bartholomew Lebowitz, priest May the 3rd 1870[43]

Charles inscribed in the back cover of the church's book of *Instructions in the Sacraments, Sacrifice, Ceremonies of the Catholic Church*.

> Charles and Mollie now and forever
> Hurrah hurrah.

Below it, Molly inscribed,

> To Charley.
> To my bosom thou art dear more dear than words can tell.
> If a fault be cherished there 'tis loving you too well.[44]

Charles's new in-laws presented them with an inscribed silver handled jar—"To Dr. C. L. Metz and wife from Joseph Clasgens, May 4, 1870." In keeping with family tradition, Francis presented his son with the *Jealous Wife* oil painting and the beautifully engraved French sword. It was the third time that the painting had been passed down from father to son as a wedding present. Family oral traditions maintain that Johannes M. Metz originally obtained the painting and sword as a "war prize" during his service as a medical officer in Napoleon's army.[45]

An aspiring archaeologist

After the wedding, Molly moved in with Charles's parents in Plainville while he completed medical school. During the summers, Charles moved home to Plainville to be with his wife and assist in his father's practice. Day after day, they rode past burial mounds and earthworks in the Little Miami

River valley. Charles never lost his childhood fascination with American Indians and the physical evidence of their past. He turned to the college library to find out what was known about them. The *Ohio Valley Historical Series* was a new seven-volume account of the early history of the area, but it did not go back far enough in time to answer the kinds of questions that Charles was asking.[46]

Charles read anything and everything he could get his hands on about the archaeology of the Ohio River valley. Most of the archaeology books Charles found in the library contained fanciful theories and distorted facts. They engendered a raging debate over the initial inhabitants of the Ohio River valley. The books were deeply rooted in the tenets of fundamental Christianity and ultraconservative politics. Most of the authors whimsically speculated that either a lost white race of giants, Danes, Hindis, Toltecs, Vikings, or a lost tribe of Israel constructed the mounds and earthworks.[47]

The controversy over the origin of the mounds and earthworks was not just an esoteric academic debate, but it was deeply rooted in the nineteenth-century genocide of the American Indian. At the time Charles was in medical school, President Andrew Johnson and Congress debated whether or not the American Indian should be exterminated. They even calculated the cost of the genocide in terms of dollars, number of people, and time needed to accomplish their complete annihilation.[48]

Congress estimated that complete annihilation of the American Indian would cost a million dollars and take ten thousand soldiers three years to accomplish. Johnson told Congress, "If the savage resists civilization, with the Ten Commandments in one hand and the sword in the other, [*sic*] demands his immediate extermination." Like their political predecessors, Johnson, Congress, and the courts of the United States considered the American Indian a lower life-form.[49]

Charles was not discouraged by the politics of the era or the plethora pseudoscientific writings about the Mound Builders. He enthusiastically read Dr. Daniel Drake's 1815 *Natural and Statistical View or Picture of Cincinnati and the Miami County*, which illustrated the exact locations of archaeological sites in the Ohio River valley. By the time Charles was in medical school, however, most of the sites Drake described had been destroyed by the construction of roads, businesses, and housing. It was apparent to

Charles that archaeological sites were rapidly disappearing from the area and there was some urgency to document them.

Charles read Caleb Atwater's 1820 *Descriptions of Antiquities Discovered in Ohio and other Western States*; the 1839 *Transactions of the Historical and Philosophical Society of Ohio* by Jacob Burnet, Timothy Walker, and William Henry Harrison; and Squier and Davis's 1848 magnum opus. These books had exemplary archaeological site descriptions and maps.

Charles was more than a little surprised to find that many of the earthworks and mounds he saw with his father were not included in the books he read. To make matters worse, he read Charles Whittlesey's 1850 *Descriptions of Ancient Works at Cincinnati* published by the Smithsonian Institution. It suggested that all of the archaeological sites in the area had been obliterated. Given the rapid increase in post–Civil War population and industrial development, Charles felt it was his responsibility to document these sites. Archaeology became more than an obsession with Charles, he felt deeply that it was his obligation to science. Charles also considered himself a scientist whose job was to carefully preserve all evidence of the past.[50]

Charles changed the focus of his reading from theoretical to methodological archaeology. As a medical student, he found Samuel Morton's 1836 *Crania Americana* particularly interesting. It used the rigors of medical science to solve archaeological problems. Morton suggested that comparisons between modern and ancient crania could be used to determine ethnicity. If the people buried in the mounds and earthworks were American Indians, then their crania should be identical to those found among modern individuals.

Although Charles was well trained in medical science, he had no professional background in archaeology. He carefully read George Gibbs's 1862 *Instructions for Archaeological Investigations in the United States*. In addition to being the first field guide on American archaeology, it alluded to the possibility, if not the probability, that artifacts dating to the last Ice Age could be found in the Ohio River valley.

Charles reasoned that if artifacts could be found in geological deposits from the Ice Age, then they would prove that American Indians had been in the United States long before the assumed 6,000-year biblical age of the earth. Previous investigations used dendrochronology (i.e., counting the annual growth rings in the cross section of a tree) to date archaeological sites in the Ohio River valley. In 1798 Rev. Manasseh Cutler counted the rings on the oldest living trees growing on a burial mound in Ohio to determine that it was at least 463 years old. Reverend Cutler's age determination was widely accepted because it did not challenge the biblical time frame.[51]

Charles found solace in Charles Lyell's 1830 *Principles of Geology: Being an Attempt to Explain the Former Changes of the Earth's Surface, by Reference to Causes Now in Operation*. Lyell traveled through Cincinnati in 1841 and examined firsthand the geology of the area. He used geological rates of erosion and mountain building to demonstrate beyond a reasonable doubt that the earth was far more than six thousand years old. He showed that the rates of geological processes today were the same as those active in the past. Charles felt confident that if he looked in the right geological deposits along the Little Miami River, he should be able to discover evidence that American Indians have always lived in the United States since time immemorial.

Charles had to set aside his archaeological readings long enough to study for his medical exams. At eight o'clock in the morning of February 23, 1871, Charles walked into his final exams with a throbbing and nauseating migraine. Fearing that they may cost him his medical career, he wrote a letter to "Molly" asking her to pray for him (see appendix A).

Madisonville

Despite his severe headache, Charles passed all of his medical exams and joined his father's practice in Plainville after graduation. On March 14, 1871, Charles and Molly purchased new office and bedroom furniture and moved into a rental property on 4616 Erie Avenue in Madisonville. It was a well-built brick house consisting of two rooms side by side downstairs, two above, and a lean-to kitchen in the back. Charles and Molly's first child was born in their new home on May 11, 1871. Father Anthony baptized her Anna Teresa Metz, in Saint Michael Church. Joseph Clasgens of New Richmond, Ohio, and Molly's aunt Frances McConn were her godparents.[52]

Charles inherited an appreciation of the arts from his parents. In the evenings, he enjoyed listening to good music and reading good literature. The downside of artistically inclined individuals such as Charles is that they tend not to spend much time or energy on housekeeping. This was the case of Charles's parents and siblings. Molly, on the other hand, was just the opposite. She kept a tidy house with everything in its proper place.[53]

1.1 The *Jealous Wife* painting by Flemish master David Teniers the Younger, ca. 1650.

1.2 Drawing of Camp Dennison, Hamilton County, Ohio, June 15, 1861.

1.3. Minié ball from Confederate brigadier general John Hunt Morgan's raid on Camp Dennison, Hamilton County, Ohio, July 14, 1863.

1.4 Brass microscope used by Charles Louis Metz in medical school and in his medical practice, ca. 1865.

1.5 Charles Louis Metz, Plainville, Hamilton County, Ohio, ca. 1871.

CHAPTER 2

The Literary and Scientific Society of Madisonville

WHILE LIVING IN MADISONVILLE on Erie Avenue in 1871, Charles made a house call to the home of Phebe Ferris. Aside from being one of Charles's first patients, the "quiet and unassuming" forty-five-year-old woman changed his life forever. They both shared a passion for archaeology and quickly became close friends and remained so until her passing at the age of seventy. Phebe recognized Charles as a moral man with a marvelous sense of humor and he could be trusted. From that day on, Charles was Phebe's personal physician.[1]

Phebe Ferris

Phebe was the daughter of Joseph Ferris. She inherited the vast Ferris family property and fortune in 1831 with the passing of her father. The Ferris family was among the earliest Euro-American settlers of the area known today as Mariemont. In 1792, just eleven years after the initial settlement of Columbia (present-day Lunken Airport), Ferris brothers, Eliphalet (1774–1859) and Joseph (1776–1831) left their home in Greenwich, Connecticut, for the Ohio River valley. They floated all of their worldly belongings down river and settled on the land between the Little Miami River and present-day Walnut Hills. They purchased 480 acres from Judge John Cleves Symmes for $2.40 per acre. This sale was quite a profit for Symmes. As a Revolutionary War veteran, he was able to acquire the former Shawnee-owned land for just $0.66 per acre from Congress.[2]

In addition to raising hogs and produce, Joseph Ferris grew and milled his own corn, which he used to make whiskey in his distillery on Whiskey Run Creek. He shipped the whiskey and smoked pork by flatboat down the Little Miami River, the Ohio River, and on to New Orleans. This business venture was very profitable because of the paucity of distilleries at that time. As a Connecticut Yankee, Joseph Ferris was very generous with his newfound wealth. He cared deeply about education. In addition to building a classic multistory colonial brick home in 1808, he built a schoolhouse for his eight children and "any others who cared to attend."[3]

As a wealthy heiress, Phebe was able to remain completely independent. While she never married, Phebe devoted her life to the study of the natural sciences. She bought and read science books and journals voraciously. She had no tolerance for uncultured thinking and lowbrow behavior. Phebe was an avid bird watcher and passionately concerned about the wanton waste of species, such as the Carolina parakeet and passenger pigeon, which were being hunted into extinction. She turned some six hundred acres of her estate into a nature preserve with a hunting ban strictly enforced by game wardens.[4]

Phebe loved all aspects of the natural sciences, but especially archaeology. While she visited and photographed archaeological sites across the United States, Mexico, and Europe, the ones on the Ferris estate were her real interest. Since she was a child, Phebe collected artifacts on the family estate and protected their find-spots with a passion akin to her love for wildlife. Phebe was especially fascinated by a place she affectionately called "Pottery Field." Recognizing it as an unusually well-preserved archaeological site, Phebe refused to let anyone who was not a professional excavate there.[5]

She showed Charles her beloved collection of artifacts from Pottery Field. As Charles enthusiastically examined the collection, Phebe explained to him that as a child she enjoyed exploring the mature old-growth beech and sugar maple forest surrounding the ruins of her father's distillery on

Whiskey Run Creek. She told Charles that the flat terrace immediately above the distillery was littered with American Indian–made pottery, stone tools, arrowheads, and the broken and charred bones of animals of all sizes. Hogs roamed the area in the autumn to forage for hickory nuts. This activity brought the artifacts to the surface.[6]

Charles knew the archaeological literature well and realized that Phebe's Pottery Field was yet another archaeological site in the Little Miami River valley, which had not been documented. Phebe appreciated that Charles's interest in her archaeological site was purely professional. She promised to take him to the site when she felt better. Phebe not only made good on her promise, she gave him permission to explore the site. This opportunity was Charles's first chance to excavate a truly significant archaeological site.

Phebe made it clear to Charles that she did not want to have any unprofessional digging on her property. It was okay if professionals assisted Charles and the digging was strictly for scientific purposes, but she did not want people digging on her property for profit. Phebe was well aware that looters and grave robbers were digging up artifacts for sale on the black market and they were destroying archaeological sites around the world at an unprecedented rate.[7]

The intellectual community of Madisonville

Given Phebe's concerns, Charles turned to the professional community of Madisonville. He invited Judge Joseph Cox, whom he had known since the Civil War; a fellow medical doctor, Frank Warren Langdon; and an attorney, Charles Frank Low, to join him in the excavation of the site. All of the men shared Charles's interest in American Indians and the archaeology of the Little Miami River valley.

Like Charles, Langdon graduated from the Miami Medical College, but a decade later. Dr. Langdon's help was especially useful. Aside from his research on the human nervous system and psychological disorders, Langdon was systematically documenting the birds and mammals of Cincinnati. His expertise in zoology was an invaluable addition given the abundance of animal bones exposed at Pottery Field.

Charles and his professional friends used their combined resources and free time to collect bone, ceramic, and stone artifacts from the site. They displayed the artifacts at the Cincinnati Industrial Expositions. While the focus of the expositions was to showcase the products of Cincinnati business owners, they also included a Department of Natural History with displays of American Indian artifacts.[8]

The Cincinnati expositions were, in part, the brainchild of Alfred Trabor Goshorn. He was asked to serve as Ohio's delegate to the Centennial Exposition in Philadelphia, a national event to celebrate America's independence from Great Britain. Given his success in Cincinnati, Goshorn was later elected the head of the Centennial Exposition.

While Charles was deeply invested in the archaeology of the Little Miami River valley, he did not let it interfere with family matters. In the autumn of 1872, Charles and Molly purchased their first home from John M. Alden, a bishop of the Walden Methodist Church in Madisonville. The small-frame house was located on Main Street. Today, it is the property between 6111 and 6113 Madison Road. Charles wasted no time moving his family and medical practice into their new home.[9]

Charles and Molly enjoyed music and theatrical plays, which regularly came to the city. In December 1872 Charles and Molly attended Ned Buntline and William F. Cody's *The Scouts on the Prairie*. It was performed on the stage of Samuel N. Pike's Opera House along with the premier of the Cincinnati Orchestra. As Charles and Molly stood in line, the predominately German-American audience shouted out "Indian yells" while waiting to purchase their tickets. Once they were in their seats, Charles and Molly watched as forty "braves and palefaces" were killed on stage.[10]

In reality, all but one of the American Indians were European-American actors who danced, shouted, and shot guns with blanks. The single exception was a six-year-old Yavapai-Apache named Wassaja, which means "signaling" or more precisely "beckoning." He was the son of Chief Cocuyevah and Thilgeya. Wassaja had been taken from his parents during a Pima raid the year before. An Italian photographer, Carlos Gentile, who worked for Buntline and Cody adopted him. Gentile gave Wassaja his English name, Carlos Montezuma. While it is not known whether or not Charles and Molly were able to meet and talk to Montezuma after the show, he did go on to become the first male Native American medical doctor in the United States. Montezuma earned his doctorate of medicine from the Chicago Medical College, Northwestern University.[11]

Charles's medical practice

Late in February 1873, Charles's father contracted pneumonia and unexpectedly died on March 4, at the age of sixty years. His older sister Anna was in New York and his younger brother Franklin was away in medical school at the time of Francis's death. His father's passing not only left Charles as the head of the Metz family, it meant that he had to assume all of his father's patients in addition to those in his own practice. That spring, Charles planted a large garden of herbs in his backyard. Like his father, Charles used the plants to make medicinal teas and tinctures. With the sudden increase in patients, they were needed to supplement his store-bought medicines.[12]

The increase in patients and caseloads took its toll on Charles's family. It was not uncommon for him to travel nonstop from patient to patient over a period of three days and often without sleep. During these times, Anna and Molly would visit her parents' farm in Vera Cruz. The family remained in contact by mail (see appendix A).

Eventually, Charles was able to get his medical rounds under control to the point he could devote more time to his family, his profession, and his passion for archaeology. With his father's additional patients, Charles's annual income had grown to $1,787.50. Although he was by no means wealthy, Charles was doing better than the average American for the time.[13]

In the autumn of 1873, the United States plunged headlong into one of its worst depressions in American history, which lasted until 1879. On June 23, 1875, Charles gave a one-year, three-thousand-dollar mortgage loan to a close relative at an interest rate of 8 percent. The loan amount was almost two years of his salary and made in the middle of the longest depression in American history. However, Charles valued his family and friends far more than money. This fact is especially clear in the letters to his wife (see appendix A).

Centennial Exposition

In March 1876, Charles and Molly's second child, Florence, died. She was less than one month old. Charles coped with the sadness for the loss of his daughter by assembling a collection of exemplary ceramic vessels from earthworks in the Little Miami River valley. He was invited to display them in the 1876 Centennial Exposition in Philadelphia. A group of dedicated ladies from Cincinnati organized the Women's Centennial Committee. In addition to creating an exhibit of contemporary artwork by local women, they also helped with the exhibition of Charles's recent archaeological discoveries.[14]

Congress appropriated almost two million dollars to fund the Centennial Exposition to celebrate the one hundredth anniversary of the signing of the Declaration of Independence. More than ten million people attended the exposition from May 10 to November 10, 1876. Thanks to Charles and his friends—Cox, Langdon, and Low—the archaeology of the Ohio River valley was well represented. Their archaeological exhibit included sixteen cases of artifacts, maps of significant earthworks, tribal territories, and impressions of petroglyphs.[15]

While the Exposition was in full swing, Charles published an article "The Mound Builders" in the August issue of *Harvest Home Magazine*. It described earthworks in Stites Grove, which included a circular enclosure with a large conical mound in the center and a smaller oval-shaped mound on the earthworks' edge. Charles wanted the magazine article to compliment the exhibition. He wanted to provide the public with an accurate and humanistic portrayal of American Indians. Unfortunately, the article and exhibition were tempered by the news of Gen. George Armstrong Custer's defeat at the battle of Greasy Grass Creek.

On June 25, 1876, Charles and the rest of the nation learned that Custer and a battalion of two hundred men had been defeated by Crazy Horse and more than three thousand Lakota, Northern Cheyenne, and Arapaho warriors in the Little Bighorn Valley, Montana. It was the most decisive American Indian victory and defeat of the U.S. Army, since St. Clair's defeat against Little Turtle and his Algonquian forces on November 4, 1791. Unfortunately, the battle of Greasy Grass, also known as Little Big

Horn, reinforced a stereotype of American Indians as wild, bloodthirsty, savages. It completely tainted Charles's goals for the Centennial Exposition. Not only did the news of Custer's defeat poison Charles's well for Ohio Valley archaeology, the malevolent stereotype of American Indians as "savages" made its way into the anthropological literature of the day.

Lewis Henry Morgan, often considered the Father of American Anthropology, believed that human history showed an evolutionary relationship between technology, social structures, systems of governance, and intellectual development. In his 1877 *Ancient Society*, Morgan defined stages of technological development from the written language of "civilizations," to the domesticated plants and animals of "barbarism," and the bow and arrow carried by "savages," such as the tribes who defeated Custer.[16]

Morgan unsuccessfully ran for the office of Commissioner of Indian Affairs. During his research on the *League of the Iroquois*, Morgan befriended a Seneca named Hasaneanda, later known as Donehogawa and Ely Parker. During the Civil War he served as a brigadier general under Ulysses S. Grant. Morgan and Parker believed that Indians should be assimilated into American society. Then President Grant disagreed because American Indians were neither citizens of the United States nor were they considered persons. Morgan's books were well read by Charles and his friends and widely discussed during lively evening conversations.[17]

The formation of the Literary and Scientific Society of Madisonville

The year of 1877 brought both joy and sadness to the Metz family. On April 24, 1877, Charles and Molly celebrated the birth of their daughter, christened Clara Isabel. Casper H. Schlotman and Caroline Berger served as her godparents. On September 7, 1877, Charles received a telegram from Hillsboro, Ohio, stating, "Your brother Frank died nine o'clock this a.m." Franklin followed in his older brother's footsteps entering Miami Medical College in 1872 and graduating with the class of 1876. After his graduation he practiced medicine in Danville, Highland County, Ohio.[18]

As a dedicated medical doctor, Franklin was still making his rounds on horseback despite severe abdominal pain, fever, and bloody diarrhea. He put his patients' health before his own. This fact haunted Charles, as he too would push the limits of his own health for his medical practice and archaeological research. Like his father, Charles suffered from a persistent cough, fever, frequent headaches, stomachaches, and shortness of breath. It is likely that he suffered from malaria, or ague as it was called then, which left him physically frail.[19]

Aside from health issues, Charles faced a financial strain on his resources. The United States and the rest of the world were engulfed in the "Long Depression." It began with the Panic of 1873 and lasted sixty-five months, making it one the longest lasting economic downturns in United States history. Approximately eighteen thousand businesses went bankrupt, including hundreds of banks, and ten states. Unemployment reached an all time high in 1878, somewhere between 8 and 14 percent.[20]

Thursday evening, April 4, 1878, Louis W. C. Casou, mayor of the incorporated village of Madisonville appointed Charles as a town councilman. This new position greatly eased the pressures of his family's financial situation. Despite the economic hard times and family concerns, Charles continued to meet weekly with his friends who shared an interest in archaeology. Their evening discussions of anthropology books and plans for new archaeological exhibitions became more than a distraction from the woes of the economy. The weekly intellectual meetings were organic and the group eventually grew into the Literary and Scientific Society of Madisonville (LSSM). See appendix B.[21]

In addition to the professional community of Madisonville, Charles turned to his friends in the Jovial Fishing and Orpheus clubs. They sang, played instruments, and competed for prizes for the best music group at the annual Cincinnati Sängerfests and the biennial Cincinnati May Music Festivals. They regularly came to Charles's home in Madisonville to play chamber music.[22]

Charles's home was full of musical instruments including a piano, two four-string banjos, a mandolin, and the Furber violin, which was passed down to Charles from his father. Molly provided refreshments, which added to the enjoyment of their soirées. In a gesture of their appreciation, the musicians presented Charles and Molly with a handsome solid-walnut, hand-carved cabinet.[23]

American society during the late nineteenth century focused on music and self-education, especially in the disciplines of science and history. As a result, literary and scientific societies grew in popularity. They consisted of groups of professionals who met regularly to present papers on literary and scientific topics. These groups were quite productive and members would publish their papers in professional journals. Given that Charles was already meeting weekly with his friends to sing, play music, and to discuss the latest anthropology books, it seemed only natural to create a formal archaeological support group.[24]

On August 6, 1878, Charles read his paper, "The Prehistoric Monuments of the Little Miami Valley" at the annual meeting of the Cincinnati Society of Natural History. His presentation included a chart of all of the archaeological sites, which he and his friends had documented over the past seven years. Charles was subsequently elected a member of the society. He used his new membership to help expand his political connections with the scientific community of the greater Cincinnati area and rally their support for archaeological preservation efforts.[25]

Charles's paper was not only well received, it was published in October 1878 in *The Journal of the Cincinnati Society of Natural History*. This article was Charles's first professional publication in archaeology. It began by emphasizing that

> The aboriginal earthworks in this vicinity are so rapidly becoming more and more indistinct from the effects of continued cultivation, the elements, the leveling for building sites, and the carting away of others for the purpose of making fills and grades, that in a few more years their sites will be obliterated and forgotten.[26]

He concluded his paper by arguing, "To the archaeologist a complete and speedy examination of this whole valley is of the utmost importance."[27]

It is historically significant that Charles's first professional archaeological article attributes the construction of the earthworks in the Little Miami River valley to Americans Indians. Albeit published in a humble outlet, this conclusion was a scientifically daring move on Charles's part because it was diametrically opposed to the view of the Smithsonian Institution. Squier and Davis, just thirty years earlier, concluded that the earthworks were "engineered" by an ancient Caucasian civilization.[28]

Charles had worked closely in the field with Frank Langdon. He, like Charles, was well trained in human anatomy and physiology. There was nothing in their seven years of examining skeletal remains from archaeological sites the Little Miami River valley that would lead them to any conclusion other than the bones were from an indigenous population.

Charles and members of the newly found LSSM exhibited their collection of artifacts from the Little Miami River valley at the annual Cincinnati Exposition and stored them at the Odd Fellows Hall. During this time, his wife and children stayed at his in-laws' farm in Vera Cruz. Between September 19 and October 12, Charles wrote a number of letters to Molly from his home in Madisonville (see appendix A).

Aside from showing his love and devotion of family, the letters also illustrate his humble lifestyle. Everyday, Charles got up at dawn, drank a cup of coffee and ate bread and butter for breakfast. He consumed the same food and drink for lunch. Every other day he would add two boiled eggs to his menu. For dinner, Charles had a glass of milk and oatmeal crackers. Twice a week, he would have steak or oysters for dinner. However, he avoided fatty meat altogether. Every night, he was in bed by ten o'clock (see appendix A).

Initial meetings of the Literary and Scientific Society of Madisonville

Charles's recent publication and new affiliation with the Cincinnati Society of Natural History put him in contact with more people with mutual interests in archaeology. By November he was able to initiate the LSSM. The first meeting was held on the evening of November 12, 1878, in the home of attorney S. F. Covington in Madisonville. Charles defined the society's mission, "to promote the social, spiritual and moral welfare of the community at large, as well as to provide a feast of reason and a flow of soul."[29]

In addition to Charles and Covington, E. A. Conkling, R. O. Collis, Joseph Cox, Frank W. Langdon, Charles F. Low, and H. B. Whetsel were in attendance. They discussed the prospects of the new club and proposed a course of lectures that could be given at the upcoming winter meetings. After the business portion of the meeting, everyone was invited to examine artifacts, which Charles, Cox, Langdon, and Low had collected from archaeological sites in the Little Miami River valley. The newly formed group adjourned and agreed to meet the following Tuesday at the home of the honorable Joseph Cox.[30]

On Tuesday evening, November 19, 1878, the Literary and Scientific Society of Madisonville had their second meeting. In addition to those who were in attendance at the first meeting, Dr. G. N. Lasher, W. Rogers, Dr. R. Stanton, and Jason H. White joined them. After examining artifacts collected by Judge Cox, Charles F. Low read an original essay on the "Ceramics of the Prehistoric Races of North America."[31]

Low's presentation included a comparative collection of American Indian pottery from the Little Miami River valley, which he compared with ceramic artifacts from more distant archaeological sites. Charles also provided examples of local pottery types. While everyone was inspecting the artifacts, Mrs. Cox interceded with an invitation for everyone to examine her collection of pottery—plates and bowls filled with "appropriate viands." The food was quickly and joyfully consumed. The group agreed to meet the following week in the home of Judge Samuel F. Hunt and the meeting was adjourned.[32]

On the following Tuesday evening, November 26, 1878, Judge Hunt, gave a lecture on "Egypt and the Pyramids." His home was filled to capacity and the lecture was considered both interesting and inspiring. Because of the huge success of the meeting, Hunt presented Charles with a green-colored *ushabti*, also known as a *shabti* or *shawabti*. The ushabti was an Egyptian funerary figurine entombed with the deceased to supply work in the afterlife. In the beginning, meeting locations were rotated among the member's homes, but as the group grew in size and became more active in the field, the meetings shifted full time to Charles's office in Madisonville.[33]

The LSSM was now well established and growing. Charles appointed himself secretary. He wrote the society's bylaws and made longhand notes in a large ledger, which included the date of the meetings, an attendance list, locations of the meetings, and minutes (e.g., topics discussed, election of affairs, etc.). Charles made an attendance sheet and an index page for the minutes of the meetings as well as their archaeological field notes (see appendix B).

Among the members was Dr. Gustav Brühl. Like Charles, Brühl was a German-American medical doctor who was passionate about archaeology and anthropology. He visited archaeological sites across the western hemisphere, from Mexico to South America. As a physician, Brühl practiced at Saint Mary's Hospital in Cincinnati, Ohio, and served as a lecturer on laryngoscopy, the visual examination of a patient's vocal cords, at Miami Medical College. Brühl was the founder and president of the Peter Claver Society for the public education of African American children. He also served as the Democratic Ohio state treasurer.

One of Brühl's sons, Theodore, was a prominent Cincinnati attorney. He assisted his father with correspondence between Charles and Dr. Rudolf Ludwig Carl Virchow in Germany. Virchow founded *Zeitschrift für Ethnologie* (Journal of Ethnology), which was published by the German Anthropological Association and the Berlin Society for Anthropology, Ethnology and Prehistory. These organizations were just two of the many societies, which he founded.

Although Virchow considered himself a professional anthropologist, he was vehemently opposed to Darwinian evolution. In 1872 he presented evidence at the Berlin Society for Anthropology, Ethnology and Prehistory, which suggested that the Neanderthal-type specimen was nothing more than a recent bone pathology (i.e., a disease, which deforms or alters bone). This position was diametrically opposed to the evolutionary interpretations of Thomas Henry Huxley and Sir Charles Lyell. In the end, Virchow was discredited, as the specimen was shown to be about forty thousand years old.

In the day, the British Royal Society, the Prussian Academy of Sciences, and the Royal Swedish Academy of Sciences considered Virchow the foremost expert on bone pathologies. Therefore, Charles wanted Virchow to examine samples of ancient bone pathologies from archaeological sites in the Little Miami River valley.

Through Brühl and his son, Theodore, Charles sent comparative samples to Virchow. Charles also sent samples of charred maize (i.e., corn).

Charles believed that certain bone pathologies resulted from a diet high in the consumption of maize, which caused dietary malnutrition. It would be almost a century later until Charles's theory was confirmed (see appendix B).

Archaeological excavations in the Little Miami River valley

In addition to the weekly meetings, members of the LSSM began to help Charles conduct test excavations of the earthworks and mounds surrounding Phebe's Pottery Field. Under Charles's direction, the group hired Matthias Britten to assist with the digging. They began with Spice Bush Mound referred to as "Group A, Mound 5" in Charles's 1878 publication. Despite the unusually cold weather that year, they were able to dig through the autumn of 1878 and the winter of 1879.[34]

In March Charles had the group dig a trench, which extended from his Mound Group A and into Pottery Field in order to understand their relationship. On March 20, their trench reached Pottery Field and the true significance of the site was discovered. It was an American Indian cemetery. Charles Low quickly penned and mailed off a description of the site on behalf of the LSSM for J. T. Short's 1879, *The North Americans of Antiquity*, a nationally recognized archaeological publication.[35]

Charles wasted no time making a formal resolution in regard to Phebe Ferris's Pottery Field. The LSSM explorations of the property suggested that the American Indian cemetery was geographically extensive and voluminous. They found that the burials were "numerous and thickly grouped." This discovery was truly significant because previous archaeological mortuary features described from the Ohio Valley were defined almost solely on the basis of isolated remains or small groups of individuals interred in earthworks, mounds, or shell heaps. Charles initially named the site the Ferris Cemetery in honor of his dear friend Phebe.[36]

Given the significance of the site, members of the LSSM pooled their financial resources and took charge of excavations of the Ferris Cemetery with Charles listed as the site "superintendent." On April 1, 1879, they began exploring the southwestern slope of the site. By April 12 Charles

Low had gridded off the site so features could be mapped in and drawn in detail.[37]

On June 23 excavations expanded into the adjacent Spice Bush Woods, which was owned by the Stites family. They dug trenches through what Charles labeled in his 1878 publication, "Group A, Mound 8" as well as four nearby circular enclosures. In terms of the number of artifacts and mortuary features, they were meager at best.[38]

Given the poor returns on the money and time they had invested, excavations resumed on the Ferris Cemetery on July 7. The summer was very mild and the autumn had been especially warm, culminating in the second warmest October of all time with an average temperature about 62°F, more than 7°F above normal. Even the winter was warm compared to the previous year. Consequently, excavations continued steadily until January 1, 1880. Approximately 360 human skeletons were exhumed, as well as 176 cache pits exposed, and about 140 earthenware vessels were recovered from the forty-foot grid.[39]

The weekly results of their excavations were presented at their Tuesday evening meetings and carefully recorded by Charles in the society's minutes. In time, their fieldwork attracted the attention of local newspapers. The contents of these articles were also recorded in the society's ledger. This activity was exactly what Phebe Ferris had hoped for—a professional archaeological excavation on her estate.[40]

2.1 Front of the Metz family home located between 6111 and 6113 Madison Road, Madisonville, Hamilton County, Ohio, ca. 1872.

2.2 Back of the Metz family home located between 6111 and 6113 Madison Road, Madisonville, Hamilton County, Ohio, ca. 1872.

2.3 An ancient Egyptian ushabti gifted to Charles Louis Metz from Literary and Scientific Society of Madisonville member Judge Hunt on November 26, 1878.

CHAPTER 3

Frederick Ward Putnam and the Peabody Museum

IN ADDITION TO ATTRACTING the attention of local newspaper reporters, the publications of the LSSM attracted the attention of Dr. Frederick Ward Putnam, considered by many as the "Father of American Archaeology." On Tuesday evening, September 9, 1879, Professor Putnam attended the group's weekly meeting along with newcomers Drs. Gustav Brühl, R. M. Byrnes, and Howard H. Hill, and members of the Ferris and Stites families, archaeological site landowners.[1]

Putnam was no stranger to the Cincinnati area. His father, Ebenezer Putnam, was a successful Cincinnati commission merchant. In 1874 Putnam served as an assistant to the Kentucky Geological Survey located in nearby Lexington. At the time of the September 9 meeting, he was returning from his third year as a civilian assistant to the U.S. Engineers in their surveys of lands west of the 100th meridian.

Peabody Museum of Archaeology and Ethnology at Harvard University

Putnam attended the meeting of the LSSM in the capacity of curator of the Peabody Museum of Archaeology and Ethnology at Harvard University.

The Peabody Museum was the brainchild of Othniel Charles Marsh, a preeminent nineteenth-century vertebrate paleontologist from upstate New York. The concept of the museum occurred to him in October 1865 while excavating a burial mound near Newark, Ohio. Afterward, Marsh wrote a letter to his philanthropic uncle, urging him to provide Harvard with the funds needed to establish the museum.[2]

Marsh's uncle was none other than George Peabody, American financier, entrepreneur, and father of modern philanthropy. Marsh's mother, Mary, was Peabody's younger sister. In 1866 George Peabody acted on Marsh's suggestion and donated $150,000 to Harvard University to establish the Peabody Museum.[3]

Jeffries Wyman was appointed the Peabody Museum's first curator and later Harvard's Hersey Professor of Anatomy. During his tenure, Wyman focused his archaeological research on shell mounds along the beaches of Florida's Atlantic coast and the banks of St. John's River. He is best known for his detailed documentation of their complex stratigraphy and pioneering work in American forensic anthropology.[4]

Wyman died unexpectedly in 1874 from what was diagnosed as a pulmonary hemorrhage, an acute and catastrophic event. Asa Gray was appointed as Wyman's replacement as "Curator *pro tern.*" Gray made it perfectly clear to Harvard that he did not want to assume the administration of the museum. Frederick Ward Putnam, who had worked with Wyman in the field, was appointed curator of the Peabody Museum in 1875, a position he held for thirty-four years, when he became honorary curator and, from 1913 to the time of his death, an honorary director.[4]

Frederick Ward Putnam

Despite the longevity of Putnam's position at the Peabody Museum, he was neither an archaeologist nor an anthropologist by training. Indeed, Putnam was a zoologist and a productive one at that. From the age of sixteen, Putnam published papers on ornithology and ichthyology. His first position, between 1856 and 1861, was curator of Ornithology in the Essex Institute of Salem. While at the Essex Institute, his curatorial responsibilities changed to include mammalogy in 1862, ichthyology (i.e., the scientific study of fish) in 1863, and all vertebrates between 1864 and 1867.[5]

In the years between 1864 and 1870, Putnam also served as the superintendent and director of the Essex Institute, curator of Ichthyology for the Boston Society of Natural History, and superintendent of the Museum East Indian Marine Society in Salem, Massachusetts. In other words, by the time Putnam arrived at the Peabody Museum, he was no stranger to the responsibilities of a curator or an institutional administrator.[6] In addition to Putnam's administration skills, he was also a prolific scholar. While at the Essex Institute, Putnam published more than fifty articles on amphibians, birds, fossils, insects, mammals, and reptiles. In 1866 he also began tinkering in anthropology. His interest in archaeology began when he serendipitously found burned earth and pottery among an accumulation of shell and fish bones.[7]

Putnam's first paper, "On an Indian grave on Winter Island, Salem, Massachusetts" was published in 1866 in the *Proceedings of the Boston Society of Natural History*. It was one of the earliest reported prehistoric American Indian mortuary features. While Putnam never lost his interest in ichthyology, it was clear that anthropology and archaeology had piqued his interests. He continued to aggressively write articles on a wide variety of topics in natural history, but Putnam also published at least one archaeology paper per year.[8]

Putnam's eclectic publication record and administrative experience led him to the director of the Museum of the Peabody Academy of Sciences, a position, which he held between 1869 and 1873. This experience made him a natural for Wyman's replacement at the Peabody Museum. As the new curator, Putnam quickly shifted his full-time interests to anthropology and archaeology.[9]

The later part of the nineteenth century saw great progress in American archaeology thanks largely to the efforts of Putnam. Perhaps his most important contribution was in the training of professional archaeologists. He became known as the "professionalizer of American archaeology." At the time Putnam first met Charles they both were well-read, self-taught archaeologists, and relative newcomers to the field. While Charles had far more archaeology field and exhibition experience, Putnam had the financial backing of the Peabody Museum and the academic clout of Harvard University. Each of them had something that the other wanted, and needed. Putnam had the academic credentials and East Coast cachet and Charles had access to one of the most important archaeological sites in eastern North America.[10]

In addition to the archaeological quid pro quo, Charles and Putnam felt strongly that American Indians had been in the Ohio Valley since the Ice Age and they both had fire in their bellies to prove it beyond a reasonable doubt. Therefore, it is not surprising that Charles and Putnam became close friends despite the fact they were political opposites—Metz a staunch Republican and Putnam a faithful Democrat.[11]

Putnam funded excavations in Trenton, New Jersey, in 1876, which produced what appeared to be European-like Paleolithic tools in a layer of gravel dating to the last Ice Age. Unfortunately, the work did not prove whether or not artifacts had found their way into the glacial gravels through natural geological processes such as slumping, overturning trees, and decaying roots. He was hopeful, however, that more convincing evidence could be found in the Little Miami River valley because of the abundant and well-preserved terraces, which dated to the last Ice Age.[12]

As a museum curator, Putnam appreciated the care that members of the LSSM took in documenting artifact provenience (i.e., the three-dimensional location), provenance (i.e., source of the raw material), and their ability to use this information for public exhibitions. Putnam presented Charles with a copy of *Grave-mounds and their contents: a manual of archaeology, as exemplified in the burials of the Celtic, the Romano-British, and the Anglo-Saxon periods* published in 1870. It was an invaluable addition to Charles's archaeology library because it provided detailed guidance on the excavation of both burial mounds and mortuary features.

In the autumn of 1878, Charles and members of the LSSM created an archaeological exhibition for the annual Cincinnati Industrial Exposition. Their artifacts, maps, and archaeological site models were displayed in the new Music Hall complex, first opened for the 1878 May Music Festival. The 1879 exposition was held in the new north and south wings, Machinery Hall and Art Hall respectively.

Charles attended the exposition with his close friends Matthias Britten and Charles Low. The last day of the exposition was October 9, 1879, after which they moved their exhibit to the Grand Lodge of the Independent Order of Odd Fellows located on the northwest corner of Third and Walnut in downtown Cincinnati. From there, the artifacts were returned to members of the group.[13]

Theoretical opposition

While Charles's archaeological research suggested that the earthworks, mounds, and village sites in the Little Miami River valley were created by the ancestors of the Shawnee, there were still people who were willing to challenge him, and in the press! In 1879 former Gen. M. F. Force published a thin book, *Some Early Notices of the Indians of Ohio: To What Race Did The Mound Builders Belong?* Force revived the Mound Builder debate arguing that they were an extensive civilization in Ohio that extended from Worthington, Ohio, to the Ohio River down the Great Miami River basin across to Portsmouth and back up the Scioto River valley to Worthington. Within this great triangle, Force believed that there were ancient defensive forts connected by what he called hilltop "signal mounds," which were in sight of one another. He argued that a message from Worthington could be sent to the Ohio River in a matter of seconds or minutes. Force used the Norwood Mound as an example of a signal mound.

Force vehemently argued that the Mound Builders were not related to the historic Shawnee because they were nomadic and there was no evidence that they built mounds. Instead, Force suggested that the Mound Builders flourished at the time of Charlemagne and were almost completely annihilated in a war with the Iroquois to the north. He believed that remnants of the Mound Builders divided themselves into two opposing groups with Illinois and Indiana being swept clean by warfare and the Ohio Mound Builders defended themselves with enclosures until they collapsed or fled southward. Force believed that the Cherokees, Creeks, and Choctaws took in those who retreated southward. The result was the creation of mounds in the southeastern United States, especially along the Gulf of Mexico.

The juxtaposition of theories between Force and members of the LSSM paralleled the competition between Harvard University's Peabody Museum and the Smithsonian Institute. While they were both seeking to discover the secrets of the Mound Builders, their interpretations of the data were dramatically different.

As a true scientist, Charles always kept an open mind. While he knew the archaeology of the Little Miami River better than anyone, Charles had no first-hand experience with the earthworks and mounds surrounding the Gulf of Mexico. Could Force's theories be right? In order to properly evaluate their relationship with the archaeology of Little Miami River valley, he traveled to Florida. In the spring of 1880, Charles visited the mounds described by Force and examined artifacts from the area. As usual, he stayed in contact with his family through letters. At 7:00 p.m., on March 18, 1880, Charles wrote Molly an affectionate letter from Macon, Georgia (see appendix A).

When Charles returned from Florida, he resumed excavation of the Ferris Cemetery site. Matthias Britten and members of the Literary and Scientific Society of Madisonville continued to excavate within the forty-square-foot-grid that Charles Low staked off in the previous year using trees as the corners of the units. Excavations conducted prior to the establishment of the grid were assigned to a large single unit. This system allowed burials and other archaeological features to be mapped in detail.

Publications of the Literary and Scientific Society of Madisonville

In April 1880 the LSSM published the "Archaeological Explorations near Madisonville, Ohio" in the *Journal of the Cincinnati Society of Natural History.* It was prepared by Charles F. Low at the request of the "publishing committee." Other members of the committee included of Joseph Cox, Charles L. Metz, and Frank W. Langdon.

The publication gave a chronicled account of the excavation of mounds and earthworks during the previous year conducted under Charles's direction. It discussed the contexts and contents of Mounds 2, 3, 4, 5, and 6 in Group A referred to in Charles's 1878 publication, as well as the discovery of the Ferris Cemetery. The report provided the dates of excavations, names of the excavators, artifact and feature provenience locations, and weather conditions. It also illustrated site stratigraphy, skeletal positions, and key artifacts such as ceramic vessels and ground-stone pipes recovered from mortuary features and maize storage pits.

One of the more subtle but notable discoveries was that not all of the earthworks and mounds were constructed for the purpose of human interment. Charles found that one of the mounds in Group A was composed entirely of sand. While the sand was locally obtained, the earthwork was likely constructed for symbolic or ceremonial purposes.

Because of the detailed reporting of the previous year's fieldwork to the Cincinnati Society of Natural History, they agreed to help fund the 1880 excavations. With this additional source of money, fieldwork was able to continue throughout the year until December 18. Charles focused on excavation "Block 12." Ultimately, it contained 239 human skeletons, about 170 cache-pits, and 75 earthenware vessels. A suite of archaeological features called "kitchen middens" were also discovered in the heads of nearby ravines.[14]

The kitchen middens were defined as refuse heaps composed of animal bones of all sizes, the shells of edible mollusks, broken pottery, and implements. Middens were thought to be the trash of past habitations. This discovery added a new dimension to the site. It suggested that some of the bodies were interred in the same areas that trash was discarded.

Where and how someone is buried and what he or she is buried with can be viewed in terms of "fossilized terminal status." In other words, while a person's station in life may change through time, death marks the termination of social status. Thus, the location of a grave and its contents provide a fossilized social status.[15]

If a person is buried in the trash, then it might suggest that he or she had a lower station in life. On the other hand, if a person died in the coldest months of winter when the ground was frozen solid, burial in a trash heap may have been more pragmatic. Decomposing organic matter keeps the ground warm and it is easy to dig in year round. If a grave is covered in trash, or a refuse pit disturbed a grave, then it might suggest that the burial population was different than the people discarding their trash.

Despite Charles's obligations to the excavation of the Ferris Cemetery and his medical practice, he took time to help out and care for his aging in-laws. On June 29, 1880, Charles wrote Molly from her parent's farm in Vera Cruz, Ohio. Eight months later, Charles and Molly's first son was born on February 7, 1881. He was christened Charles Wilbur Metz on February 13. Ferdinand Blasie and Anna Berger Schlotman agreed to be his godparents (see appendix A).

A return to Florida

By 1881 the LSSM had assembled a large number of shell artifacts from the Ferris Cemetery and the mounds and earthworks in the surrounding area. While freshwater mussels and snails were easily compared to those still living in the Little Miami and Ohio rivers, there were also many bivalve and gastropod shells that appeared to be marine in origin. One genus that caught Charles's attention was Busycon, whelks native to the Gulf of Mexico.

Charles remembered seeing similar whelks in the shell mounds and on the beaches of the Gulf Coast during his 1880 trip to Florida. In order to be certain, Charles again departed for Florida on March 17, 1881, but this time he was accompanied by Charles Low. The purpose of this trip was to make a comparative marine shell collection and reexamine the mounds of the area. As usual, Charles diligently wrote letters to his wife along the way (see appendix A).

On March 19 Charles and Low arrived in Macon, Georgia. They stepped out of the Union Passenger Depot and found the Brown's Hotel across the street. It stood on Fourth Street, today's Martin Luther King Jr. Boulevard, at Plum Street. While the hotel was built around 1856, it burned down in 1878 and had been recently rebuilt prior to their visit. Once Charles settled into his recently renovated room, he wrote another letter to Molly (see appendix A).

Charles and Low reached Jacksonville, Florida, on March 21, 1881, where they checked into the Duval Hotel located on the northwest corner of Forsyth and Hogan Streets. It was in a historic part of the town, near the place where Lewis Zachariah Hogans is said to have built the first homestead in Jacksonville. His house stood on Forsyth Street, immediately west of the Duval Hotel. Charles wrote another love letter to Molly from his hotel room, which also indicated an abundance of shells in the area (see appendix A).

Discontent and financial strain

When Charles returned to Ohio, he found members of the LSSM feeling the bodily and financial pressures of the sustained excavation of the Ferris Cemetery. Despite the significant archaeological discoveries from their fieldwork in the preceding years and the added financial support from the Cincinnati Society of Natural History, members of the LSSM had grown weary of archaeology. Furthermore, it was becoming clear to Charles that some of the members viewed archaeology more of a potential money-maker than a scientific or intellectual exercise. Rather than making money, the excavations were costing them money and much, much, more.[16]

This situation is not all that surprising given that archaeology is a physically demanding science. It also takes a great deal of time and money to conduct fieldwork, carefully make maps of the excavations, features, and artifact find-spots. Additionally, all of the artifacts and field data had to be processed the in the laboratory. Then there is an enormous commitment of time needed to write up the results for publication. If that is not enough, archaeology requires a profound emotional stamina. Archaeological theories and interpretations inevitably fall under the critical, and often scathing, scrutiny of peers and the public. Not all of the LSSM members had skins as thick or pockets as deep as Charles and Low.

To make matters worse, America was teetering on the edge of yet another economic depression, which lasted from March 1882 to May 1885. Railroad construction was on the decline resulting in weakened iron and steel industries. While this depression was not as severe as the economic downturn of 1873, it was nevertheless a hardship on Cincinnati businesses because prices for services and goods were dependent on the railroad.[17]

Charles was more than a little concerned. Without the financial and physical support of the LSSM, the excavations would have to be shut down. All of Charles's efforts to thoroughly document the Ferris Cemetery site were now threatened. He quickly turned to his friend Frederick Ward Putnam who agreed to visit the site. Somewhat relieved, Charles decided to spend some time helping his in-laws with their wheat harvest. He wrote Molly a letter from their farm in Vera Cruz, Ohio, in the evening of June 27. In addition to giving her an update on his health and that of their extended family, Charles asked Molly if she had "noticed the comet in the northern sky" (see appendix A).

In the dark countryside of Vera Cruz, Charles was able to see the Great Comet of 1881, discovered by John Tebbutt, an amateur astronomer in Australia. It was the first comet in history to be photographed thanks to advances in photography, which used sensitive dry gelatin plates. Thus, its discovery on May 22, 1881, made it into newspapers around the world. In the dark nighttime countryside of Vera Cruz, Ohio, Charles was able to first see the comet on the evening of June 22, 1881. It was greenish in color, except the core, which was yellow and seemed to change to orange in time.[18]

Putnam returns to Cincinnati

Charles returned to Cincinnati in time to meet Putnam in July 1881. He was genuinely impressed with the excavation of the Ferris Cemetery site and the sheer volume of artifacts and human skeletal remains it had produced. Putnam made suggestions to Charles, Charles Low, and Frank Langdon on how best to document them. He also put them in contact with Lucien Carr, who also advised them on the best metric data to collect from the human skeletal remains. Putnam promised Charles that the Peabody Museum would provide enough funding to ensure that excavations could continue. He said the money could be used to purchase equipment and hire workers to do the digging. However, Putnam added the stipulation that Harvard would acquire all of the notes, artifacts, and human skeletal remains in exchange for the funding. Charles readily agreed.

Putnam returned to Cincinnati in September to make sure all was going well. He was pleased to learn that the additional funding from Harvard allowed Charles to excavate at the site through the autumn. The trip also allowed Putnam to collect the first installment of artifacts, human remains, field notes, and maps from the 1881 field season. E. A. Conkling, Charles Metz, P. P. Lane, and Charles Low presented Putnam with additional specimens from the site for the Peabody Museum's collection.

1881 publications

In October 1881 "The Madisonville Pre-Historic Cemetery: Anthropological Notes" was published in the *Journal of the Cincinnati Society of Natural History*. While Frank Langdon is listed as the author, it was prepared together with Charles and Charles Low and edited by Putnam and Carr of the Peabody Museum. It is important to note that this publication is the first time the name "Madisonville" was used for the Ferris Cemetery site.

The article presented detailed descriptions and measurements of the human bones so they could be compared to specimens from other archaeological sites and known tribes. It also discussed and illustrated significant bone pathologies from disease and malnutrition. Perhaps the most interesting pathologies resulted from trauma. Langdon presented direct evidence of violence, perhaps warfare. There were numerous examples of cranial trauma from strong blows to the head, broken bones, arrowheads embedded in bone, and a skullcap carved into a bowl.

Langdon's article was closely followed by Charles's *magnum opus*, "The Prehistoric Monuments of Anderson Township, Hamilton County, Ohio" published in the December issue of the *Journal of the Cincinnati Society of Natural History*. It was the culmination of all his years of archaeological fieldwork in the lower Little Miami River valley. The publication documented the exact location of earthen mounds, stone mounds, earthen enclosures, stone enclosures, "circumvallation" earthworks, prehistoric campsites, village sites, cemeteries, and workshops. It was accompanied by a detailed map, which used the international archaeological symbols of the day. The paper also noted the geographical errors of previous archaeologists who had published reports about this region. This publication became the foundation for all future archaeological work in the area.

Once again, Charles passionately expressed his concerns that archaeological sites in the Little Miami River valley were being "destroyed by curiosity-hunters who have no other object or desire seemingly than to destroy that which, to the archaeologist and ethnologist, is of the greatest importance." As with all of the LSSM publications, it was a group effort. William Archer and Charles Low helped Charles with the drafting of the map and Frank Langdon helped with the editing. Notwithstanding all of these significant contributions to Ohio Valley archaeology, future fieldwork was going to proceed under guidance of Frederick Ward Putnam and under the auspices of the Peabody Museum.

Putnam's protégé

Charles was eager to become Putnam's protégé. Together, they planned the 1882 summer excavations at the Ferris Cemetery site, but now they were going to be under the auspices of Harvard's Peabody Museum. Unfortunately, some of the members of the LSSM did not take this new alliance well. Instead of embracing the new East Coast academic sponsorship, funding, and additional help in the field, disgruntled members began to sell artifacts from the site.[19]

Ultimately, large collections from the Ferris Cemetery were sold to the Cincinnati Art Museum, the Cincinnati Museum of Natural History, and the Smithsonian Institution. Smaller collections were also sold to other museums across the country and around the world. This situation was

Phebe Ferris's worst nightmare coming true. To make matters worse, Charles had promised her from the start that artifacts from the site would not be sold for profit. Unfortunately, it was a promise that he was unable to keep.[20]

Putnam arrived at the Ferris Cemetery site on May 2, 1882, and excavated with Charles until May 16. During this time he opened a large trapezoidal-shaped excavation on the extreme eastern margin of the Ferris property. This excavation square later became known as the "Putnam block." Charles made a map of the excavation, which exposed eight burial features and a number of maize storage pits. Putnam and Charles also re-examined the earthen enclosures on the Stites' property, northeast of the Ferris Cemetery.[21]

Before departing, Putnam asked Charles to change the focus of his archaeological fieldwork to a group of earthworks and mounds located on the Turner family farm seven kilometers (about four miles) immediately east and upstream from the Ferris Cemetery site. He also requested that Charles and Charles Low write periodically to keep him informed about their progress and findings. They were more than happy to comply with Putnam's request because the earthworks and mounds were sitting on top of a rich sand and gravel deposit and aggregate miners were eager to acquire the property. If the earthworks and mounds were not salvaged soon, then their contents would be lost forever.

The Turner site

The Turner site was a complex of geometric earthworks, mounds, and village, which covered more than 165 hectares (407 acres) on the eastern side of a shallow crossing of the Little Miami River, less than thirteen kilometers (eight miles) from the Ohio River confluence, in Anderson Township, Hamilton County, Ohio. Despite its location and large size, the Turner site was completely overlooked by Squier and Davis in their 1848 publication, *Ancient Monuments of the Mississippi Valley*.[22]

All of the maps and site data published by Squier and Davis of archaeological sites in southwestern Ohio were actually reproductions of Gen. William Henry Lytle's surveys made during the late eighteenth and early nineteenth centuries. Charles knew that Lytle's surveys missed the site because his primary interests were hilltop earthworks, which resembled military fortifications.[23]

Despite the fact that Lytle, Squier, and Davis missed the site completely, Turner had been subsequently surveyed during the first half of the nineteenth century. Unfortunately, the exact locations, dimensions, and orientations of the earthworks, mounds, and village were obfuscated by a plethora of geographic errors. In 1839 the first geographic dimensions of the Turner site complex were reported by T. C. Day in *The Antiquities of the Miami Valley*.[24]

Day described the Turner site as an earthen "fort" carved from the third alluvial bottom, enclosing approximately four acres with an internal earthen wall about three feet in height and two hundred yards in diameter, and an eastern opening thirty-six yards wide bounded by two semicircular ditches—a northern ditch five hundred feet long and a southern ditch two hundred feet long, both eighty feet wide at the top, forty feet wide at the bottom, thirty feet deep, and free of vegetation. Day was particularly impressed by a "causeway" three hundred feet long and one hundred feet wide gradually descending from the fort to the alluvial bottom with a partial earthen wall approximately seven feet high, forty feet wide, and seventy-five feet long at the base.[25]

In 1850 Charles Whittlesey published a map of the earthworks and mounds in his *Descriptions of Ancient Works in Ohio*. Whittlesey labeled Day's fort "earthwork A" and called his causeway a "turnpike" and labeled it "earthwork g." He also mapped a mound within earthwork A, which he labeled "c," a cluster of six mounds two to four feet high labeled "m," two earthen walls labeled "f" and "t," and a circular enclosure labeled "earthwork B."[26]

Charles was troubled by the fact many of Whittlesey's measurements differed from Day's. For example, Whittlesey measured the diameter of earthwork A as approximately 470 feet, the turnpike (earthwork g, Day's causeway) as 600 feet in length, and he also described an internal "drain or gutter," illustrated in his cross-sections a-b and c-d.[27]

In July 1878 Charles resurveyed Day's fort, Whittlesey's earthwork A, and found discrepancies in their measurements (e.g., 39 feet in height, 625 feet in basal circumference). Charles also noted that Whittlesey wrongly plotted the Turner group of earthworks and mounds in Clermont County, Ohio, and "erroneously described" them "as being one mile north, instead of one mile east, of Newtown." Charles was the first archaeologist to correctly locate the earthworks and mounds in Anderson Township, Hamilton County, Ohio, and use the term "Turner" to describe them. He named the site after then property owner Michael Turner.[28]

In Charles's 1878 article, "The Prehistoric Monuments of the Little Miami Valley," he identified earthwork 1 enclosing a mound, Whittlesey's earthwork A, mound c, and turnpike g, a "circumvallation" earthwork labeled 2, and three of Whittlesey's cluster of six mounds labeled 3, 4, and 5. In his 1881 essay, "The Prehistoric Monuments of Anderson Township, Hamilton County, Ohio," Charles expanded the site boundaries to include two inhumations, a circular earthwork enclosing a mound labeled 23, a mound labeled 21, an elongated earthwork labeled 11, and two additional mounds labeled 10 and 22.[29]

Given all of the time Charles spent surveying and mapping the Turner site, he was anxious to begin excavations in the summer of 1882, which continued through the early winter. On August 30 Charles Low recorded in his field notebook that the dig produced "a large sheet of mica, a perforated sheet of copper (eight by four inches), and large quantities of pearl beads, copper scrolls [*sic*], spools, and shell beads." Similar artifacts were discovered a month later. On September 9 Charles wrote Putnam about the discovery of seven heat-damaged human shaped ceramic figurines, pottery with the "image of fish or alligator," many fragments of mica, a copper bracelet, and small copper beads all "found in a circular depression" (see appendix B).

On October 6 Charles wrote Putnam another letter about their progress at the Turner site. The letter included a sketch of what he believed to be an "altar" showing a coffin-like box. The altar was a mortuary feature today known as Hopewell crematory basins. On October 23, 1882, Charles entered in his field notes that several other altars had been found—one almost two and a half feet in length and more than a foot and a half wide. He reported another one about three feet wide and two feet deep. Charles also found a skeleton in one of the altars.[30]

By November 6 Charles reported to Putnam that he had begun to excavate what he called "the Whittlesey mound." Charles hired Mr. Hosbrook, a civil engineer, make a plat map of the entire site. He reported that the weather was delightful—dry and warm—and without frost. Charles also noted that the peas were in bloom and "altogether we are having a remarkable autumn."

On November 18 Charles provided Putnam with a detailed report on the Whittlesey enclosure. By November 26 Charles had alerted Putnam that they had completed their 1882 field season. The letter also included an accounting of his monthly expenses (see appendix B).

The Turner and Ferris Cemetery excavations made it apparent to Putnam that Charles could direct multiple concurrent archaeological projects in addition to caring for his family and patients. It was now time to expand their archaeological surface surveys and excavations to other locations in the Little Miami River valley.[31]

3.1. An exotic, shell tempered, Mississippian vessel (beaker) excavated by Charles Louis Metz from the Madisonville site (Ferris Cemetery), ca. 800 to 1600 C.E.

3.2. Brass magnifying glass used by Charles Louis Metz to examine artifacts and read small print.

CHAPTER 4

The Cost of Archaeology

In 1883 Putnam wanted Charles to continue his investigation of the earthworks and mounds of the Turner site, but he also wanted him to begin examining the other archaeological sites reported in his 1881 publication. For Charles, this was a great opportunity to conduct a systematic and spatial comparison of archaeological sites in the Little Miami River valley. He believed different sites served different functions. Some of the sites were likely used for ceremonies, others as habitations, and some for mortuary activities. As in the years before, Charles diligently kept Putnam informed about his 1883 fieldwork. Charles's letters provided Putnam with a first-person view of the discoveries from the perspective of the excavator (see appendix B).

Initiation of the 1883 field season was delayed by a devastating flood, which began on February 11. It shut down the railway and freight businesses. The Northern Railroad Freight Depot in Cincinnati was inundated. Between thirty thousand and forty thousand people lost their jobs and the city had to borrow one hundred thousand dollars from the Ohio legislature. Property damage was estimated to be in the millions of dollars.

The Little Miami River valley archaeological survey

By February 21 the floodwaters receded and Charles and his crew began to examine the earthworks and mounds along the Little Miami River. He diligently recorded his findings, documenting their progress in a series of notes and letters. On March 16 Charles sent Putnam a letter confirming the discovery of a "mass of iron" from Mound Number 4 (see appendix B).

The mass of iron turned out to be one of the more interesting discoveries at the Turner site. It was meteoric in origin. The mineral composition of the artifact was identical to the meteoric iron found in the Hopewell Mounds suggesting they were from the same meteor fall.

In addition to the Turner site, Charles began an exploration of Hahn Field located on the Little Miami River almost directly across from the Ferris Cemetery. While both sites contained shell tempered pottery, the decorations, handles, and shapes were dissimilar. Also the settings of the two sites were quite different. The Ferris Cemetery sat atop a high terrace and the Hahn Field site was on a small rise in the floodplain. While both sites contained European trade goods such as Spanish iron, the Hahn Field site was dominated by shell-tempered pottery and triangular arrowheads that were stylistically different than those found at the Ferris Cemetery.[1]

On April 15, 1883, Charles reported to Putnam that he found a large copper earring perhaps two and a half or three inches in diameter. He also discussed plans to excavate a "mound located in the great work above Milford." Charles was referring to the Milford Earthworks originally described by Squier and Davis in 1848 (see appendix B).

Charles's continuing fieldwork in the Little Miami River valley began to positively impact local attitudes about American Indians. His enthusiasm for American Indian culture had become contagious in Cincinnati and beyond. It created a synergy of enthusiasm about American Indians, especially among the German-American community.

Buffalo Bill in Cincinnati

Buffalo Bill Cody and his Wild West, Rocky Mountain, and Prairie Exhibition rolled into town on June 2, 1883. Cody set up his Wild West reenactment on the Bank Street Grounds located on the corner of Bank Street and McLaren Avenue. It was a field used by the Cincinnati Red Stockings, an American Association baseball team. The Wild West show was a welcome break for baseball fans as the team was in third place, five games behind the Philadelphia Athletics.[2]

Cody's crew quickly transformed the baseball field into "a small but complete picture of Western life." A whitewashed fence was set up in the infield for horse racing. Eight bison, a herd of elk, Texas longhorn steers, and Mexican burros were allowed to roam within the enclosure. Cooking and dining tents were located in right field and Plains tipis filled center field.[3]

Charles took a break from his fieldwork to take his family to see Cody's show. They waited in the hot summer sun for almost two hours to get tickets. Sharpshooter Dr. William Frank Carver and horseback rider Buck Taylor joined Cody as stars of the show. The Metz family watched attentively as Carver and Cody exhibited their skills with a gun by breaking glass balls thrown into the air. Cody himself broke two with one shot. Taylor rode around the arena on a wall-eyed calico horse. As the band played, the Metz family watched almost four hours as dozens of Lakota and Pawnee rode, shot, and whooped their way around the Bank Street Grounds. The "warring savages," as they were called, wearing eagle feathers and painted faces attacked the real Deadwood stagecoach and "heroic" cowboys.[4]

Cody's Wild West show glorified Manifest Destiny and justified the suppression of American Indians in the name of population growth and westward expansion. While the controlled chaos was wildly entertaining, it created a negative American Indian stereotype. It was diametrically opposed to the image Charles wanted the public to have about the beloved people he spent so much time studying. However, like other German-American families, the Metz's cherished any chance to see American Indians.

Fieldwork resumes

Following Cody's Wild West Show, Charles resumed work at the Sand Ridge site as well as writing progress reports to Putnam. On June 6, 1883, he wrote a letter to Putnam about an important discovery at the Ferris Cemetery site by his close colleague H. B. Whetsel. It was a "copper cross." Although it was unknown at the time whether it was manufactured from European or North American copper, the symbol of a crucifix suggested contact with a Roman Catholic Jesuit priest. Charles also added that he had recovered numerous pieces of mica and fifteen copper beads strung with buckskin near the head of an individual at the Turner site (see appendix B).

On June 23 Charles wrote another letter to Putnam about his explorations of the Camden earthworks and burial mound. He included a report and illustration of the mound's structure. Of particular interest was Charles's description of a spool-shaped copper earring found in direct association with a small child. By accident, one of them fell to the floor exposing the ornament's interior. Charles closely examined the broken earring and found that it had been manufactured by hammering sheet copper around a wooden preform, which remained inside the ornament. His letter represents the first detailed description of the manufacture of Hopewell spool-shaped copper earrings (see appendix B).

On July 2 Charles wrote a letter to Putnam about the administration of the Cowden estate, which included the Fort Ancient burial mounds, earthworks, and villages. He suggested that it was valued at about five thousand dollars and less than the heirs of the estate had been asking for the property. Charles also let Putnam know that artifacts from the burial mounds at the Sand Ridge site were on their way to the Peabody Museum. Among the specimens were two small bone fishhooks. Charles's letter was followed by a detailed report of the Sand Ridge site excavations (see appendix B).

Charles's July 20 letter to Putnam included a report on the Sand Ridge site. It concluded that the site was different, yet similar, to both the Ferris Cemetery and the Turner site. The Sand Ridge site pottery was better made than specimens from the Turner site, but not as well made as that from the Ferris Cemetery. The pottery from the Turner site was tempered with crushed volcanic and metamorphic rock, while the pottery from Sand Ridge was manufactured with crushed limestone. The pottery from the Ferris Cemetery was tempered with crushed mussel shell. Although there was no way to determine exactly how old the sites were, it seemed to Charles as if the different pottery types represented different stages of technological development (see appendix B).

On July 22 Charles wrote a letter to Putnam about his chance meeting with Henry A. Shepherd, "an attorney-at-law residing at Hillsboro, Ohio." At the time, Shepherd, was working on a new book, *Popular History of the State of Ohio*. He explained to Charles that the book was going to focus on the "antiquities of the state of Ohio" and include full descriptions, illustrations, and maps of the earthworks of the Mound Builders as well as their burial mounds, cemeteries, defensive fortifications, sacred enclosures, and tombs. Shepherd wanted to include Charles's archaeological discoveries in the Little Miami River valley. The book was eventually published in 1887 and reprinted in 1889 and 1890 by J. C. Yorston and Company in Cincinnati (see appendix B).

By August 13 Charles had moved his excavations one mile downstream near the mouth of the Little Miami River, an area known then as Stites Grove. The site was named after Benjamin Stites who purchased the land from John Cleves Symmes. He acquired all of the land between the Little Miami and Great Miami rivers from Congress in 1792, also known as the Miami Purchase. Charles reported to Putnam on August 15 that he had discovered ground stone artifacts including a gorget and two pestles, ceramic vessels, and a stone pipe. Although it was not known at the time, the site was near the location of a historic Algonquian village inhabited by the Delaware and Shawnee (see appendix B).

Eleventh Cincinnati Industrial Exposition

Charles took a break from fieldwork in order to participate in the Eleventh Cincinnati Industrial Exposition held in Music Hall between September 5 and October 6. He was awarded a silver medal for his educational display of comparative artifacts from the Little Miami River valley. The Board of Trade, Chamber of Commerce, and Ohio Mechanics Institute presented it to him.[5]

During the exposition, Charles led an "Archaeological Exploration Party," which included Frederick Ward Putnam, Douglas Putnam, and Charles Low to examine the earthworks and mounds in the Scioto River valley. Charles sent Molly postcards from Bainbridge, Ohio, on September 19, and from Chillicothe, Ohio, on September 20, 1883. He wrote Molly that they had "arrived, stopping at the Albright House. This afternoon we go to Hopetown. My lungs are becoming fuller and I breathe very much easier than I did" (see appendix A).

Return to the Turner site

Following the exposition, Charles returned to his fieldwork at the Turner site. On October 22, he wrote a letter to Putnam about the discovery of "an extensive hearth beneath which were six furnaces or ovens" in Turner Mound Number 3. Charles believed the features were used to cremate human remains. The cremation of a human body requires a prolonged and extremely high-temperature fire to remove soft tissue and leave behind only fragments of mineral bone and teeth (see appendix B).

Charles wrote a series of letters to Putnam between October 29 and November 18 concerning the remarkable crematory features at the Turner site. Charles believed that in addition to open-air cremation, American Indians created more elaborate crematories with large arches, which appeared to have served as flues or chimneys. He sent Putnam samples of the mica and bone-filled ash from the features. Mica is a mineral, which remains stable at temperatures as high as 900°C (1,650°F). This property was undoubtedly an important aspect of its use in mortuary ceremonies, perhaps as an allegory for an immortal life force (see appendix B).

In order to maintain the relentless fieldwork, Charles had to dip into his personal funds to make sure that the workers were paid. At one point, Charles found himself in a bit of a panic because he was spending more than he was earning. He asked Putnam for a short-term loan of five hundred dollars to keep the fieldwork going. Putnam did not hesitate to help Charles and ensure that the work proceeded uninterrupted (see appendix B).

Once Charles was able to recoup the money from his medical practice, he repaid Putnam. As a gesture of thanks for the prompt repayment of the loan, Putnam sent Charles a rare copy of the *Transactions of the American Antiquarian Society, Volume 1* published in 1820. He inscribed it on the first page, "To Dr. C. L. Metz Madisonville Ohio from the Peabody Museum Cambridge Mas. F. W. Putnam Curator of the Museum Nov. 1883."

Charles was deeply touched by Putnam's gift and inspired to continue fieldwork through the end of the year. On December 2 Charles wrote a letter to Putnam describing yet another important discovery at the Turner site. By excavating Turner Mound Number 3 in cross-section, Charles was able to determine that it was "composed of from six to eight small mounds. These small mounds were eventually covered over forming one large tumulus." Each of the individual mounds contained "a scatter of charcoal and ashes" and "numerous pieces of burned human bones" (see appendix B).

The 1883 field season was a huge success. Charles had discovered a variety of American Indian mortuary features and expanded the geographic range of his archaeological survey. However, the financial demands of a prolonged survey and multiple excavations were growing at a rate, which exceeded the available funding. To make matters worse, the country was falling deeper into a prolonged recession.

Krakatoa, the flood, and panic of 1884

On August 27, 1883, a series of catastrophic volcanic explosions on the island of Krakatoa sent ash twenty-seven kilometers (seventeen miles) into the atmosphere. The eruption caused the average summer temperatures in the Little Miami River valley to fall more than 2°F and create severe winters, which lasted until 1888. Thus, the winter of 1883/84 was raw and brutal.

The resulting severe arctic outbreak sent temperatures down to -10°F with more than ten days of temperatures below 0°F. The ground and all bodies of water were frozen solid. These conditions brought fieldwork at the Turner site to a halt. In the warmth of his home in Madisonville, Charles wrote Putnam a letter on January 20, 1884, updating him about his field crew and their salaries.

Archaeological fieldwork did not stop Charles and Molly from expanding their family. On Tuesday, January 29, 1884, Charles and Molly's daughter, Beatrice Amelia, was born. Had Florence survived, Beatrice would have been their fourth daughter. Charles and Molly were now a family of six with four children living at home—Beatrice, a newborn; Charles Wilbur, age three; Clara Isabel, age seven; and Anna Teresa, age thirteen.

Beatrice was born into troubled times. Not long after her birth, the Ohio River and its tributaries—the Great and Little Miami rivers—began to rise as a result of rapidly melting snow and ice on top of rain. By Saturday, February 23, Cincinnati was inundated by the Ohio River at an unprecedented height of seventy-one feet above the low-water mark and five feet higher than the flood of 1883. Large numbers of people were homeless and without a way to stay warm.[6]

To complicate the extreme weather problems created by the eruption of Krakatoa, Cincinnati, the United States, and Europe were in an economic panic and still reeling from the depression of 1873. By 1884 Europe had completely depleted their gold reserves. The U.S. Treasury allowed the national banks in New York to halt all of their investments and call in all of their outstanding loans. More than ten thousand investment firms failed.[7]

In Cincinnati, high unemployment and a high crime rate combined with extremely poor working conditions and a corrupt local government exacerbated the economic downturn of 1884. On March 27 a guilty cold-blooded killer, William Berner, was convicted of manslaughter instead of murder in the first degree. Given the corruption in the criminal justice system of the time, popular opinion was that this murderer would walk away free and clear. This situation was intolerable to the citizens of Cincinnati.[8]

On Friday, March 28, one of the worst riots in American history erupted in response to the corruption. More than ten thousand people faced the Ohio National Guard. They shot into the crowd killing five protesters. In response to the killings, the protesters set fire to the Hamilton County courthouse on Saturday, March 29. They also prevented the fire department from reaching the burning building. The courthouse was a total loss. The protesters then began to loot and destroy businesses in the area. The National Guard responded by shooting to death fifty-one protesters and injuring more than three hundred others. By Sunday, March 30, the National Guard had retaken control of the city.[9]

The economic panic of 1884 and the protest riots downtown made it difficult for Charles to conduct archaeological fieldwork in the spring of 1884. In a letter to Putnam on April 22, Charles noted that he felt "broken down considerably . . . by continued exposure to the weather and loss of sleep."

Charles also wrote Putnam that he had brought his mother from Springfield, Ohio, to his home in Madisonville. At the time she was suffering from a terminal cancer. If that was not bad enough, Charles's mother-in-law had come to visit his mother, took ill, and died in his home on Sunday, April 13, 1884. In spite of these troubles, Charles managed to include in the letter "a sketch with accurate measurements" of a burial mound with "encircling walls of the (mound) group" (see appendix B).

Working with the Smithsonian Institution

For a brief episode Charles's relationship with Putnam was strained as artifact collections from his excavations started to show up for sale at other institutions. Some of Charles's field workers, as well as disgruntled members of the LSSM, were selling artifacts and collections to museums behind his back. Furthermore, they were claiming that Charles had collected the artifacts firsthand.

Putnam wrote a letter to Charles about this situation. On July 25, 1884, Charles responded. Charles emphasized,

> I never signed any paper or authorized any person whatever to sign my name to anything and should the S.I. (Smithsonian Institution) people have my name signed to any circular or paper in regard to the matter in question it is a fraud. There is no other man by the name of Metz that is engaged in archaeology in this part of the state (see appendix B).

Charles knew that his old colleague Judge Cox had gone to Washington D.C. and met with representatives of the Smithsonian Institution two weeks earlier and discussed his fieldwork with Charles at the Turner site. Charles wrote, "the Judge is the only man that I feel anxious about for he may act as an escort" (see appendix B).

Charles did admit to Putnam that he had written a letter to Spencer Fullerton Baird who had been serving as the second secretary of the Smithsonian Institution since 1878. Charles wrote Baird that he had a collection of artifacts from the Turner site and said,

> it was for sale and told him what I had in it and also told him that there were only two collections of similar bones and horn implements from the same locality and they were in the Peabody Museum and the other in the Society of Natural History of Cincinnati (see appendix B).

Aside from explaining his dealings with the Smithsonian Institution, Charles updated Putnam on their access to the Sand Ridge, Stites Grove, Turner, and Turpin sites. However, These archaeological matters were dwarfed by the loss of Charles's beloved mother, Babette. She died on July 28, 1884, just three days after penning his letter to Putnam. She was only sixty-five years old.

Once again, Charles turned to archaeology to help him grieve for his loss. He quickly made plans to study the Milford earthworks and mounds described by Squier and Davis in 1848. On August 2 he wrote Putnam a letter about expanding the geographic range of his fieldwork, extending from the Little Miami–Ohio River confluence area up to the East Fork of the Little Miami River (see appendix B).

As a result of artifact sales to the Smithsonian by Charles's LSSM colleagues, Cyrus Thomas contacted him directly. Thomas was the director of Mound Exploration at the Smithsonian Institution. He spent his archaeological career studying burial mounds and earthworks in the Midwestern United States.[10] Like Charles and Putnam, he believed American Indians rather than a "lost race" of Europeans built them.

Charles made arrangements for Thomas to visit Cincinnati and examine the archaeological sites in the Little Miami River firsthand. Charles wanted to remain loyal to Putnam and the Peabody Museum, but his financial situation was becoming desperate. On August 7, 1884, Charles explained to Putnam in a letter that his monetary problems were so bad that he might have to sell artifacts to Thomas and the Smithsonian to ensure that archaeological fieldwork continues in the Little Miami River valley.[11]

Charles wrote a letter to Putnam explaining,

> I would like to save my collection for the Peabody but I need the money and should Thomas give me my price I will sell to him only I do hate to see them get things that come from the places in which we are so much interested namely the Ferris Woods, the Sand Ridge, and Hahn Field that I would sell to the Peabody Museum on monthly or quarterly installments (see appendix B).

Putnam responded to Charles's letter with a check in the amount of three hundred dollars, which was sent to ensure that his excavations could continue.

The Cost of Archaeology 73

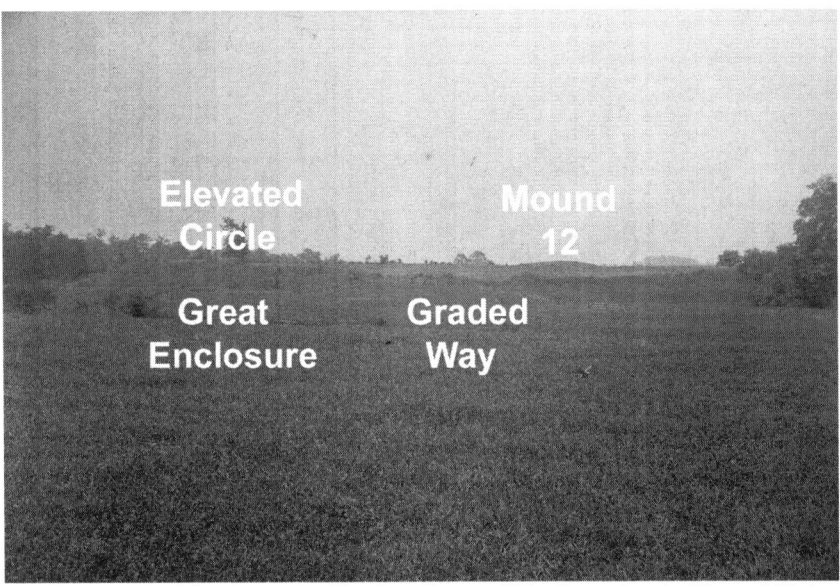

4.1 Photograph of the Turner site, Hamilton County, Ohio, illustrating the Elevated Circle, Mound 12, Graded Way, and the Great Enclosure, ca. 1883.

4.2. Photograph of the Turner site, Hamilton County, Ohio, illustrating the Graded Way and Turner farmhouse, ca. 1883.

CHAPTER 5

AAAS and Beyond

In 1884 Putnam was secretary of the American Association for the Advancement of Science (AAAS). The AAAS was created on September 20, 1848, from the Association of American Geologists and Naturalists. The purpose of the society was to promote scientific discussions and collaboration. It was the premier science organization in the United States and one of the foremost in the world.

American Association for the Advancement of Science (AAAS)

Charles was completely transparent when it came to Cyrus Thomas and the Smithsonian. On August 10 Charles wrote a letter to Putnam about Thomas's Cincinnati visit.[1] Much to Charles's chagrin, Thomas stayed at his home in Madisonville having been unsatisfied with his accommodations at the Burnet House in Cincinnati.

Charles was clearly of two minds when it came to Thomas.

> He is a sharp old coon and I think means us no good. He said he would not interfere with us in any way and then with the next breath tells me that he is going to open a mound at Foster's Crossing,

which is about 15 miles above here on the Little Miami River about 8 miles this way from Ft. Ancient. I shall keep him in tow as long as he is about here (see appendix B).

In the same missive Charles wrote, "He is a good man, an old Quaker of a most excellent family." At the end of the letter, Charles also requested that Putnam endorse him for membership in the American Association for the Advancement of Science (AAAS) (see appendix B).

The Thirty-third annual meeting of the AAAS was going to be held in Philadelphia in September. Charles wanted to present a paper in the Anthropology session about his work on American Indian mortuary features at the Turner site. Membership in the AAAS and a presentation at the annual meeting was a great honor for Charles and a turning point in his archaeological career. It meant for the first time Charles would be nationally recognized as a professional archaeologist.

On August 18 Charles sent another letter to Putnam updating him on Thomas's activities in Ohio.

Professor Thomas has not turned up as he promised and I haven't seen anything of him since he was here on Saturday evening. On inquiry I cannot learn of his whereabouts. He is somewhere in Ohio and that is all I know (see appendix B).

Charles also wanted Putnam to know that work at the Turner site was "progressing." Six days later, Charles wrote Putnam about Cyrus Thomas.

Professor Thomas has kept remarkably quiet since he has been in Ohio. I cannot learn anything of his whereabouts nor do the Cincinnati men know of him (see appendix B).

With the excavations at the Turner site picking up momentum, Charles began to wonder if he could afford to take time to travel to Philadelphia for the AAAS meeting. He wrote Putnam a letter about his concerns on August 24.

Can I leave to go to Philadelphia just at the time when I should be at the Mound everyday. . . . My chances to be present at the Philadelphia meeting are growing slim and slimmer. I am not well. My family is sick and I shall have to forego the pleasure of seeing you again until you again come to Madisonville (see appendix B).

Putnam was able to convince Charles that discussing the scientific significance of their archaeological findings at the AAAS meeting would be far more important than missing a few days in the field. Charles agreed and set out on the long train journey to Philadelphia with his close friend Charles Low. They arrived on September 4 at the Hotel Lafayette in Philadelphia. Charles wrote Molly a letter from the hotel.

> Professor Putnam . . . offered me one thousand dollars for my collection and $300. Three hundred dollars a year for my services as long as we worked together and when times are a little better he will give me more. I have not yet accepted Putnam's offer (see appendix A).

In addition to Putnam, Charles met with Alexander Graham Bell and John Wesley Powell at the Lafayette Hotel. Powell was a decorated Civil War hero, having lost his right arm to a minié ball at the battle of Shiloh. After the war, he became a celebrity for his western expeditions to the Rocky Mountains and down the Green and Colorado rivers. His expedition through the Grand Canyon brought him international acclaim. At the time of the AAAS meeting, Powell was serving as the director of the U.S. Geological Survey and the Bureau of Ethnology at the Smithsonian Institution. He presented two papers in the Anthropology session, "The Three Culture Periods" and "Mythology of the Wintuns."[2]

Bell was no stranger to anthropology or American Indians. The Mohawk chief Onwanonsyshon, also known as George Henry Martin Johnson, made Bell an honorary chief for translating the Mohawk language into written symbols. As professor of Vocal Physiology at Boston University, he trained students on how to teach deaf mutes to speak. He was best known, however, for the story of the telephone and the phrase, "Watson, come here! I want to see you!" Bell obtained a patent for his telephone on March 7, 1876, which was first successfully used on March 10, 1876. His paper in the Anthropology session was "Upon the evolution of a race of deaf mutes in America."

Putnam's paper in the Anthropology session was "Archaeological Explorations by the Peabody Museum of American Archaeology and Ethnology Communicated by the Trustees of the Museum." It was the perfect segue for Charles's presentation, "Description of Human Remains in the Intrusive Pit in the Large Mound of the Turner Group, Little Miami River Valley, Ohio During the Explorations of Messrs Metz and Putnam." Charles's paper was well received and he had firsthand contact with the most well-known anthropologists and archaeologists in the United States.[3]

Charles used the East Coast meeting as an excuse to visit his sister, Maria Anna, in New York. He wrote Molly a letter on September 6.

> I start for New York this a.m. and will be back here Monday a.m. and will be in Washington Tuesday and home Thursday evening . . . the meeting is one of great success and there were 2,000 people (see appendix A).

Similar sentiments were expressed in Charles's letter to Molly on September 8 from New York. He also emphasized Putnam's promise to resolve the financial burdens associated with the archaeological survey and excavation of archaeological sites in the Little Miami River valley.

> I get Professor Putnam's offer in writing tomorrow so as to make it binding on the Peabody Museum. I think the offer is better than $1,200.00 don't you (see appendix A).

On September 9 Putnam made good on his offer and drew up a legal binding contract to resolve Charles's financial problems associated with his archaeological survey and excavations. Putnam officially offered Charles twelve hundred dollars per year to work for Harvard University and the Museum of American Archaeology and Ethnology.

> F. W. Putnam, a curator of the Peabody Museum, shall allow twenty-five dollars ($25.00) on each monthly bill, from August 1, 1884, an account of the explorations in Ohio to Dr. C. L. Metz for his services as agent of the Museum (see appendix B).

Henceforth, Charles was officially an employee of the Harvard University and the Museum of American Archaeology and Ethnology.

Carl Schurz and the American Indian

With the Harvard contract in hand, Charles wasted no time following the meeting to resume his fieldwork with Putnam on Ohio Valley earthworks and mounds. In fact, the positive response from other archaeologists attending the AAAS meeting reinforced the significance of their research. On October 5 Charles wrote Molly a letter about his excavations with Putnam in the Scioto River valley (see appendix A).

On October 9 Charles, Putnam, and their assistant Britten arrived at the Warner House (hotel) in Chillicothe, Ohio. The hotel was rebuilt in 1854 following a devastating fire in 1851. It was subsequently known under a variety of monikers such as the Valley House and the Emmitt House reflecting changes in ownership. Jake Warner, who renamed it the Warner House, later remodeled it. Charles wrote Molly a letter about his meeting with Carl Schurz at the Warner House.

> Carl Schurz speaks here tonight. I spoke to him, for he nearly fell over me in the Barber Shop of the Warner House (see appendix A).

Schurz was giving a political presentation on American Indians. Carl Schurz was a German immigrant from Wisconsin and the person responsible for organizing the members of the German-American Turner Society to advocate against slavery and support the Republican Party and the nomination of Abraham Lincoln at the Republican Convention. Schurz was so close to Lincoln that he was given a personally inscribed copy of the Lincoln-Douglas debates. Between 1877 and 1881, Schurz met with tribal leaders and representatives at the White House along with President Rutherford B. Hayes. Unfortunately, they made promises to the tribal leaders that they could not possibly keep.[4]

In October 1884 Schurz was speaking in Chillicothe about his efforts to reduce the corruption and racism that American Indian tribes were experiencing. His solution, however, was to force them onto reservation lands with little or no food or water resources making their economic and cultural development almost impossible. Schurz's proposal would further alienate tribes from the United States making it impossible for them to become voting citizens.[5]

While Schurz was trying to convince Charles, Britton, Putnam, and the rest of the Chillicothe audience that his plans for American Indians were in their best interest, the U.S. Supreme Court was deciding on whether or not they could be citizens. John Elk, a Winnebago, had renounced his tribal affiliation and used the Citizenship Clause to proclaim himself a citizen of the United States.[6]

From the earliest days of European colonization, American Indians were defined as "non-persons." This definition was deeply rooted in the Greek and Roman traditions of law and order where only free, that is, non-enslaved people with a certain amount of wealth were considered "citizens" with certain special rights. The United States was forced to address the issue in April 1879, when Ponca chief Maⁿchú-Naⁿzhí (Standing Bear), sued Gen. George R. Crook for a writ of habeas corpus in the district court in Omaha, Nebraska.

Speaking in his own defense, Standing Bear raised his right hand and said, "That hand is not the color of yours, but if I prick it, the blood will flow, and I shall feel pain. The blood is of the same color as yours. God made me, and I am a man." On May 12, 1879, Judge Elmer S. Dundy ruled that an Indian is a "person" under the law and is entitled to the rights and protection of the United States. He further stated, "The right of expatriation is a natural, inherent and inalienable right and extends to the Indian as well as to the more fortunate white race."[7]

Given the 1879 court decision and the Thirty-ninth Congress's use of the Citizenship Clause as an extension of the Civil Rights Act of 1866, John Elk believed that he had the right to American citizenship and the right to vote. The Civil Rights Act granted citizenship to all persons born in the United States that were "not subject to any foreign power." On April 5, 1880, John Elk registered to vote in Omaha, Nebraska. Charles Wilkins, the registrar of voters, denied him the right to vote.[8]

The Supreme Court had to decide if an American Indian was a citizen under the Fourteenth Amendment of the Constitution if they were born in the United States, renounced their tribal allegiance, and resided among "whites." A complicating factor was that the Office of Indian Affairs, a division of the War Department, originally governed American Indians. That office was transferred to the Department of the Interior in 1849.[9]

The U.S. Supreme Court ultimately ruled that while Congress regulated commerce with American Indians within the boundaries the United States and its territories, tribes were in fact alien nations. Tribes were considered nations within a nation. Tribes dealt with the United States on all legal matters through treaties and acts of Congress. It was assumed that American Indians could not be loyal to both their tribe and the United States. Thus, Elk was not considered an American citizen at the time of his birth. Because of the 1884 ruling, American Indians were excluded from citizenship until the Indian Citizenship Act of 1924.[10]

Pleasant distractions

William Henry Holmes contacted Charles about his archaeological research in the Little Miami River valley. At the time, Holmes was working under John Wesley Powell as an assistant geologist for the U.S. Geological Survey. In 1882 Holmes was appointed an honorary curator of Aboriginal Ceramics at the Smithsonian's National Museum. Although Holmes's specialty at the time was Mexico and the American southwest, he was interested in acquiring museum quality specimens of pottery from the Little Miami River valley.[11]

On October 12 Charles wrote Putnam about a letter he received from Holmes. He informed Charles that the Bureau of Ethnology wanted to appropriate artifact collections from the Little Miami River valley for the upcoming New Orleans Exposition. Holmes also explained that he had only one month to make the purchase (see appendix B).

On October 19, 1882, Buffalo Bill Cody returned to Cincinnati. Cody found that the Union Association owned the Bank Street Grounds where the Wild West Show performed the previous year. He decided to set up in the new Cincinnati Baseball Grounds located on the block created by Findlay Street, Western Avenue, York Street, and McLean Avenue, less than a mile away from the old ballpark. As in the previous year, Charles took his family to watch hours of cowboys, Indians, bison, trick horses, and sharpshooters performing in series of open-air western plays. Charles's real passion was to see and meet the American Indians in the show. He liked the fact Cody treated them with equal respect as the other performers.

More family matters

Since his father, Francis, passed away, Charles was viewed as the *paterfamilias* of the Metz family. His relatives turned to him for everything from their medical care to helping them out with their financial woes. Given the panic of 1884, the monetary matters of his family continued to loom large. They confused Charles's fame with fortune. While he was now an archaeological celebrity, he had to borrow money to help them. On November 13, Charles reluctantly wrote a letter to Putnam about a one-year loan of between four hundred and five hundred dollars to help save his relatives' property.

Putnam was more than happy to help out his friend and archaeological partner. With his family money problems in order, Charles was able to resume fieldwork at the Turner site. Unlike the previous winter, the weather was unusually warm, which allowed Charles to excavate throughout the year.

On December 11 Charles wrote a letter updating Putnam on his excavations at the Turner and Hahn Field sites. Of particular note was the discovery of "a fossil elephant's tooth (not a mastodon's)" at what he referred to as "the schoolteacher's, Mr. Durham's mound" (see appendix B).

The elephant tooth was the molar from an extinct species of mammoth (*Mammuthus sp.*). Its presence in the Broadwell Mound was, indeed, an unusual and unexpected find. The mound was constructed on a deposit of glacial outwash, which dated to the last Ice Age. While mammoth remains are not common, they do occur as isolated fossils in the sand and gravel deposits underlying the mound. It is quite possible that American Indians collected the tooth from a natural exposure. It is also possible, however, that the tooth was collected from Big Bone Lick, Kentucky, some thirty kilometers (nineteen miles) downstream from the mound. Mammoth teeth commonly occur in the gravel bars of Big Bone Lick Creek and its tributary Gum Branch.

In addition to a mammoth molar, the base of the Durham's mound contained abundant post-holes, pottery, and a heavily burned surface. On December 12 Charles wrote Putnam another letter updating him about their continuing excavations at the Broadwell and Durham's mounds (see appendix B).

The winter brought health problems to the Ohio River valley and to the Metz family. A number of diseases were in epidemic proportions in 1884 including cholera and smallpox. Children were especially vulnerable to diphtheria, scarlet fever, and whooping cough. There were also a plethora of gastrointestinal infections resulting from spoiled food and impure water.[12]

On December 31 Charles sent Putnam an update on his excavation of a small mound at the Hahn Field site. He also discussed his future plans to begin work at the Sand Ridge site. Charles also wrote Putnam about the health of his daughter.

> I was pained to learn of the illness of your daughter and sincerely hope that the patient is convalescing. My little people have fared very well so far. There is but little illness among the people at the present time (see appendix B).

1884 Ferris Cemetery publication

By the end of 1884 it had become apparent to Charles that one of the emotional costs of archaeology was delayed gratification. While the thrill of the chase and the excitement of discovery provided immediate satisfaction, archaeological analysis and the publication of their significance in high-impact peer-reviewed journals took years of patience, study, and extensive editing. Nowhere was this situation more apparent than the publication of the Ferris Cemetery excavations, which began in the 1871.

Charles and Putnam published the results of their fieldwork at the Ferris Cemetery in the *The Sixteenth and Seventeenth Annual Reports of the Trustees of the Peabody Museum of America and Ethnology*. It was one of three volumes, which included all of the reports of Jeffries Wyman, the first curator; those of Asa Gray, the interim curator; and seven years of Putnam's reports as curator.[13]

From the outset Putnam stated that he was deeply indebted to "Dr. C. L. Metz and Dr. Frank W. Langdon" for their careful exploration, description, and illustration of the Ferris Cemetery site. It was published in three parts "under the editorship of Mr. C. F. Low." Putnam also noted that the site had "become famous in American archaeology."[14]

In the volume Charles and Putnam described the size of the Ferris Cemetery site as extending over more than fifteen acres. They reported that about three acres had been excavated "foot by foot," an area that contained "over six hundred skeletons" and associated grave goods. Charles's descriptions of bone pathologies were considered the most significant aspect of the research.[15]

Charles and Putnam provided an inventory of the grave goods, which included small decorated and undecorated cooking pots, vessels with human faces, similar to those found in Missouri and Arkansas mounds, vessels with salamanders, and double pots. They also described numerous flaked-stone arrowheads, drills, and scrapers, ground-stone pipes and celts, and pitted-stones apparently used for cracking nuts. Copper beads and cut sheets of copper were also found among the human remains.[16]

Charles and Putnam emphasized that the "ash-pits" were every bit as important as the mortuary features in understanding American Indian culture. Indeed, nothing is more telling of past human behavior than what people discarded as trash. Garbage not only contains food remains, it also provides direct evidence of human livelihood as well as clues to social, economic, and political class. While it is not very romantic, Charles and Putnam were well aware that archaeology was basically the study of the garbage of dead people.[17]

Household garbage was found in approximately four hundred ash-filled pits underlying the mortuary features and in "three areas about fifty feet in diameter." Charles and Putnam called these areas kitchen middens that were "several feet in thickness" and "at the head of a small ravine." Because the midden "contained the same character of materials found in the pits," they correctly surmised that, "it evidently belongs to the same period" as the ash pit features in the cemetery.[18]

The ash pits began as circular to bell-shaped maize storage pits, which extended three to four feet into the well-drained underlying sand and gravel deposit. The floors of the pits were lined with hickory bark, which held large woven bags of maize. They were then covered with hickory bark to divert water away from the maize. The pits and their contents were sealed with a clay cap and covered with leaves, which protected them from discovery of scavenging animals and rival tribes.[19]

While the village was seasonally abandoned, warring tribes could starve the village to death by burning their winter food reserves. This situation was evident in two pits filled with "several bushels" of carbonized corn "covered with bark, twigs, and matting, which were also burnt." "Above the corn, the pit was filled with the usual mass of ashes, containing animal bones, shells and other things." When the pits were no longer suitable for storing maize, they were recycled into trash pits and in some cases used to bury the dead.[20]

Charles and Putnam reported finding human skeletons at the bottom pits, beneath a "mass of ashes, animal remains and potsherds." They speculated that the bodies might have been placed in the pits as a temporary grave and later "removed for final burial in mounds or other places." It is also possible, however, that the individuals were buried in the winter when the ground was frozen solid or the bodies were members of a lower social class. Charles and Putnam considered this scenario more likely because the skeletons were covered beneath undisturbed layers of ashes and animal remains "as found in the other pits."[21]

In addition to ash (i.e., hearth cleanings) the pits also contained large potsherds and the bones of fish, reptiles, birds, and mammals. The bones of elk, deer, and bear were "generally broken" suggesting they were used as food. Charles and Putnam noted that some of the pits contained "about half a bushel of such bones." They also observed that more than one hundred shells of several species of freshwater mussels were removed from a single pit. Some of the mussel shells were perforated for use as a hoe and others were ground to make temper for pottery.[22]

Charles and Putnam also described, "a large number of implements made of bones and of deer and elk antlers." Large elk antlers were ground and shaped into digging implements for agricultural purposes. Leg bones of deer and elk were grooved longitudinally to create sharp beveled edges for use as a drawknife to process large animal hides. These "beamers" occurred in the ash pits in various stages of manufacture and use.[23]

Other bone implements included awls used in leatherwork and sewing fabrics made from plant fibers such as milkweed and rattlesnake master. Cut and polished bird bones were shaped into beads, flutes, and whistles, some of which had "tally" marks. Bone harpoons and fishhooks were found in various stages of manufacture and use.[24]

Putnam concluded the report by stating that the Peabody Museum will pay for "a portion of the expenses of exploration" and "receive its share of all that is obtained as the work of excavation proceeds." He added that Charles and his colleagues E. A. Conkling, P. P. Lane, and Charles F. Low, were "working with care and wisdom" and were "preventing the random exploration of prehistoric sites in the vicinity," and were "stopping to a certain extent the wanton destruction of mounds and other important ancient works by mere curiosity hunters, or by dealers in relics."[25]

Determining antiquity

In 1885 there were still many people who believed that American Indians were relatively recent inhabitants in North America, postdating biblical times. Despite Charles and Putnam's scholarly research, which was independently verified by Cyrus Thomas and Henry Schoolcraft, there were still people who believed that the earthworks and mounds of the Ohio River valley were created by two waves of migration from the Old World—a group of people arriving from Mesopotamia sometime around 3000–2000 BCE and a group arriving from Israel in 590 BCE. This scenario was published in the *Book of Mormon* in 1830. It further suggested that all evidence of these early inhabitants were destroyed by warfare around 385 ACE. By 1885 this interpretation of the Ohio Valley's past had become more of an item of religious faith rather than a scientific fact.

Charles had no way to determine the absolute age of the archaeological sites in the Little Miami River valley. He knew they had to be older than the age of trees growing on top of them. Charles also knew that an archaeological site had to be younger than the geological age of the site's surface. While it was safe to assume that deeper meant older, there was no way to ascertain exactly how much older.

Charles had identified a few archaeological sites, which contained sixteenth- and seventeenth-century Spanish- and French-made trade goods such as cut sheets of copper, gunflints, iron axes, celts, pot fragments, and glass beads, but most of the sites had none. He assumed that archaeological sites without European trade goods were more than four hundred years old, but he could not determine if they were hundreds, thousands, or tens of thousands of years older.

Some of the archaeological sites Charles documented had elaborate earthworks, some had burial mounds, some had both earthworks and burial mounds, some had mounds without burials, and some had no mounds or earthworks. Some of the sites contained earthenware pottery and others had none. Some of the sites covered hectares and others were less than a quarter acre in size.

Charles had lingering questions about the contemporaneity of these sites. Did they represent different activity areas or an increase in population through time? Did different American Indian tribes with different technologies create these sites or did they represent a single tribe developing new technologies over a long period of time? Or were both of these theories possible? In order to help answer these questions, he chose to focus his field research on the Hahn Field site.

Back to the Hahn Field site

The Hahn Field site was located in the floodplain immediately across the Little Miami River and within eyesight of the Ferris Cemetery. Both sites had European trade goods, pits filled with ashes and garbage, and shell-tempered pottery with similar rims, handles, and decorated surfaces. These similarities suggested that the sites were contemporary despite their different geological settings.

While Charles was anxious to excavate the Hahn Field site, the elements were not cooperating. On January 31, 1885, Charles wrote a letter to Putnam about the poor weather conditions. He also briefly discussed his search for "stone graves" with his assistant Britten in Remington, Ohio (see appendix B).

The mortuary feature Charles referred to in his letter was a stone box grave or coffin of limestone placed in a rectangular pattern. Their occurrence in the Little Miami River valley was of particular interest because they suggested a cultural connection with Muskogean-speaking people in the Southeast especially in the Cumberland River valley.

The cold weather continued through the month of March making fieldwork difficult and sometimes impossible. February temperatures dropped to -10° F and were still in the single digits and teens in the first half of March. Charles made the most of this downtime seeking permission from the landowners to excavate. On March 2 he wrote a letter to Putnam about how the weather was delaying his work at the Hahn Field site.

> It has been thawing for four days past. The snow is gone but it is very muddy and soft and on account of this will delay work for a day or two yet (see appendix B).

While the poor weather did not permit excavations, it was dry enough to conduct a surface survey of the Turner site. On March 7 Charles wrote to Putnam about his discovery of a new burial mound. "I have found another small mound near the Marriott Mound back of the Whittlesey work and it should be explored had we but the means to do it with" (see appendix B).

Charles also included with his letter a new book, which he called "a literary curiosity *The Book of Algoonah*," written by a resident of Madisonville. Charles referred to the author as "very intelligent yet he talks queer and claims that the book is a spiritual revelation or something of that sort" (see appendix B).

While Charles worked diligently to demonstrate that American Indians were the architects of the earthworks and burial mounds of the Little Miami River valley, far-fetched theories about an ancient white race continued to emerge. Among them was *The Book of Algoonah: Being a Concise*

Account of the History of the Early People of the Continent of America Known as Mound Builders published January 1, 1884, by Mezzina Roth. The book was a fanciful, self-indulgent, fictional account of "the land of the Mezzina Roth" where mounds were built by an ancient white race along "the great river."

On March 8 Charles wrote a letter to Putnam about his progress on the excavation of a burial mound at the Hahn Field site. On March 18, Charles wrote another letter to Putnam letting him know they had completed the excavation. Given that the results were more than a little disappointing, Charles wrote Putnam a letter on March 29 explaining that they would be shifting their focus back to the Hahn Field village site. He also inquired, "When can we expect to see the 18th annual report of the museum" (see appendix B).

Charles was anxious to see the eighteenth volume of *Annual Reports of the Trustees of the Peabody Museum of America and Ethnology*. He and Putnam had submitted their paper "Account of Continued Explorations of Mounds in Ohio," for publication. However, the eighteenth volume was going to be combined with the nineteenth and was not scheduled for publication until spring 1886.

On April 2 and 3 Charles wrote two letters to Putnam about his recent discoveries at the Hahn Field site. He discovered mortuary features similar to those found at the Ferris Cemetery site.

> Ash pits exactly similar to the ones in the Ferris Woods with burials over them . . . two skeletons . . . over the skull of one was an inverted vessel . . . along with fragments of . . . grooved bone . . . several perforated unio shells . . . fragments of pipes . . . almost a cartload of animal remains (see appendix B).

Charles also noted that he was especially on the lookout "for bones exhibiting marks of disease or injury" (see appendix B).

Like most archaeologists, Charles was constantly looking for sources of funding to support his fieldwork. In April he learned that Orlando Smith, president of the Cincinnati, Washington, and Baltimore Railroad (CWBRR); president of the Columbus and Cincinnati Midland Railroad (CCMRR); and vice president of the Baltimore and Ohio Railroad (B&ORR) was interested in Ohio Valley archaeology.[26]

Smith's family moved to Chillicothe, Ohio, in 1852 from Lewiston, Maine, where he became fascinated with the earthworks and mounds of the Scioto River valley. In addition to his railroad work, Smith had an active military career beginning with his command of an Ohio Militia Company known as the "Chillicothe Greys." During the Civil War he served as a Union colonel in the Seventy-third Ohio Infantry and a brigade in the XI Corps.[27]

On April 20, Charles wrote a letter to Putnam about Smith's interest in archaeology and the possibility of obtaining free railroad passes.

> B & O Railroad . . . passes were issued to Major Powell and three others of the S.I (Smithsonian Institution). . . . I learned however that Mr. Orland Smith, the president of the C.W.B.R.R. was somewhat interested in archaeology. I called on some of his friends with the photographs and I have since learned that he is very anxious to see the photographs also (see appendix B).

Charles's letter of April 20 also suggests that there was a clear competition between the two intellectual powerhouses in the east—the Peabody Museum of American Archaeology and Ethnology and the Smithsonian Bureau of Ethnology. Selling artifacts and information during hard economic times pulled Charles and his LSSM colleagues into the archaeological competition between these institutions. Both of them were genuinely concerned that the mounds and earthworks of the Ohio River valley were being destroyed at an alarming rate by sand and gravel mining and construction activities and they were working hard to dismiss the pseudoscientific explanations about their origin. However, both the Peabody and Smithsonian were dependent upon the same local fieldworkers for the acquisition of artifacts and archaeological data.

This situation broke the foundation of the LSSM. On April 23 Charles wrote a "confidential" letter to Putnam about Charles Low's dealings with the Smithsonian. In addition to artifacts, they were trying to acquire the field notes of the excavations funded by the Peabody Museum.

> Low . . . had sold his collection to the S.I. (Smithsonian Institution) and that Professor Holmes would be on to arrange the packing of the material of the Ferris Woods. He also demanded all of the field notes of the exploration conducted by the L&S Society of this place (Literary & Scientific Society of Madisonville). Now I claim the field notes as my exclusive property since the L&S Society has been dissolved and I refuse to give them up (see appendix B).

In addition to copies of the *Sixteenth and Seventeenth Annual Reports of the Trustees of the Peabody Museum of America and Ethnology*, Putnam gave Charles recordings of traditional American Indian music made by Alice Cunningham Fletcher. Thanks to Thomas Edison's 1878 patented mechanical phonograph cylinder, Fletcher was able to record and reproduce music in the field.

Fletcher was yet another of Putnam's protégés who was passionate about studying and documenting traditional American Indian culture. Like Charles, she worked on the earthworks and mounds of the Ohio River valley for the Peabody Museum of America and Ethnology. In 1881 the Peabody Museum paid Fletcher, an assistant in ethnology; Thomas Tibbles, a journalist; and Susette Bright Eyes La Flesche, an interpreter, to travel to the Dakota Territory, live with the Lakota, and record their music. La Flesche had served as a spokeswoman and interpreter for Standing Bear in his landmark civil rights trial and Tibbles was the journalist who wrote about the trial. In later years, Fletcher became a second mother for La Flesche's son, Francis.[28]

On May 21 Charles wrote a letter to Putnam about wrapping up work at the Hahn Field and Sand Ridge sites and how he used Fletcher's recordings to help persuade site landowners to allow him to excavate on their property. He also discussed the discovery of stone mounds above "Symmes Station" and on the "high hills along the Little Miami River" (see appendix B).

As Charles penned his letter to Putnam on Saturday, March 21, at 1:30 p.m., Sullivan's Printing Company located on 19 Sixth Street in downtown Cincinnati was engulfed in flames. It was a sweatshop that employed young girls. Despite the employees pulling an alarm, which quickly brought a company of fire engines to the building, the fire killed seventeen people in fifteen minutes, including young girls. A can of benzene had fallen into an elevator shaft and exploded. Eight girls jumped from fifth story windows, but only three survived. John Sullivan, a cousin of the owner, was able to rescue two girls, but he became trapped and died trying to save more.[29]

News of the fire and loss of so many lives, especially young girls, made Charles think about his own family's safety. He also thought that if he had been there some of the lives might have been saved. In spite of all of his other obligations, Charles made the decision to enlist as a member of the Madisonville Hook and Ladder Company.

On May 29 Charles wrote Putnam a letter about field prospects for the summer. At the time Charles was working "along the Little Miami River . . . in Loveland" and at "Foster's Crossing between Remington and Ft. Ancient." He wanted to move onto the excavation of burial "mounds about Newtown," which were closer to home (see appendix B).

On June 2 Charles wrote another letter to Putnam inquiring about the possibility of doing more fieldwork at the Turner site. He also gave Putnam a heads up that the artifacts from the Hahn Field site and burial mound were on their way to the Peabody Museum. Charles also continued to ask Putnam, "when will the 18th annual report of the museum be ready" (see appendix B). The slow progress of journal publication reinforced that to Charles that an archaeologist must be patient and understand that gratification from the discipline was always delayed.

5.1. Chillicothe Fairground Mound, Ross County, Ohio. Left to right: Mr. Douglas, Mr. Charles Low, Charles Louis Metz, Frederick Ward Putnam, ca. 1884.

CHAPTER 6

Turning Back the Hands of Time

In 1885 Charles expanded his excavations in the Little Miami River valley upstream and downstream from the Ferris Cemetery site. His previously published archaeological surveys identified a village site and burial mound on the Turpin family farm. He also knew that workman had exposed about fifty human skeletons while digging a cellar for the Turpin farmhouse in 1800.[1]

The Turpin Farm site

The Turpin Farm site was located on a glacial terrace on the same side of the river as Hahn Field, less than a mile downstream. Charles found abundant human bones, flaked-stone artifacts, and shell-tempered pottery in the plowed fields of the farm. The designs, rims, and handles of the pottery were slightly different from those found at the Hahn Field site and Ferris Cemetery, which suggested to Charles that the site either represented a different tribe or an occupation of a different age.

On June 6, 1885, Charles wrote a letter to Putnam informing him that he was excavating the Turpin Farm village site and planning to move his focus to the Sand Ridge site.[2] He told Putnam that they had already recovered two pipes, a quantity of shell beads, a long chisel shaped stone, and a vase. Charles also let Putnam know that he was keeping his eye on the Smithsonian Institution archaeologists who were also digging in the valley (see appendix B).

Moreover, Charles explained to Putnam that his youngest brother, who had recently moved "to Madisonville with his family," was excavating with their most reliable crew member Britten. Charles's youngest brother was thirty-four-year-old Julius Alphonse Metz. He was born in 1851 in the Metz family home in Plainville, Ohio. Julius was the co-owner with A. W. Siegbahn of the Rainbow Steam Dye Works in Springfield, Ohio. His help at the Turpin Farm site was invaluable as Charles was becoming ill.

As usual, Charles did his best to hide the fact he was sick to his family and to Harvard. On June 7 Charles wrote a letter to Putnam updating him on their progress at the Turpin Farm site. Among the recent discoveries, he described an arrowhead made from the tip of a deer's antler tine stuck "in the dorsal vertebrae of one of the skeletons . . . similar to many we found in the Ferris Woods ash pits." This was a significant finding because it suggested that the two sites were culturally similar (see appendix B).

On June 11 Charles wrote another letter updating Putnam about his work at the Turpin Farm site and the arrival of Harvard student assistant, McKerron. At that juncture, Charles had found even more cultural similarities between Turpin Farm, the Ferris Cemetery, and Hahn Field including the size and nature of features they referred to as "ash pits" and zoomorphic applications on the rim of shell-tempered ceramic vessels. These included a bear's head, a crested duck's head, and a lizard (more likely a salamander) (see appendix B).

In a second letter written on June 11, Charles wrote a letter to Putnam about Charles Low's impression of the Peabody Museum in comparison with the Smithsonian Institution. Low described the Peabody Museum as "the crown jewel of them all." He went on to state "the S.I. (Smithsonian Institution) is a junk shop in comparison." Low also complained that the Smithsonian's "oil painting of the Serpent Mound by Mrs. McLean representing a frog making frantic efforts to escape the open jaws of a serpent" was preposterous (see appendix B).

Charles's health

Charles's health was getting worse so he took a brief break from work to visit with Molly's family in Vera Cruz, Ohio. On June 27, he wrote a letter to Molly about his stay on the farm.

> I have been shucking wheat and carrying it when my back gave out and I had to layup. My diarrhea had stopped. Mother (Molly's mother) cured it with a quart of good buttermilk yesterday morning. My fever comes on every day but it's getting shorter in the attacks. My voice is getting better but my cough is more troublesome . . . if I should not be as well as I expect by next Wednesday I might stay up here a little longer (see appendix A).

In the letter Charles also asked Molly if she "noticed the comet in the northern sky?" Astronomical wonders such as comets and meteor showers were sights to behold on the dark, moonless summer evenings of Vera Cruz, Ohio. Five comets were discovered and named in 1885. Additionally, the Andromedids meteor shower was created as the earth passed through the tail of Biela's Comet. Spectacular meteor showers, several thousand per hour, could be seen as the comet was breaking apart in the summer of 1885 (see appendix A).

On June 29 Charles wrote a letter to Putnam informing him that artifacts from the Turpin Farm site were on their way. He also mentions that "soapstone pottery" was discovered in a mound on the Turpin Farm. The pottery was actually fragments of a stone bowl carved from a soft metamorphic rock commonly known as steatite (i.e., dunite, serpentinite, or pyrophyllite). These rocks are composed mostly of talc, with lesser quantities of green mica (chlorite) and amphibole. In the Ohio Valley, steatite was also used to make jewelry, pipes, and atlatl weights (i.e., spear thrower weights) also known as banner-stones (see appendix B).

On August 1 Charles wrote a letter to Putnam accounting for his fieldwork expenses and to let him know that the contents of three burial mounds and associated field notes would be shipped to the Peabody Museum in the "coming week."

Later that day, Charles received a letter from Putnam about a possible fellowship in the American Association for the Advancement of Science (AAAS). Putnam had penned the letter following the 1885 AAAS meeting in Ann Arbor, Michigan. Charles quickly wrote a second letter on August 1 in response to Putnam's. He asked Putnam, "What are the requirements that are necessary to become a fellow of the AAAS? Am I eligible" (see appendix B).

Charles was more than qualified. He was a meritorious member of the

AAAS and in good standing for a period of four years. Also, Charles had made significant contributions to anthropology and archaeology, provided service to the LSSM and the Cincinnati Natural History Society, and his public archaeology exhibitions and presentations helped communicate and interpret anthropology and archaeology to the public. Thus, Putnam was more than happy to nominate Charles (see appendix B).

Charles explained to Putnam that although he was "convalescing from a severe cold," he was in the process of excavating a burial mound, which stood next to the Turpin homestead. Charles also assured Putnam that he was keeping up with the bookkeeping duties associated with the expenses of archaeological fieldwork (see appendix B).

In a quick and undated letter, Charles wrote Putnam about his fieldwork expenditures and failing health. He also let Putnam know about his planned attendance at the upcoming AAAS meeting.

> I leave for Buffalo on the evening of the 16th if nothing prevents my going. I am not well and anxious to get away for a rest (see appendix B).

On August 17 while Charles was in New York, he wrote a letter to Putnam ensuring him that his brother Julius was making sure the fieldwork continued. He noted that, "My health has at times been very bad always the result of losing rest at night." At the time, Charles felt well enough to plan a new expedition to Chillicothe to excavate the Harness mound (see appendix B).

Unfortunately, Charles had misdiagnosed himself. He clearly had more than a cold. By August 27 Charles's condition had taken a turn for the worse. Julius wrote a letter to Putnam informing him of Charles's condition.

> I write informing you of his serious illness. The doctor was taken down with an acute attack of dysentery, which has acquired a serious form.

Charles had a high fever, abdominal pain, and his intestines and colon had become inflamed. He also had a severe case of bloody diarrhea (see appendix B).

Putnam replied to Julius, expressing his deepest concern about his "dear friend's" serious condition. Charles had long been plagued by a cough and fever, most likely a reoccurring case of malaria then known as ague. At the time, however, it was not known whether or not he actually had malaria, or another malady such as tuberculosis, then called consumption, or pneumonia.

On August 30 Julius wrote a letter to Putnam, updating him on Charles's condition.

> The doctor is slowly improving. He rested easy the greater part of the night and has gained a little strength. He is able to converse a little and expects to improve during today (see appendix B).

Despite his weakened condition, Charles wrote a letter to Putnam the next day, Monday, August 31, about his slow recovery.

> I have been very sick during the last week or so seriously that some of my kind friends felt greatly alarmed. As about myself I knew very little as I was unconscious most of the time until Friday night. At 4:00 p.m. my family thought I was dying. I regained consciousness at that time and found the Doctor rubbing my body. I am yet very weak and have no control of my bowels. Today I am being fed ice and limewater and milk every two hours (see appendix B).

While Charles was improving, he was still sick. On September 2 Julius wrote a letter to Putnam about his brother's condition.

> His condition has been one of slow improvement . . . the doctor is still troubled with circumscribed inflammation at the head of the colon. The fever is about gone and general condition improved (see appendix B).

By September 5 Charles was able to sit up and write a letter to Putnam.

> I suffered all night and the ulcers in my bowels are yet very sore and Dr. McKenzie says it will be some time before I am well. Today I will remain in bed and not get up at all (see appendix B).

Charles assured Putnam that work at the Turpin site was progressing under the direction of his brother. Indeed, he described the discovery of unusual dwelling features at the Turpin Farm site.

> In the present excavations we are finding peculiar trenches from 10 to 20 feet long in the bottom of which are little circular pockets three to four inches apart. The trench is usually filled with black soil and many of the pockets with ashes (see appendix B).

Unbeknownst to Julius Metz, he had discovered wall trenches, an initial building stage in the construction of a house.

After being sick in bed for two months, Charles was finally able to travel again and return to the Turpin Farm site. On October 8 Charles wrote a letter to Putnam about his recent discovery of "stone graves found on the Kendall farm near Madisonville." He noted that they "differed greatly from any others that we have found in this vicinity" (see appendix B).

An American Paleolithic

While doctors did not know with any degree of certainty exactly what malady Charles suffered from, his self-diagnosis was a severe case of dysentery. Having seen firsthand epidemic levels of dysentery during the Civil War at Camp Dennison, he knew that sanitation issues increased the risk of contracting the disease. While Charles did not know the specific infecting parasite or bacteria that caused dysentery, he did know that it was caused by drinking water contaminated from human feces.

Charles believed that sewage from his family privy had leached into the well where they drew drinking water. Since the early 1800s, human waste was disposed of in an outhouse located behind the home and in a chamber pot located in the bedroom. While Cincinnati had a working storm sewer system by 1828, its sole purpose was to prevent flooding and ponding on the streets. The storm sewers were eventually converted to sewers that carried wastewater to the Ohio River, but not until 1897. In 1885, the outhouse and chamber pot were the primary means of human waste disposal.

Charles could not change the method of disposing the family's sewage, but he could change their source of drinking water. In order to prevent this situation from occurring again, Charles decided to have a cistern built. A waterproof cistern could catch and store rainwater that would be impervious to sewage contamination.

Charles hired a group of workmen to dig a pit for the cistern. During the course of excavations, a flaked-stone artifact was found in the underlying glacial gravels at a depth of eight feet. Given that the gravel dated to the Ice Age, the artifact also had to date to the Ice Age.

On October 28 Charles wrote a letter to Putnam about the serendipitous discovery of the artifact. He described it as

> an implement of flint dug from a depth of eight feet from the surface when the men were digging my cistern. The implement came from a stratum of coarse gravel eight feet from the surface, and two feet above this in the clay a smooth stone was found which was water worn (see appendix B).

John Conyers made the first discovery of a flaked-stone artifact in glacial gravels along with mammoth bones in a London gravel pit in 1690. Like the artifact found by Conyers, Charles had discovered a teardrop-shaped, flaked-stone tool with sharp edges and a pointed tip. Furthermore, the artifact was similar to those found by Dr. Charles Conrad Abbott in glacial gravel near Trenton, New Jersey, in 1875. While the exact age of the glacial gravels was not known, the deposit was located about a mile (1.6 km) from the Little Miami River and almost a 100 feet (approximately 30 meters) higher suggesting a great antiquity for the artifact.[3]

Charles knew that the greatest critic of the discovery would be his old friend William Henry Holmes at the Smithsonian Institution and the Bureau of American Ethnology. He was not only an archaeologist, but Holmes was also trained in geology. He had previously rejected all of Putnam's claims for an American Paleolithic as nothing more than the manufactured rejects of more recent stone tool and weaponry production.

Holmes's systematic reexamination of the American Paleolithic find spots showed that they were, at most, a few thousand years old. Holmes also argued that making comparisons between European Paleolithic artifacts with those found in America was defective science. While Charles was concerned about the criticisms that Holmes would make about his discovery, he also knew that he had the academic support of Charles Abbott, Lucien Carr, Frederick Putnam, Nathaniel Shaler, J. D. Whitney, and even Warren King Moorehead.[4]

Given the inevitable scientific controversy, Putnam cautiously questioned Charles about the provenience of the artifact. Charles responded to Putnam's query in a letter written on November 4, 1885. He explained,

> the flint implement came from the gravel at the bottom of the cistern and that it was not pushed down from the surface while digging. . . . I am positive it came from the coarse gravel in the bottom of the cistern (see appendix B).

Charles's letter was written on the same day that Putnam displayed the artifact at the annual meeting of the Boston Society of Natural History. It was, in fact, a Clovis spear point preform. That is, it was a flaked-stone spear point in the early stage of manufacture. While Clovis spear points were not recognized as artifacts that dated to the last Ice Age in 1885, Clovis spear points were later confirmed as evidence that American Indians lived in the Western Hemisphere for almost fourteen thousand years. Charles's discovery was made more than forty years before a comparable spear point was found in association with mammoth bones in Clovis, New Mexico.

Pipe dreams

In addition to Charles's research on the presence of American Indians in the Western Hemisphere during the Ice Age, he was also passionate about their mortuary behavior, demography, and bone pathologies. Anthropomorphic sculptures provided him with evidence of body decoration, hairstyles, posture, stature, and in some cases health issues.

On October 31 Charles wrote Putnam about the discovery of a new and unusual ground-stone pipe.

> Oh Doctor we have found the baby and it is a darling. The darling baby proved to be a large stone pipe resembling a human figure in a squatting position. It is of compact sandstone almost six inches in height and four inches across the base. It resembles figure 148, page 248 in Squire [sic] and Davis in the head, the head and headgear, the nose not so prominent however. It is somewhat like figure 149 Squire Davis, but in a more upright position resembling a person squatting in the act of defecation. The arms are thrown backwards and extend at the full length. The hands spread out as if supporting the buttocks and the body is leaning forward and resting on the flexed knees (see appendix B).

The pipe illustrated on page 248, figure 148, of Squier and Davis's 1848 *Ancient Monuments of the Mississippi Valley: Comprising the Results of Extensive Original Surveys and Explorations* was that of a human figure bent over a rock with the smoking bowl in the middle of the back and a stem-hole in the buttocks. The head of the figure exhibits a scalplock similar to that worn historically by the Shawnee. The face was decorated with a hawk eye design often referred to as a "weeping eye" motif.

Facial symbolism was commonplace on artifacts from archaeological sites in the Mississippi River valley and the southeastern United States. It was also common among Muskogean-speaking tribes such as the Chickasaw, Choctaw, and Creek. The discovery of the pipe in the Little Miami River valley suggested that there likely was contact between American Indians living in those regions.

A large snake was wrapped around the neck of the figure. It is possible that the serpent was the Shawnee snake clan symbol. The Shawnee is the only tribe with the snake as a patrician name, known as *Manato*. Historically, the snake clan symbol was often used as a Shawnee tribal sign on eighteenth-century treaties. Snakes were common motifs on copper pendants and engraved bone artifacts excavated from the Ferris Cemetery. It is possible that the site represents a Shawnee Snake Town cemetery, similar to that documented during the late eighteenth century.[5]

It is also possible that the snake was symbolically associated with water. The snake is a culturally significant symbol associated with indigenous creation stories about water. For the southern Iroquoian-speaking Cherokee, Uktena, the Thunder Spirit, is a horned snake that lives in water and rain with lightning as its tongue. Other Cherokee stories related to water include the Snake Dance; Snake Boy; Snake Man; Uksuhi, the blackracer; and Gulegi, the blackrat snake.[6]

There were similar stories among Algonquian speakers such as the Ojibwa. Nanabozho was an Ojibwa warrior who encountered the great serpent at his home, Manitou Lake (i.e., Lake Superior). The great serpent made the sound of thunder by pounding water against the shore and before he died he caused a great flood in an attempt to kill all living things. Comparable creation stories are found among the Shawnee, including the tradition of a devastating flood caused by a great copper-headed serpent.[7]

On November 1 Charles wrote a letter to Putnam letting him know that the package of two ground-stone pipes was on its way to the Peabody Museum. They were so important to Charles that he insured the package for one hundred dollars. He also wrote Putnam that the largest pipe had been photographed "in case it gets lost we will know at least what it looked like" (see appendix B).

Charles let Putnam know that Charles "Low has seen the pipe this a.m. I let him see it after he promised me that he would not speak of it to anyone even Judge Cox. Britten is so worked up over the find that I am afraid he will get his "feet freezed" as he styled it and have a sore head to go to work tomorrow" (see appendix B).

Charles informed Putnam that the *Cincinnati Enquirer* had an article, which stated that, "Mr. John Cone Kimball of the Peabody Museum of Cambridge, Massachusetts was the guest of Mrs. Florence Conkling." In 1885 John Cone Kimball worked as a student field assistant for the Peabody Museum. Like Charles, he had a close personal relationship with Putnam who called him "his friend and pupil." Putnam often sent him alone to work with artifact collectors and fieldworkers. Kimball was particularly valuable in the field because he knew how to use a camera and photo-documented archaeological sites, artifacts, and features.[8]

On November 3 Charles wrote a letter to Putnam to inform him that he was allowing the anthropomorphic pipe to dry before he shipped it to the Peabody Museum.

> I still have the carved pipe here and as the moisture is drying out it appears to have a reddish cast probably the material from which it is made is compact red sandstone (see appendix B).

Interestingly, Charles described the pipe as having been made of "compact red sandstone." The pipe illustrated by Squier and Davis from Chillicothe was also described as being made of "compact red sandstone" suggesting that it may have been made by the same tribe or perhaps the same artist.

On November 13 Charles wrote a letter to Putnam giving him an update on his student assistant, Kimball, and the discovery of another pipe fragment. Charles also informed Putnam that he still was not feeling well and that he was fighting an epidemic of scarlatina. Also known as scarlet fever, scarlatina is a bacterial infection that results in a sandpaper-textured rash, a strawberry-textured tongue, a high fever (greater than 101 degrees Fahrenheit), nausea, vomiting, headache, swollen glands, and body aches.[9]

In the 1880s scarlatina was pandemic in the United States as well as Europe. Children ages five to fifteen years old were particularly vulnerable. At the time, scarlet fever was one of the most common infectious childhood diseases, which resulted in death. Fatality rates were more than 30 percent, which was more than measles, diphtheria, and pertussis. In 1885, antibiotics were not available to Charles. Without them, children often developed rheumatic fever, kidney problems, and eventually died. Even today, there is no vaccine for humans against scarlet fever.

On November 13 Charles wrote a letter to Putnam.

> Scarlatina is proceeding epidemically in this region and I have from 16 to 20 calls a day besides a number of confinements, which cause me to lose my night's rest (see appendix B).

On the evening after Charles penned his letter to Putnam, there was a reoccurrence of the great Andromedid meteor shower. The *American Journal of Science* reported that there were so many meteors that some observers could not accurately count the number of meteors per minute. Others reported seeing more than 230 per minute. It was estimated that about 75,000 meteors fell per hour.

On November 24 Charles wrote a letter to Putnam updating him on his recent fieldwork, the discovery of a new ceramic pipe, and a possible heart condition.

> Since writing to you my previous letter I have been again housed up and feel troubled with a severe neuralgia in my left side localizing itself in the region of my heart. Sometimes in my neck, arms back and face (see appendix B).

Charles's neuralgia produced a sharp, stabbing, spasm. The pain wrapped around his chest and intensified during exertion. At this juncture, it was not known whether the neuralgia was from an injury he experienced in the field or if it was actually a symptom of a more serious cardiac issue.

On December 1 and 5, Charles wrote letters to Putnam about the cold weather and the possibility of funding next years' field season and personnel. He provided an update on his health.

> I am greatly improved as regards my health. I have concluded to do quiet all night work and attend to office and day calls during the wintertime (see appendix B).

While much of the 1885 fieldwork focused on the Hahn Field and the Turpin Farm, Charles was anxious to return to the Turner site. He was also hoping that his close friend and mentor, Frederick Ward Putnam, would join him in the field, excavating together, side by side. Charles was also hoping that serendipity would strike again and more artifacts would turn up in the demonstrably Ice Age sediments.

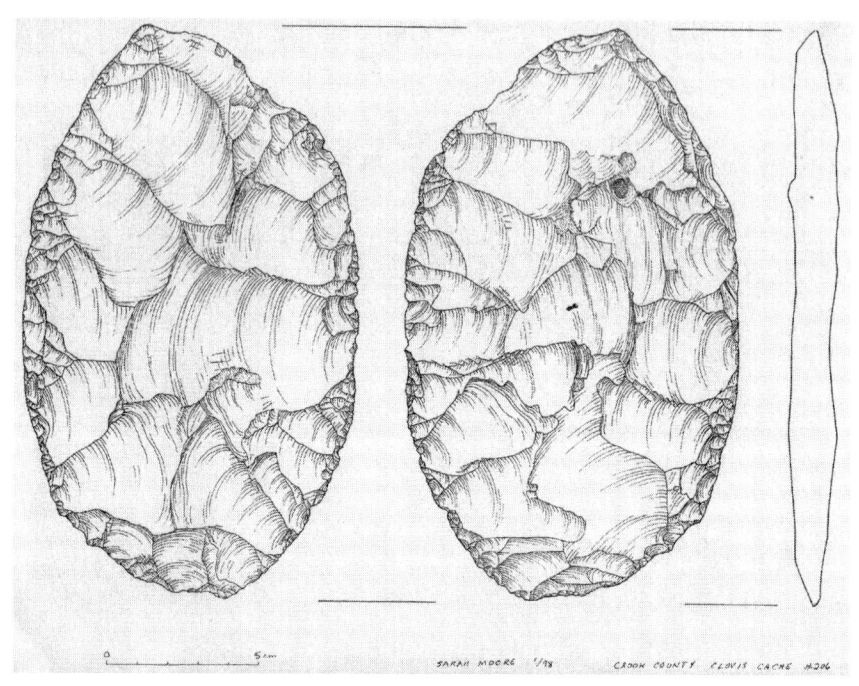

6.1. Clovis spear-point preform similar to those found by Charles Louis Metz in Madisonville and Loveland, Hamilton County, Ohio, ca. 13,500 years old.

CHAPTER 7

Revisiting the Turner Site

THE 1886 NEW YEAR began with extremely cold weather. Temperatures plummeted down to -12°F during the first two weeks of January. For Charles, it was a good time to stay inside, sit around the fire with his family, play music, sing, plan fieldwork, and read the most recent archaeological publications.

The Eighteenth Report of the Peabody Museum

In January 1886 Charles and Putnam's "Explorations in Ohio: Conducted for the Peabody Museum of American Archaeology and Ethnology, In Connection with Harvard University" was published. It focused on their exploration of a mound on the property of Benjamin Marriott in October 1884. His farm adjoined Michael Turner's land and the mound was undoubtedly part of the Turner site. It was located immediately west of a large burial mound and circular earthwork on the Turner farm.[1]

Charles named the mound Marriott Mound Number 1, as it was one of two mounds on the property. The Marriott family used the second mound as a family cemetery, thus it could not be excavated. It was also known as the "Cemetery Mound." Marriott Mound Number 1 was about sixty feet in diameter, but it had been reduced to a height of two feet by a century of plowing. Like the burial mounds on the Turner farm, it was covered with stream-worn limestone slabs.[2]

Charles and Putnam completely excavated the mound to its base. They found an ash-filled burned clay basin in the center of the mound floor. It was likely a crematory basin. Artifacts recovered from the mound included perforated black bear canine teeth with freshwater pearl inlays, bone awls, flaked-stone dart and spear points made of chert and slate, a flaked-stone knife hafted in antler handle, long narrow blades manufactured from a beautifully colored Flint Ridge chert, copper spool-shaped ear rings, and a large rectangular copper "breastplate" with a finely woven fabric adhering to it.[3]

The breastplate was manufactured from cold-hammered native copper. Buried in the carbonate-rich ground over a long period of time, percolating acidic groundwater gradually decomposed the surface of the plate. This process formed two copper carbonate minerals on the plates' surface—a deep blue mineral called azurite and a bright green mineral called malachite. Woven plant fabric adhering to the plate was preserved in this mineralization process.

Perhaps the most significant aspect of the Marriott Mound was the discovery of large postholes located fourteen to twenty-two feet from the central basin. While they could not determine whether or not the postholes "projected through the mound," Charles reported that they were similar to those found beneath the mounds on the Turner farm. They were exceptionally well preserved because iron-rich groundwater and oxidizing bacteria mineralized the decomposing wood and bark with a layer of the iron mineral goethite. The posts were likely the remains of "a wooden structure," which predated the mound's construction. The patterns of the postholes were extensive and complex demonstrating that the structures were far more complicated than a single-room building.[4]

On Methods of Archaeological Research in America

Putnam's "On Methods of Archaeological Research in America" was published in the 1886 *Johns Hopkins University Circular*. It was a written version of a paper he presented to Johns Hopkins University on December 16, 1885. The university was interested in the scientific methods used by Putnam in the excavation of archaeological sites in the Ohio Valley. Like Charles, Putnam went out of his way to emphasize that American Indians were by no means recent inhabitants in America.[5]

Putnam emphasized that it was important to understand the artistic and economic conditions of American Indians "from a period before the glacial epoch" to the present. His discussion used the three levels of cultural complexity defined by Lewis Henry Morgan in 1877—savagery, barbarism, and civilization. He argued that over thousands of years, American Indians developed comprehensive social organizations and made great advances in art. Putnam explained that the spatial and temporal variation in their symbols and artwork had "deep ethnological significance and can be classed no longer as mere coincidences." For Putnam, these artistic and symbolic patterns demonstrated that American Indians "were not the homogeneous people generally supposed."[6]

Putnam stressed that only the recent archaeological fieldwork in the Ohio River valley followed "perfect scientific methods." All of the facts had to be "properly correlated" in order to draw deductions about American Indians before European contact. He went on to assert, "that the day had passed when a simple collector of relics of the past could be called an archaeologist." Putnam further argued, "nothing can be learned" from artifact collectors because they do not record "the exact conditions under which every object was obtained and its association with other things." Thus it was impossible "to draw conclusions of any scientific value."[7]

Putnam's presentation and publication used Charles's archaeological research as an example of modern archaeological field techniques. He detailed the methods, which Charles used investigating the archaeology of the Little Miami River valley. Putnam explained that all of the archaeological sites such as burial mounds, earthworks, and villages were trenched with "vertical walls" and "sliced" to the base. He noted that these surfaces were then drawn, photographed, and measurements taken in the cardinal directions.[8]

Putnam placed an emphasis on the recovery of human skeletal remains, the documentation of their association with artifacts and features, and their comparative laboratory study with remains from other sites. Putnam stated, "Deductions of importance can be drawn only from material obtained by such methods."[9]

Putnam concluded his paper with "an appeal to all archaeologists to follow the same principles, which are followed in other departments of science." He demanded that we should "not be satisfied with partial results." Only "conscientious and thorough work" will lead to the discovery of the "origin and connections" of pre-European contact American Indians, "and their distribution and routes of migration over the continent."[10]

Long days of winter

The brutally cold weather meant that there was an increase in illnesses among Charles's family and patients. While the cold did not cause illness, people stayed inside their homes for prolonged periods of time. Their homes were heated by burning coal or wood with little or no ventilation. This form of heat created extremely dry air, which dried out sinus passages making it easy to contract a virus. Also, viruses are more active and resilient in extremely cold weather.

On January 7, 1886, Charles wrote a letter to Putnam about the increase of sickness among his family and patients.

Wilbur, and Beatrice, the baby, were quite ill. . . . Measles prevailing as an epidemic, scarlatina bronchitis and fevers prevailing with numerous other cares thrown in as a variety (see appendix B).

Charles also noted that his dear friend, Phebe Ferris, "has had too much Christmas and may be classified as having a head of *malade imaginaire*." Le malade imaginaire was a reference to the three-act 1673 comedic ballet by the French playwright Moliére. Phebe Ferris was suffering from a case of melancholy. She felt lonely after the holiday season and she loved to listen to Charles talk about his most recent archaeological exploits. He always had a way to cheer her up and was more than happy to do so.

Although Charles could not get to the field, the cold weather gave him time to pack up the artifacts and field notes from the previous year. On January 19 Charles wrote a letter to Putnam about his latest shipment. Among the shell and copper artifacts, which he boxed-up was a specimen of "carbonized matting of the basket pleating." He wrote that, "it is well preserved" (see appendix B).

Ancient basketry is extremely rare because plant fibers quickly decompose in the moist ground. In the Ohio River valley ancient basketry only survives in dusty dry caves and rockshelters. It can also be preserved when the fibers are reduced to carbon in a smoky fire. Carbon is an inert element, which does not decay when buried in the ground. Once the fibers become pure carbon, they are forever preserved, albeit extremely fragile.

On February 13, Charles wrote a letter to Putnam about funding for the upcoming field season.

> We have but a moment left before the spring plowing begins and the men are anxious to go to work at once. We should have our own team. One could be purchased for less than $150.00 and the keeping would not exceed $4.00 per week thereby saving considerable in the way of that expense. Four or five men would be a sufficient force (see appendix B).

On February 22, 1886, Charles wrote a letter to Putnam following his recent attendance at the Ohio State Archaeological and Historical Society (OSAHS) meeting. Ohio governor George Hoadly championed the incorporation of the OSAHS in 1885 "to promote knowledge of archaeology and history in Ohio." It was a revitalized organization started by former Civil War brigadier general Roeliff Brinkerhoff in 1875. The second president of the OSAHS was Rutherford B. Hayes, an outspoken Republican civil rights advocate. As president of the United States, he appointed Carl Schurz as Secretary of the Interior in charge of the Bureau of Indian Affairs. In 1881 Hayes told Congress, "In short, nothing should be left undone to show the Indians that the Government of the United States regards their rights as equally sacred with those of its citizens"[11]

Charles wrote that, "I attended the meeting of the State Archaeological and Historical Society last week at Columbus." In addition to discussing "that a committee be appointed to present the matter to the legislature and secure an appropriation for the purpose of purchasing the ancient monuments especially Ft. Ancient, Ft. Hill, the Serpent, Alligator and Forts on the Miami River and at Hamilton," the OSAHS also considered the preservation of the Marietta Mound and enclosure (see appendix B).

While Charles "was greatly disappointed in the so-called archaeological collection at the State University. . . . Poor arrangement ala Smithsonian," he was especially excited about meeting "Professor Wright" at the meeting (see appendix B).

George Frederick Wright was a professor at the Oberlin Theological Seminar where he earned a Masters of Arts in 1859. He later received a Doctorate of Divinity from Brown University and a Doctorate of Law from Drury College in 1887. Between 1881 and 1882 he served as an assistant geologist for the Pennsylvania Geological Survey. At the time Charles met Wright he was working as an assistant geologist for the U.S. Geological Survey under the directorship of John Wesley Powell. Wright was also serving as president of the OSAHS.[12]

Wright had traveled around the world many times and developed an eclectic interest in archaeology, biology, geology, history, and religion. Despite his divinity training, Wright was a staunch Darwinist and a defender of "theistic evolution." In 1884 he published, *The Glacial Boundary in Ohio, Indiana, and Kentucky*. At the OSAHS meeting, Wright told Charles about his desire to demonstrate beyond a reasonable doubt that American Indians were in North America during the Ice Age. In this vein, he shared a common theoretical ground with Charles and Putnam.[13]

Fieldwork at the Turner site

Charles and Putnam were anxious to resume excavations at the Turner site. Archaeologically, one of the most interesting aspects of the Turner site was Charles's discovery of heavy minerals such as copper, gold, and silver in the burial mounds. In a single feature, referred to as "the central altar" at the base of Mound 3, Charles found a plethora of cut, hammered, and artistically shaped copper and silver artifacts, hammered copper and gold nuggets, and unaltered copper nuggets. Mound 3 was the largest of seven connected mounds within a large earthen enclosure. Despite the fact it had been plowed repeatedly over the past century, it was fourteen feet high and one hundred feet in diameter. It was completely encased in limestone slabs.[14]

At the time, archaeologists believed that copper, silver, and gold artifacts made their way into the Ohio River valley from long distance trade or direct procurement from sources in the Great Lakes region (Michigan, Minnesota, and Wisconsin), southern Canada (Ontario, Quebec, and Manitoba), or the Appalachian Mountains of Georgia, Maryland, North and South Carolina, Tennessee, and Virginia. Charles had also discovered artifacts manufactured from Busycon, Fulgar, Marginella, and Strombus shells from the Atlantic coast and volcanic glass from western Wyoming and eastern Idaho at the Turner site, so long distance procurement seemed like a reasonable possibility.

It was more likely, however, that the copper, gold, and silver came from local sand and gravel deposits. Precious metals are especially abundant in nearby Stonelick Creek and Brushy Fork. Copper nuggets weighing more than five kilograms and gold and silver nuggets weighing more than three deadweight ton have been found in the streambeds. Charles discovered other local rocks and fossils at the Turner site. He found a cache of local invertebrate Ordovician fossils at the center of Mound 4 including brachiopods (*Platystrophia ponderosa*), horn corals (*Grewingkia canadensis*), and stream-worn, bituminous coal cobbles, which were common in the gravel bars of the Ohio River.[15]

On April 19 Charles wrote a letter to Putnam about the results of his recent archaeological survey of the Little Miami River valley. He noted that "There are so many places where mounds are located four to ten in a group." Charles also inquired about the return of Putnam's twenty-one-year-old student, William Baker Nickerson, to the Peabody Museum (see appendix B).

Nickerson, along with John Cone Kimball and Cordelia A. Studley were the first archaeology students in the United States. They studied archaeology at Harvard University under the tutelage and mentorship of Putnam between 1883 and 1887. He taught them firsthand archaeological field and laboratory methods and how to interpret data.

On May 6 Charles wrote a letter to Putnam about beginning fieldwork at the Turner site.

> Britten and my brother are camped in the old Marriott house on the riverbank near the Whittlesey work. Hoping that you will be enabled to carry on the work with at least two men this summer and that we shall make some food finds right along (see appendix B).

On May 16 Charles wrote another letter to Putnam about the discovery of two new groups of stone mounds.

> On most every prominent point along the East Fork of the Little Miami River are stone graves and at one place on the Stone Lick Creek are probably about 100 (see appendix B).

He also inquired about Putnam's opinion of Wright's intention to investigate the occurrence of American Indian artifacts in Ice Age deposits.

On June 25 Charles wrote a letter to Putnam about the ongoing fieldwork at the Turner site and his plans to attend the August AAAS meeting in Buffalo with his fifteen-year-old daughter, Annie (Anna Teresa).

I propose to attend the Buffalo meeting of the AAAS and shall be accompanied by my daughter Annie. I have many relatives living at Buffalo whom I propose to visit (see appendix B).

The June 16 issue of the *Clermont Courier* included an article about Charles's archaeological research in the Little Miami River valley, which greatly disturbed him. On July 8 Charles enclosed a copy of the article along with a letter to Putnam. Charles wrote that "The last half is especially bad and if not they have something especially valuable in their mounds and will go to digging themselves (see appendix B)."

Charles sought Putnam's advice about how to respond to the article.

Do you not think it advisable to sent a communication to the *Courier* stating the object of the exploration; what becomes of the finds, how they are arranged for study and that they are not bartered for in the market. That the work we are doing is paid by money contributed by individuals and this is in the interest of archaeological science (see appendix B).

Charles was trying to systematically examine burial mounds, earthworks, and village sites in the Little Miami River valley before plowing, construction, and sand and gravel mining destroyed them. He was concerned that the article, which discussed the lucrative artifact market and the intrinsic value of gold and silver artifacts, would prompt grave robbers and artifact hunters to dig in the mounds.

Charles understood that once the ground was disturbed, it could never be returned to its original state. In other words, the archaeological record is finite—not renewable. His goal was to preserve all of the contents of the mounds as well as their documentation such as field notes, maps, and photographs in museums and universities so many future generations of archaeologists could study them.

On July 20 Charles wrote a letter to Putnam about the AAAS.

I have received the certificate of election as a Fellow (of the AAAS) several days ago. Thanks. Will try and be at the Buffalo meeting if all goes right here (see appendix B).

He also explained to Putnam that bone preservation was highly degraded in the stone mounds. American Indians living in the Little Miami River valley commonly used limestone in their mortuary features. Charles found that many of the mounds in the Little Miami River valley were covered with stream-worn slabs of limestone. Over the centuries, the stones were covered with wind-blown sediment and vegetation giving the appearance of an earthen mound. Mounds on the hilltops, however, lost most if not all of the soil beneath the stone slabs, creating what appeared as mounds of limestone. Without soil encasing the contents of mounds, bone tissues quickly decomposed.

On July 26, Charles wrote another letter to Putnam reaffirming the poor condition of bone in the hilltop stone mounds. Charles explained to Putnam that he decided to abandon his work on hilltop stone mounds stating, "I should go to work on a mound in the valley having lost faith in the mounds on the high places." He did note, however, "I have a region of stone graves in reserve for you to explore when you come out" (see appendix B).

Thirty-fifth annual meeting of the AAAS

The Thirty-fifth annual meeting of the AAAS was held in August in Buffalo, New York. Charles and his daughter Anna traveled to Buffalo, New York, by train. In addition to visiting relatives, Anna wanted to visit Amherst College. Since 1846 it was a well-known medical school and it had a hospital for teaching purposes. Millard Fillmore, the thirteenth president of the United States was an alumnus. By 1886 women had entered the medical profession. Indeed, Cincinnati resident Elizabeth Blackwell was the first woman to receive a medical degree in the United States on January 23, 1849.[16]

While Anna visited Amherst College, Charles met with Putnam and attended the Anthropology session of the AAAS meeting. Although Charles did not present a paper at the meeting, his work was discussed in Putnam's conference presentation, "The Diversity of the Mounds and Earthworks in the United States."

On August 19 Charles wrote a letter to Molly about their travel in New York and Canada. He let her know that their daughter was making good use of their time.

> Anna goes to Amherst to stay today. She is just having a good time. ... Anna gets good ideas and will make a good traveler before long. ... It does not take her long to find out things. Anna has seen many new things yesterday and today she shall see more (see appendix B).

Charles also explained that, "Professor Putnam wants us to stay until after the meeting and stop over at Dayton, Ohio and visit the Soldier's Home." The Soldiers Home in Dayton, Ohio, which Charles mentioned in his letter, was a hospital and nursing home established following the Civil War for disabled Union veterans.

The home provided veterans with large, beautifully decorated reading-rooms filled with flowering plants and colorful pictures and paintings. There was also a military cemetery filled with white marble tombstones in a hundred-acre grove on the west side of the home. In 1877 Rutherford B. Hayes dedicated a fifty-foot high white marble monument of a Union private for the cemetery. It was inscribed with the words "To our fallen comrades and these were honorable men in their generation."[17]

Archaeological field camp

On September 4 Putnam and Charles set up a field camp along the Little Miami River along with Putnam's student protégé and photographer John Cone Kimball, Charles Low, Matthias Britten, and Thomas Ryan. Britten and Ryan had worked with Charles over the previous five years. They set up two tents for files, maps, and equipment, and three for sleeping.

The news going round camp was that Chiricahua Apache chief Geronimo had surrendered to Gen. Nelson Miles at Skeleton Canyon, Arizona, after thirty years of defending his homeland. His laying down of arms brought an end to the Indian Wars. At Fort Bowie, Arizona, Geronimo and his men were loaded into the boxcars of a train bound for Florida.[18]

Back at the Turner site, Putnam excavated twenty-five graves, most of which were stone lined and included grave goods such as copper pins and breast plates, flaked-stone blades, ground-coal celts, large conch shell vessels, mica, perforated bear canine teeth, shell beads, and spool-shaped copper ear ornaments held in skeletal hands. Putnam also uncovered what he labeled cache pits, which had been dug to a depth of three feet into the underlying sand and gravel deposit. They were surrounded by postholes.[19]

In order to maximize their time in the field, Charles excavated seven different mortuary features. Like those excavated by Putnam, the graves were stone lined and contained bone awls and needles, mica, shell beads, and spool-shaped copper ear ornaments. Charles also discovered that not all of the skeletons were complete. He found evidence of reburials, partial cremations, and complete cremations. Charles also found postholes around most of the graves suggesting preexisting structures.[20]

From the Turner site, Charles, Putnam, and their workforce moved their camp upstream to excavate a mound on the farm of Robert McCafferty in Vera Cruz, Brown County, Ohio. The mound was about sixty feet in diameter, three feet high, and situated on high ground above a permanent spring, about 140 feet south from a smaller mound. The height of mounds had been greatly reduced by plowing.[21]

Like the Turner site, they found an intrusive burial. Below the interment, Charles and Putnam discovered a polished celt, four large spear points, potsherds, and a ten-inch layer of ashes. One of the more interesting discoveries was an enclosure of some sixty closely spaced post molds beneath the ashes and six to eight feet from the center of the mound. The remains suggested that a structure had burned to the ground prior to the mound's construction.[22]

On October 2 Charles and Putnam returned to the Turner site to determine the nature and relationship of the site's most prominent features—the elevated circle, graded way, and the great oval. They occurred on a second glacial terrace. Charles and Putnam discovered that segments of the terrace had been prehistorically excavated and sculpted to create the elevated circle and graded way. In other words, American Indians had the ability to modify their landscape at a very large scale, thousands of years ago.[23]

The geometric design and location of the Turner earthworks suggested that they were, at least in part, hydraulic features. The graded way dammed water from Turner's primary stream and the south ditch of the elevated circle diverted water into the great enclosure. Additional water was diverted into this area from limestone lined features that Charles and Putnam described as a "drain or gutter" within the earthen enclosures of the elevated circle and graded way. This system of managing water was undoubtedly an important aspect of agriculture at the Turner site. Because it is underlain by porous sand and gravel, it would have been seasonally drought prone.[24]

Charles received a letter from Putnam explaining that his student assistant, Nickerson, was on his way to the Turner site to assist Charles in the field. On October 23 Charles responded in a letter to Putnam about his concerns.

I do not know what to say about Nickerson coming out here. I candidly think that he is not nor never will be an archaeologist. Adopting archaeology for a profession seems to me a very queer idea. He was out here. He made very little out of the opportunity. He would pay no attention to what suggestions I made (see appendix B).

As it turned out, Charles was correct about Nickerson's career path. He quit archaeology and sought regular employment. Putnam used his financial situation to call for the University Foundation "to form scholarships, by which means might be at hand for the support of deserving students or assistants." While Nickerson "evinced an aptitude for archaeological research," there simply was no funding available to support him in the discipline. While Charles had become a well-recognized archaeologist, he had his medical profession to support his family. At the time, archaeology alone could not support Nickerson's livelihood.[25]

Although Charles continued to excavate at the Turner site after Putnam's departure, the landowner had imposed some restrictions on where he could work. On October 24 Charles wrote a letter to Putnam to let him know that, "Mr. Turner refuses to allow us to dig in the field west of the road. He says we can go into it all we want next Summer" (see appendix B).

The day after Charles wrote his letter to Putnam, news reached Cincinnati that Geronimo and fourteen of his men arrived in Florida. They were supposed to be imprisoned at Fort Marion in St. Augustine, Florida, but the citizens of Pensacola Bay petitioned the government to have them incarcerated at Fort Pickens as tourist attraction for the city. For Geronimo and his men, it was no vacation. In spite of the signed terms of their surrender, they were forced to do hard labor as hundreds of tourists gawked at them.[26]

Charles continued to excavate at the Turner site. On November 4 he wrote a letter to Putnam about an interesting discovery at the Turner site. He was able to confirm his previous suspicion that the Turner burial mounds were in fact built on top of a large village site, which included a suite of complex structures. In the letter, Charles described the contents of the mound.

> This mound contains an enormous quantity of animal remains, fragments of pottery, shells some with perforations, fragments of burned masses of clay. In fact, the mound seems as far as we have

gone to have been made of all kinds of refuse—a veritable kitchen midden (see appendix B).

Fort Ancient

By November Charles had a growing concern that the Fort Ancient earthworks and mounds located on a ridge 270 feet above the Little Miami River in Warren County, Ohio were endangered. The Fort Ancient earthwork was three and one-half miles long and enclosed one hundred acres making it the largest hilltop earthwork in the United States. The site was also considered significant because it contained a village with artifacts that resembled those recovered from the Ferris Cemetery and burial mounds similar to the Turner site.

On November 6 Charles wrote a letter to Putnam about the possibility of the Peabody Museum's purchase of the Fort Ancient site.

> I have been looking up the Ft. Ancient matter. . . . I think $6,000.00 will buy the whole Fort from both parties together with enough slope to protect the work (see appendix B).

On November 9 Charles and Molly's sixth child was born, Ethel Helen. She was named after Putnam's daughter, Ethel. The next day, Charles penned a letter to Putnam about her birth. He delightfully wrote that "Yesterday Mrs. Metz presented me with a little daughter. Both mother and child are doing well" (see appendix B).

On November 15, Charles wrote another letter to Putnam about the possibility of the Peabody acquiring the Fort Ancient site.

> What do you think about Ft. Ancient? Can you not get it now? Is it not more important than the serpent. . . . Will not some moneyed individual immortalize himself or herself by advancing $10,000.00 to save one of the greatest monuments on the American Continent? Had I but the means Peabody should have Ft. Ancient for Thanksgiving present. . . . The Cowden heirs won the land enclosed in the Fort except a few acres at the north end and all of the land forming the slopes of the hill 291 acres in all. This they will sell at $30.00 per acre if taken altogether. . . . Mr. Rich has not yet made a proposition as yet and he may come to terms at about $50.00 to $75.00 per acre (see appendix B).

Charles explained to Putnam that the Rich family property included the hillsides of Fort Ancient and a number of significant mortuary features. Clinton Cowden, however, was the principal owner of Fort Ancient. When he passed, Alfred Cowden and the Dunham family were the principal heirs of the vast majority of the site. They were working closely with Warren King Moorehead and Gerard Fowke to find a means to purchase the site. Fowke and Moorehead were considered at the very least competitors and more realistically the nemeses of Charles and Putnam.

Unlike Charles, Moorehead was independently wealthy. His grandfather, Joseph Warren King, developed a fortune selling black powder to the United States during the Civil War. He owned the King's Powder Mills, which Morgan's raiders failed to destroy. Moorehead pursued an academic career in archaeology at Denison University. He eventually dropped out of college and became a professional artifact collector. Despite his relationship with Thomas Wilson at the Smithsonian Institution, he ignored the proper archaeological field methods of the time. His goal was to increase his personal collection of artifacts, thus the professional community largely dismissed his interpretations.[27]

Fowke on the other hand was an academically trained geologist. He worked for the Smithsonian Institution and focused on the geology of the Ohio River valley. He was best known for his careful documentation of Flint Ridge, a significant source of colorful chert used by American Indians for more than thirteen thousand years for the production of flaked-stone tools and weapons.[28]

Between November 16 and 27 Charles wrote brief letters to Putnam detailing his work and findings at the Turner site. On November 28 Charles wrote a third letter to Putnam about the occurrence of stone-lined graves in the Little Miami River valley. He believed, "that wherever we find limestone laying on the surface they mark either a burial or other place that has been used for some purpose or another." Charles also explained to Putnam that he and his men were "now working in two places" (see appendix B).

Charles was careful not to overwork and under pay his men. He was keenly aware that laborers were unionizing across the country, beginning with the Knights of Labor. By 1886 the Knights of Labor membership had reached almost a million people from the working class. In 1886 they had been involved with a number of strikes, including some of which were violent. Thus, Charles went out of his way to take care of his fieldworkers. He also wanted to make sure he could count on them the following year.

On December 18 Charles updated Putnam about the status of his fieldwork and health. He noted that "I have stopped all work on account of the weather. Am convalescing rapidly from my throat trouble." Charles also inquired about the possibility of obtaining Christmas money for his fieldworkers. He noted that "they want some for Christmas" (see appendix B).

In addition to the welfare of his fieldworkers, Charles was also concerned about those who could not fend for themselves. The first of January 1887 Charles paid his membership fee for the year for Ohio State Society for the Prevention of Cruelty to Children and Animals. He was also reelected as a Madisonville School trustee for a period of three more years.

Charles did not abandon his concerns about the potential loss of Fort Ancient. On January 31, 1887, Charles wrote to Putnam and asked, "What about Ft. Ancient?" He also wanted Putnam to know that his student, Kimball, was doing well. Charles wrote, "that Mr. Kimball is yet among the living and getting the photographs ready to send on" (see appendix B).

Competition

On April 20 Charles wrote Putnam a letter about the recent publication of two new books which discussed the archaeology of the Little Miami River valley.

> I sent you a copy of Shephard's *Antiquity's of Ohio* [sic] in which much of the three last Peabody Museum reports is embodied. . . . I met Dr. Gustav Brühl of Cincinnati who has just returned from Yucatan and the Myan [sic] Country. . . . The doctor thinks that the Myans have been overestimated by many writers. Dr. Brühl is waiting on publishing a book in German. The doctor said that he should have published in English instead of German (see appendix B).

The book written in German was Gustav Brühl's 516-page *Die Culturvolker Alt-Amerika's* (Culture of the Americas) published in 1887 by the Cincinnati-based Benziger Brothers' Press. Brühl was a close friend of Charles, a fellow doctor, and a member of the LSSM. Unfortunately, he used the book as a forum to argue that the architects of the burial mounds and earthworks of the Little Miami River valley were the builders of pyramids in Mesoamerica, a throwback to the days of William Henry Harrison.

Ice Age archaeology

During the warmer months of 1887, Charles surveyed the west fork of the Little Miami River. He discovered a tear-dropped shaped flaked stone tool in the glacial gravels of a terrace lining the valley. It was similar in appearance and context to the one discovered next to his home in 1885. This time, however, it was located at a depth of thirty feet below the surface and "in close proximity to mastodon bones." The artifact was another Clovis spear point preform. Charles had found the evidence he and Putnam were looking for: American Indians had, indeed, been in the Little Miami River valley during the last Ice Age. Although there was no way to determine the age of the artifact, it was at least thirteen thousand years old.[29]

Completing the Turner Site excavations

Charles's fieldwork continued through the end of the decade, as did the size of his family. On August 21, 1889, their seventh child was born, Julia Marie. She was the fifth surviving daughter. With their brother, Charles Wilbur, they were now a family of eight.

Three days after the birth of Marie, Charles wrote a letter to Putnam that there was some urgency to complete the work at the Turner site.

> Mr. Turner is confined to his bed and cannot last more than two or three weeks. We must make haste to get through with the Turner work this fall. It will be our last chance (see appendix B).

On August 26, 1889, Charles emphasized the growing importance of the Turner site in his letter to Putnam. He wrote about his recent discoveries, which were among the most significant finds at site during the past decade.

> Another hit has been made today in the discovery of a small altar containing numerous relics such as perforated shark's teeth, copper beads, copper earrings, oblong copper ornaments, one or two copper buttons, two little cones of meteoric iron, one flat pin of bone finally carved and representing the Central American carved figu-

rines more closely than anything I have yet seen from here, numerous pieces of cylindrical bone carved, and mica (see appendix B).

While the copper and meteoric iron were likely procured locally, the perforated sharks teeth and mica were undoubtedly from exchange, trade, or long distance procurement. Although Putnam was anxious to see the latest findings from the Turner site, the owner passed away.

Putnam wrote in a letter to Charles on September 26.

> So the poor old man has gone at last. With the horrible disease that he had, we can only be thankful for him. Please give my sympathy to his son. . . . How do you find Saville, and how does he take hold now that he is left by himself so much? I hope to make a good archaeologist of him, and trust that you are doing your part in putting him through in the right way (see appendix B).

Putnam was referring to Marshall Howard Saville, an archaeology student from Rockport, Massachusetts. In 1889 he was Putnam's assistant curator of Ohio Valley archaeology at the Peabody Museum. With his timely help, work continued at the Turner site. Saville was able to fill the gaps when Charles could not be on site. He explained this situation in a letter to Putnam a letter on October 2.

> I have been suffering from a carbuncle on my neck and in consequence I have not been at the camp since the 21st but shall go up tomorrow and after that daily (see appendix B).

Looking ahead

As the year came to a close, Charles and Putnam were looking forward to the possibility of showing their archaeological discoveries to an international audience at the upcoming World's Fair. It was going to celebrate the four hundredth anniversary of Christopher Columbus's landing in the Western Hemisphere. While the exact time and place had not been set, the cities of Chicago, New York, Saint Louis, and Washington D.C. were being bantered about. Ultimately, Congress would make the final decision on the basis of available funding.[30]

122 *American Indian Archaeology of the Little Miami River Valley*

7.1. Families of Charles Louis Metz and Frederick Ward Putnam at the Great Serpent Mound, Peebles, Adams County, Ohio, ca. 1887.

CHAPTER 8

The World's Columbian Exposition

By 1890 Charles and Molly had six children living at home with them—Anna Teresa, age nineteen; Clara Isabel, age thirteen; Charles Wilbur, age nine; Beatrice Amelia, age six; Ethel Helen, age four; and the baby, Julia Marie, age one. Additionally, the number of Charles's patients who made office visits had grown and he had a new partner—Arthur Knight, M.D. He needed a new doctors' office and a new in-office pharmacy.[1]

Charles also wanted to maximize the time he spent at home with his family. His solution was to build a new home that accommodated his growing family and medical practice. Charles's plan was to move their wooden frame house to the back of their Madisonville lot facing what was then Julian Street, today's Prentice Street, to make room for a new and much larger and more permanent stone and brick house facing Madisonville's main street, Madison Road.[2]

Planning the World's Fair

As construction on Charles's new home and office was underway, Putnam was appointed president of the World's Columbian Commission and chief of the Department of Ethnology and Archaeology for the exposition. In

1890 he turned to Charles to create an exhibition on Ohio archaeology for the exposition. Putnam knew that Charles had many years of experience creating models of archaeological sites and exhibitions of American Indian artifacts. Although Charles knew that it would take years of hard work to put an exhibition together for the World's Fair, he thought it would be a chance to educate an international audience about the true nature and accomplishments of American Indians in the Ohio River valley.

World's fairs were immensely popular and extremely lucrative during the second half of the nineteenth century. More than ten million people attended the Centennial Exhibition of 1876 in Philadelphia and more than twenty-eight million people attended the Exposition Universelle of 1889 in Paris. They brought the cultures of the world to the working class who could not afford international travel, but did have enough money to bring their family to a World's Fair.[3]

In 1889 Congress began reviewing proposals from major cities across the United States for the venue of the World's Fair. On February 24, 1890, they awarded it to Chicago. Mayor DeWitt C. Cregier, Lyman Gage, Andrew McNally, George Pullman, and Charles Schwab raised five million dollars for the fair and they convinced Congress that they could raise another five million dollars. Of course, the sympathy factor for Chicago did not hurt. The great fire of 1871 was still in the memory of most Americans as well as the 1886 Haymarket Square bombing. Having the World's Fair in Chicago would help the city recover from the national perception of a city in ruin. Because only twenty-eight years had passed since the Civil War, it also would give the United States a chance to heal as one nation.[4]

While Chicago demonstrated that they had the ability to raise millions of dollars, Congress insisted that city supporters would have to work together with at least two representatives from each state and territory under the direction of retired army colonel George Davis. The theme of the fair was going to be the celebration of the Columbian quadricentennial.[5]

Given the phenomenal success of the Paris Exposition Universelle of 1889, Chicago decided to use it as a template for their World's Fair. They even borrowed, in part, the name of the fair—the Columbian Exposition. One of the key components of the Paris Universal Exposition's popularity was its anthropological perspective of "civilization." Exhibits of modern civilization, such as the Eiffel Tower, juxtaposed "primitive" villages and indigenous people from French colonies in Africa and Asia. The exhibits were recreated with the assistance of the most renowned European anthropologists of the day. They filled the exhibits with ethnographic and archaeological artifacts.[6]

Davis turned to George Brown Goode, a taxonomist and the assistant secretary of the Smithsonian Institution to help him repeat the success of the Exposition Universelle. Goode had experience organizing the popular Philadelphia Exposition and he had a strong interest in the history of American science. Goode believed that the World's Fair should be designed as an "encyclopedia of civilization" that would be juxtaposed by American Indian exhibitions and other examples of what he called "primitive human beings." Given that the Indian Wars had officially ended with Geronimo's surrender, the idea seemed both plausible and peaceable.[7]

Goode studied at Harvard and, like Putnam, was a trained ichthyologist. Goode asked Putnam to be in charge of the fair's anthropological and archaeological exhibition. Goode wanted American Indian culture and technology, past and present, to serve as a stark contrast to the civilized people of Chicago. In order to accomplish this task, Putnam turned to German anthropologist, Franz Uri Boas, later known as the father of American Anthropology for help. Boas was asked to direct almost one hundred "assistants" and create living exhibits of American Indians "in their natural conditions of life."[8]

Working with Warren King Moorehead

In order to have a successful anthropological exhibition at the Chicago World's Fair, Charles and Putnam were forced to work closely with people and institutions, which were their scientific rivals and, at times, nemeses. This situation meant that they would be working side by side at the national level with the Smithsonian Institution and at the local level with Warren King Moorehead.

Like Charles, Moorehead had been interested in archaeology since he was a schoolboy. Because he was independently wealthy, Moorehead could fund large-scale excavations and amass enormous collections of pristine artifacts as exemplified by his extravagant personal display at the 1888 Cincinnati Centennial Exposition. With support from his friends at the Smithsonian, Moorehead entered the University of Pennsylvania under the mentorship of world famous vertebrate paleontologist, Edward Drinker Cope.

Today, it might seem unusual for someone interested in archaeology to enter an academic program of vertebrate paleontology. However, it is important to remember that paleontology is the study of past life. As humans are living things with backbones, evidence of ancient human life fell under the auspices of vertebrate paleontology. In this regard, we may think of archaeology as glorified paleontology and artifacts and features as nothing more than trace fossils. It was not until fairly recently that anthropology claimed archaeology as a sub-discipline.

Moorehead's time as a college student was brief. He did not like being overshadowed by Cope and thought it was beneath him to write papers that would be read by only one person. Morehead dropped out of school and began to work on a series of public lectures and publications.[9]

In 1890, at the age of twenty-four, Moorehead published a somewhat successful novel, *Wanneta: The Sioux*. It attracted the attention of Maurice M. Milton, the general manager of the *Illustrated American*, the latest "weekly news magazine" published in New York. The fledgling magazine wanted to exploit the national enthusiasm associated with the upcoming World's Fair.

Milton was especially interested in anthropological and archaeological articles about the American Indians. He offered Moorehead a contract to write an article about the Ghost Dance as it was being practiced at the Pine Ridge Indian Reservation, South Dakota. Moorehead agreed to be a "special correspondent" for the magazine.[10]

Moorehead had a family friend at Pine Ridge, U.S. Marshall George Bartlett. He had been employed at the Kings Powder Company, Moorehead's family business in Xenia. In February 1890 Bartlett offered to show Moorehead around Pine Ridge and introduce him to the tribal leaders of the Lakota Nation. Moorehead was especially keen on the idea as Bartlett spoke some Lakota.[11]

At Pine Ridge Moorehead found that Bartlett was true to his word. He took Moorehead from camp to camp introducing him to Lakota elders including the chief of the Oglala, Mapíya Lúta, (Red Cloud). They were always warmly welcomed. Moorehead's pleasant visit at Pine Ridge quickly took a downturn as he was engulfed in a mass of journalists.[12]

The reporters were from the *Chicago Tribune, Dakotan, Frank Leslie's*

Illustrated Newspaper, Harper's Weekly, New York Times, Omaha Daily Bee, Washington Post, and the *Yankton Press*. They were in search of a flashy career changing news story about an Indian uprising and the outbreak of a new Indian war that threatened national security on the eve of the World's Fair. Even though there was no truth to the matter, headlines in Cincinnati newspapers throughout the month of November 1890 were about the impending Indian war.[13]

The Ghost Dance was a religious ritual. Instead of writing about the true nature of the ceremony, newspaper reporters claimed it was a war dance and call to arms. They distorted the ceremony's true meaning with fictionalized field sketches, distorted and staged photographs, and menacing captions to support their claims. On December 6, 1890, *Harper's Weekly* ran a copy of Frederic Remington's, *Ghost Dance by the Ogallala Sioux at Pine Ridge Agency, Dakota*.[14]

By December 15 word had spread across the United States that the Indian police murdered the Hunkpapa's spiritual leader, Sitting Bull. His death was a devastating loss to the Lakota and reached far beyond Pine Ridge. Sitting Bull had won the hearts of people all over the world during his tour with Buffalo Bill's Wild West Show, which featured his adopted daughter from Cincinnati, Annie Oakley.[15]

With Bartlett as his interpreter, Moorehead was the only reporter on the scene who understood that the Ghost Dance was, in fact, a peaceful religious ceremony and not a call to war. Much to his credit, Moorehead's field reports to Milton were more anthropological and academic than those of the newspaper journalists.[16]

While Moorehead believed that all American Indians should be fully assimilated into American society, he was sympathetic with the Lakota, their way of life, and their religious beliefs. Rather than inciting a national panic about a fictionalized Indian war, Moorehead asked his readers for a "greater cultural understanding" of Lakota culture.[17]

On Christmas Eve, December 24, 1890, Benjamin Harrison issued an official Presidential Proclamation recognizing Chicago as the official location of the next World's Fair. It was widely known that the Lakota would be a crucial component of the fair. That fact did not sit well with the Seventh Cavalry Regiment. The idea of inviting the very people who killed Custer and members of the Seventh Cavalry to a World's Fair was infuriating.[18]

It had only been fourteen years since the battle of Little Big Horn and members of the Seventh Cavalry were hungry for revenge. The highly sensationalized and fictionalized public reporting of an Indian uprising at Pine Ridge was all they needed to justify their heavy-handed dealings with the Lakota. One last decisive and victorious battle with the Lakota would help the Seventh Cavalry finally set the record straight.[19]

It was clear to Gen. John Rutter Brooke that Moorehead's reporting to the *Illustrated American* was supportive of the Lakota and it could be used to prejudice his planned military actions with President Harrison, Congress, and the citizens of the United States. They were all heavily invested in the upcoming World's Fair. On December 28, 1890, Brooke had Moorehead escorted off the reservation and put on a train "under armed military escort."[20]

The next morning, with Moorehead out of the way, Col. James W. Forsyth and the Seventh Cavalry, serving under the orders of General Brooke, slaughtered at Wounded Knee, South Dakota, upward of 300 innocent unarmed Lakota men, women, and children who meant no harm. Moorehead had managed to give his camera to a fellow correspondent who used it to take photographs of the atrocity—the bodies of more than 150 Lakota men, women, and children morbidly frozen in the snow. Brooke also got his way with Congress. Rather than being convicted of war crimes, some twenty members of the Seventh Cavalry were awarded the Congressional Medal of Honor for their roles in the massacre.[21]

Conflicts with Moorehead

Moorehead returned to Ohio to begin work on the upcoming Columbian Exposition. However, he also continued his employment with the *Illustrated American*. In January 1891 Putnam appointed Moorehead as a "field assistant" to work at Fort Ancient and a number of other sites in the Little Miami River valley. Although Putnam consistently encouraged Moorehead to work with Charles, they avoided one another. Charles and Moorehead were like oil and water in social and economic class, ethnicity, and education. Moorehead especially resented the fact Charles was known as Dr. Metz and he was known as Mr. Moorehead.[22]

In March Charles received word that Charles Low, his dear friend and close companion in the field, had died. On March 17, 1891, he wrote a heartfelt eulogy, which was sent to the members of the LSSM that their longtime secretary and cofounder had passed away.

> In the death of C. F. Low we recognize the loss of one of the most active and efficient members of this Society. He was one of its founders and has contributed much to make it celebrated throughout civilized World (see appendix B).

While Putnam was sympathetic about the loss of Charles Low, the pressure of planning the World's Fair was emotionally consuming him. On April 20, 1891, Putnam hastily wrote a letter to Charles stating, "My trials are about as much as I can stand just at the present."[23]

In May 1891 Putnam wrote a letter to Charles formally appointing him a "Special Assistant" to the World's Columbian Exposition. Putnam was very concerned that the massacre at Wounded Knee may have tainted the public's appeal for the World's Fair. He told Charles, "I am anxious for you to stir up an interest in Ohio in favor of the Exposition." Putnam also emphasized that he wanted Charles to help develop a "thorough representation" of Ohio archaeology.[24]

Putnam was in the process of making a relief map of the Great Serpent Mound in Adams County, Ohio, for the exhibition and he wanted Charles to make a comparable one for the Turner earthworks and mounds. Because Congress was closely monitoring all of their expenditures, Putnam asked Charles to carefully document all expenses "entered in detail even to a postage stamp.[25]

The next time Putnam wrote Charles it was on a new and embossed letterhead, which included a listing of the multiple affiliations including the "World's Columbian Exposition, Chicago, 1893," and the "Department of Ethnology and Archaeology, Peabody Museum of Archaeology, Cambridge, Massachusetts," (see appendix B).

Putnam sent a second letter to Charles on July 3, but on Peabody Museum stationary. It included a twenty-five-dollar check for Charles's monthly Harvard salary and a notice that new stationary for the World's Columbian Exposition was being created for him. It would include his official title, "Special Assistant in Charge of Archaeological Work in Ohio."[26]

Having Charles in charge of all of the archaeological fieldwork in Ohio did not bode well with Moorehead. Likewise, Charles was not happy about having to work with Moorehead. Aside from the German Catholic–Scots-Irish Protestant rivalry, which was commonplace in Ohio at the time, Charles could not stand the way Moorehead cavalierly ignored the scientific field methods of the day.

Moorehead would brag before public audiences that he could completely excavate a burial mound in a morning's work. Charles felt that Moorehead was destroying the archaeological record of the Ohio River valley just to obtain specimens for his personal collection. Although Putnam was of the same opinion, he agreed to work with Moorehead in order for the World's Fair to be a success.

On July 27, 1891, Putnam wrote Charles a lengthy letter about his concerns.

> Now in relation to work in the field, it is my wish to have you conduct an exploration for the World's Fair. . . . Mr. Moorehead will call upon you at Madisonville on his way out so as to have everything perfectly harmonious and satisfactory between you. Moorehead is working fully in the interest of the Museum and the World's Fair, and I want everything to be smooth and harmonious between you. He is ready to work under your general guidance (see appendix B).

Even though Moorehead was independently wealthy, he refused to be out of pocket even for the most mundane of expenses. On August 7, 1891, Putnam wrote Charles about Moorehead's complaints.

> Mr. Moorehead telegraphed me that he only had two tents one of which was small and that he could not stow his party away in them. He asked permission to purchase another. I did not understand what had become of all our tents but supposed some misfortune had befallen them and authorized him to purchase another one as low as possible. I see now that you still have two good tents on hand, and if you can stop Mr. Moorehead's purchase and send him one of these it will be a good thing, as I do not like to get such a stock of canvas stored away to rot. . . . I have telegraphed Moorehead now to stop the purchase and get the tent from you, but it may be too late, unless you know where he was buying one (see appendix B).

Aside from his dealings with Moorehead, Putnam also wrote Charles about the upcoming exhibition.

> The plan mentioned in a previous letter relating to an archaeological map of the Little Miami Valley ... an enlarged copy of the whole valley and then locate the various work upon it, so as to show the full archaeology from the implements in the gravel to the old fireplaces in the river bottom and the earth-works, mounds, village sites, burial-places, etc. We could then have a careful drawing made of the whole map (see appendix B).

Putnam also wrote Charles about his archaeological survey at Fort Hill and to make a model of the site, comparable to one, which was made for the Serpent Mound site in Adams County, Ohio. Fort Hill, described in Putnam's letter, is an earthen enclosure excavated in 1846 by Squier and Davis and described in their 1848 *Ancient Monuments of the Mississippi Valley*.

The earthwork is similar to Fort Ancient. It is 2,627 meters (8,619 feet) long, 10 meters (30 feet) wide, and between 2 and 5 meters high (6-15 feet) with 39 openings. The enclosure is located on a hilltop about 150 meters (500 feet) above Ohio Brush Creek and more than 240 meters (800 feet) above the Ohio River.

Putnam sent Moorehead to work at the Hopewell and Mound City sites in Ross County, Ohio. They included more than twenty burial mounds and earthworks located along the Scioto River about six kilometers (four miles) north of Chillicothe. Like Fort Hill, Squier and Davis originally excavated the sites in the 1840s. They found that the mounds were built on top of crematory basins.

On September 2, 1891, Moorehead wrote a letter to Putnam and copied Charles from the home of Levi Anderson on the west side of Chillicothe. Moorehead again asked Putnam for more money, including payment for his mother's services.

> We got provisions cheap. My Mom for the most part works for $5.00 per week and board, some of the men at $1.00 per day and board, and my right-hand man gets $1.50. I shall use every endeavor to keep expenses within the bounds of reason. Please consider this request and let me hear from you at your earliest convenience (see appendix B).

Building the anthropology and archaeology exhibitions

The location of the World's Fair was originally planned for Chicago's lakefront, but the real estate was just too expensive to acquire. Instead, a poorly used marshy area known as Jackson Park was chosen as the location. The fair was originally scheduled to open in 1892, but the added cost of using the swampy location caused delays in the construction pushing back the opening day to May 1, 1893. While the exhibition buildings were under construction in Chicago, Charles and Molly were busy expanding their family at home in Madisonville. Their son, George Francis, was born on January 25, 1892.[27]

Back in Chicago, more than six hundred acres were needed to construct more than two hundred buildings including fourteen main structures with more than sixty-three million square feet of floor space. Eighty acres were needed to build the Midway Plaisance, a mile-long entertainment strip where Putnam planned to have "living displays" of American anthropology. Putnam's Apache student assistant, Antonio, played a key role in planning the exhibition.[28]

Antonio was the grandson of the great Chiricahua chief, Cochise. He had been captured by General Crook's troops in southern Arizona and sent to Fort Monroe in Hampton, Virginia, where he learned to read voraciously. At the age of eighteen, Antonio met Putnam who offered him a scholarship in anthropology at Harvard University. With funding from the Peabody Museum, Antonio was able to travel throughout the west and secure ethnological exhibits for the World's Fair.[29]

In order to meet the four hundredth anniversary of Columbus's arrival in the Western Hemisphere, the fair's dedication ceremonies were held on October 21, 1892. However, the dank wetlands of Jackson Park still had to be carefully transformed into an island paradise with series of pools, lagoons, and waterways connected to Lake Michigan. Once completed, they would provide visitors with an additional means of transportation and cool spots during the humid summer months of 1893.[30]

In keeping with the Exposition Universelle template, the main buildings would be constructed in the academic neoclassical style taught at the École des Beaux-Arts in Paris to exemplify harmony, logic, and uniformity. The Court of Honor buildings would be covered in brilliant white stucco, which would contrast a colossal gold covered statue of the Republic, which faced the railroad terminal at the fair's gates.[31]

Opening day

Early on a cold and cloudy Monday morning, May 1, 1893, Charles sat anxiously side-by-side along with other fair dignitaries, politicians, and foreign delegates. Behind them was a growing mass of more than three hundred thousand people who had paid fifty cents to see the grand opening ceremony. The crowd pushed their way toward the grandstand on the east side of the golden-domed Administration Building. They were waiting for President Grover Cleveland and Spanish nobles to arrive by carriage from the Lexington Hotel in downtown Chicago. Around 9:00 a.m., their procession of seventy-six carriages and their military escort headed south on Michigan Avenue and to the fairground.[32]

Charles felt the ground tremble with the uproar of the crowd as members of the procession took the stage. George R. Davis, director general of the Columbian Exposition, walked alongside President Cleveland who was followed by Vice President Stevenson, Secretary of State Gresham, Secretary of the Treasury Carlisle, Secretary of the Navy Herbert, Secretary of the Interior Smith, Secretary of Agriculture Morton, Putnam, and the other administrators of the World's Fair. Spanish notables, including the Duke of Veragua and his family, direct lineal descendants of Christopher Columbus, followed them. They sat next to President Cleveland. The president's cabinet, governors, national commissioners, and senators and congressmen also sat on the platform.

Once everyone was seated, an orchestra of more than two hundred musicians, conducted by Theodore Thomas, began to play Professor Paine's *Columbian March and Hymn*. Thomas was the founder and first music director of the Chicago Symphony Orchestra. Charles knew him best as the director of the Cincinnati College of Music from 1878 to 1879, and as the conductor of Cincinnati's biennial May festivals, which he regularly attended.

Afterward, Davis made the following announcement:

According to the official program for today's exercises, I have the pleasure of introducing the Reverend W. H. Milburn, chaplain of the senate of the United States, who will offer the invocation.[33]

Charles and Putnam removed their hats and bowed their head as they listened to Milburn's prayer. Davis then introduced Jessie Couthoui who read William Augustus Croffut's "The Prophecy." Much to Charles's delight, the orchestra began to play Wagner's overture *Rienzi* at the end of Couthoui's reading. Afterward, Davis stood and thanked Charles, Putnam, and all of those who worked on the World's Columbian Exposition. He then introduced the president of the United States.[34]

> And now, Mr. President, in this central city of this great republic on the continent discovered by Columbus, whose distinguished descendants are present as the honored guests of our nation, it only remains for you, if in your opinion the Exposition here presented is commensurate in dignity with what the world should expect of our great country, to direct that it shall be opened to the public, and when you touch this magic key the ponderous machinery will start in its revolution, and the activities of the Exposition will begin.[35]

President Cleveland gave a brief speech in which summarized the fair.

> We have made and here gathered together objects of use and beauty, the products of American skill and invention; but we have also made men who rule themselves. It is an exalted mission in which we and our guests from other lands are engaged, as we cooperate in the inauguration of an enterprise devoted to human enlightenment; and in the undertaking we here enter upon, we exemplify in the noblest sense the brotherhood of nations. Let us hold fast to the meaning that underlies this ceremony, and let us not lose the impressiveness of this moment. As by a touch the machinery that gives life to this vast Exposition is set in motion, so at the same instant let our hopes and aspirations awaken forces, which in all time to come shall influence the welfare, the dignity and the freedom of mankind.[36]

At the end of his speech, President Cleveland pushed down on a gold and ivory Morse telegraph key sitting on the podium. It served as a switch, which signaled the electrical crew to start Nikola Tesla's engines and power up more than two hundred thousand incandescent lights.[37]

With the backing of George Westinghouse, Nikola Tesla had outbid Thomas Edison and J. P. Morgan for powering the fair. As the lights illuminated the fairgrounds, the orchestra began playing "My Country Tis of Thee" and Charles and Putnam and the rest of the crowd proudly sang along. Afterward, they attended a special luncheon. This event was the second time Charles sat and listened to a president of the United States give a speech.[38]

The exhibitions

Charles's Ohio archaeology exhibition was displayed in a specially built Anthropology Building. Archaeological site and artifact displays were arranged from primitive to complex to illustrate human evolution and technological development. Although Putnam had paid Moorehead to work on the Ohio archaeology exhibition, he decided to disassociate himself from Putnam and Charles and create his own exhibition. Moorehead wanted the sole distinction of being the go-to guy on Ohio archaeology. As proof of his expertise, Moorehead sold copies of his 1892 book, *Primitive Man in Ohio*.

Although Moorehead's book highlighted from pages two to four Charles's discovery of evidence that American Indians were in the Little Miami River valley during that Ice Age, he openly complained about the Ohio exhibition. Moorehead claimed that the artifacts in Charles's exhibition were "decidedly crude and insignificant" when compared to his personal collection. Moorehead believed the aesthetic quality and market value of his artifacts was far more meaningful to the public than scientific evidence of past cultures and technologies.[39]

In addition to the Ohio archaeology exhibition, Putnam had forty-three American Indian exhibits located in thirty-one different buildings. At least thirteen of the exhibits featured live performers and living encampments. Putnam's pageant was arranged geographically with American Indians portraying daily life.[40]

American Indian habitations also lined the Midway Plaisance alongside the centerpiece of the fair, a gigantic Ferris wheel known as the Chicago Wheel. It was more than 80 meters (264 feet) high and rivaled Paris's Eiffel Tower. Ponca chief Macunajin (Standing Bear), who successfully argued in U.S. District Court in 1879 that American Indians were persons, proudly rode the Ferris wheel in his full regalia and headdress.[41]

Chippewa, Chiricahua Apache, Choctaw, Coahuila, Cree, Iroquois, Kwakiutl, Lakota, Menominee, Moqui, Navajo, Papago, Penobscot, Passamaquoddy, Winnebago, Yaqui, and Zuni encampments were located along the eastern shore of the South Pond. An Inuit village with twelve families living in bark-covered homes was set along the North Pond. More than sixty Dine' (Navajo), Haudenosaunee (Iroquois), Lakota, Potawatomi, Modoc, and Winnebago occupied the Midway Plaisance. They sang and danced as well as cooked and cleaned in their temporary homes. Haudenosaunee birch-bark longhouses and a Kwakiutl Kwakwa̱ka'wakw cedar house and totem pole from Tsax̱is, British Columbia, was situated next to the Anthropology Building along with a large collection of ethnographic artifacts and Haudenosaunee and Kwakiutl families.[42]

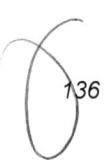

Despite the battle of the Little Big Horn and the recent massacre at Wounded Knee, the Lakota and Crow were well represented at the fair where they walked freely among the tourists. Indeed, Rain-in-the-Face, who cut out the heart of Gen. George Armstrong Custer's brother, Capt. Tom Custer, attracted enormous crowds of tourists. His image even appeared on Columbian Exposition tickets along with images of Christopher Columbus, Benjamin Franklin, Abraham Lincoln, George Washington, and George Frederic Handel. One of the most treasured souvenirs of the Columbian Exposition was Rain-in-the-Face's autograph on a ticket with his image.[43]

Rain-in-the-Face greeted visitors near the entrance of Sitting Bull's Cabin exhibit. Sitting Bull's home, the log cabin where he was murdered, was placed on the Midway Plaisance. The cabin exhibition was extremely popular with tourists because it included American Indian veterans from the Indian Wars including the battle of the Little Big Horn. In addition to Rain-in-the-Face, Kicking Bear, No Neck, Red Cloud, Rocky Bear, Two Strike, Young Bull, and Young Man Afraid of His Horses greeted visitors, demonstrated various art works, dances, songs, and posed for pictures. Some of the Oglala Lakota even said they saw "the spirit of Sitting Bull in the cabin."[44]

Thomas John Morgan, Jr., was an outspoken critic of Putnam's living exhibitions of American Indians. Morgan was the founder of the United Labor Party, a political activist, and a candidate for the Socialist Party of America. He used his political cachet to oppose Putnam's portrayal of contemporary American Indian livelihood. Morgan believed the exhibition was a direct contradiction to the progressive theme of the exposition. He pulled his financial support from Putnam and gave it to the Office of Indian Affairs. They used the money to create an American Indian School exhibition, which focused on social progress.[45]

Putnam's living exhibitions did create the impression of static American Indian cultures frozen in time. American Indians had accomplished a phenomenal number of academic achievements that went far beyond the average American. In 1893 most Americans were not educated beyond the eighth grade and 14 percent of those fourteen years old and over were unable to read or write in any language. In contrast, American Indians were college graduates, book authors, newspaper editors, and medical doctors. For example, Wampanoag Caleb Cheeshahteaumuck was a Harvard graduate and published his first book in 1665. In 1828 Cherokee Elias Boudinot became editor of the *Cherokee Phoenix*, a newspaper that used the Cherokee syllabary. In 1854 Cherokee John Rollin Ridge published *The Life and Adventures of Joaquin Murieta, the Celebrated California Bandit.* In 1889 Omaha Susan LaFlesche, Dakota Charles Eastman, and Yavapai Carlos Montezuma graduated from medical school.

In comparison to the exhibitions of the Peabody Museum, the Smithsonian's were much smaller and displayed in the Government Building. Smithsonian ethnological curator Dr. Otis Tufton Mason, who worked closely with Goode, installed them. He kept the evolutionary theme and did not duplicate the exhibits of the Peabody Museum. Instead, Mason illustrated a step-wise evolution of culture, using technology as a marker of a culture's stage of development. He organized American Indian cultures based on geographic linguistic areas.[46]

In addition to archaeological and ethnological artifacts, Mason used drawings, photographs, and seventy life-sized American Indian mannequins in Hupa, Kiowa, Kutchin, Navajo, Lakota, and Zuni regalia. The figures were positioned as if they were making silver jewelry, spinning plant fiber, and weaving fabric.[47]

Buffalo Bill's Wild West and Congress of Rough Riders of the World

Representatives of American Indian tribes across the country demanded of the organizers of the World's Fair in writing that "the perpetuation of any Wild West show at the expense of the dignity and interest of the Indian Nations will, by you, be neither encouraged nor countenanced." Both Putnam and Davis, the director general of the World's Columbian Exposition, responded assuring them that there would no degrading Wild West shows on the fairgrounds. What they could not control, however, was what went on the other side of the entrance gates.[48]

Putnam and Davis forbade William Frederick Cody from participating in the World's Fair. However, their ban did not stop the innovative entrepreneur from capturing a significant portion of the profits. Cody and his partner, Nate Salsbury, rented fourteen acres next to the fair's southwest gate on Chicago's Sixty-third Street. They built a grandstand with eighteen thousand seats and a campground for more than five hundred employees, including Annie Oakley, about two hundred American Indians, and more than three hundred cowboys, European equestrians, and soldiers.[49]

Cody charged $0.50 to see historical reenactments, skilled horseback riding, and sharpshooting. His performances went on twice a day, rain or shine. So many people attended Cody's Wild West show that an elevated train station had to be built at the entrance of his arena to control the foot traffic. Among those in attendance were Presidents Benjamin Harrison and Grover Cleveland and European nobility.[50]

Part of Cody's economic success was attributed to copious endorsements by the Nation's top newspaper journalists who declared his show a "Wild West Reality" and "a correct representation of life on the Plains." They coincided nicely with "The Significance of the Frontier in American History," a professional paper read at the concurrent Historical Congress by the well-known American historian Frederick Jackson Turner. He professed that Cody's Wild West show was a true reflection of the end of the American frontier.[51]

Because Cody's show was not located on the fairgrounds, he did not have to share his profits. Even without Cody's contribution, the World's Fair was an economic success. It provided the Chicago working class a source of much-needed money during one of the most serious economic downturns the country had ever experienced. The Panic of 1893 was an economic depression that occurred when United States banks funded overbuilt railroads, which resulted in their failure. Americans no longer trusted paper money, stocks, or bonds.[52]

Returning to the fair

On the morning of September 3, 1893, Charles boarded a train bound for Chicago with two of his older children—Clara Isabel and Charles Wilbur. He wrote a letter to Molly from the train. He noted, "At this time 11:00 a.m., we are speeding through Indiana at the rate of fifty miles an hour. We see apples on the trees," (see appendix A).

Charles wrote another letter to Molly on the evening of September 5, from Mrs. Ording's boardinghouse in Chicago.

> Mrs. Ording is the pleasantness and kindest, nicest woman we ever met. She cannot do enough for us and we are so glad we came here. She cannot do enough for Clara and Wilbur. . . . We came in at 9 o'clock tonight and Mrs. Ording insisted on getting us a luncheon (see appendix A).

Mrs. Ording's was but one of more than eight hundred boardinghouses and hotels built and equipped especially for visitors of the World's Fair.

Charles also told Molly that he took Clara and Wilbur to the "Castle." There were two castles at the World's Fair. Mercifully, the one Charles took his children to see was a sixteenth-century, medieval, German Castle with a fifteen-foot-wide moat and two drawbridges. The building housed German ethnographic artifacts, artwork, and weapons. The other castle was a block-long building built on Chicago's Sixty-third Street by a psychopathic killer, the infamous Dr. Herman Webster Mudgett, alias, Dr. Henry Howard Holmes. He was one of the worst serial killers in American history. Mudgett worked his way through the University of Michigan Medical School by stealing and selling corpses for anatomy and physiology classes. He eventually earned enough money to build his three-story castle just in time for the World's Fair.[53]

Mudgett's castle was located on the same street as Cody's Wild West Show and designed to serve as a boardinghouse for visitors to the fair. His castle included boutiques, personal offices, shops, and living quarters. Unfortunately, it also contained an airtight vault, dissecting tables, torture chambers, as well as acid vats, lime pits, and a crematorium for mutilating and disposing bodies. Mudgett murdered at least fifty visitors during the World's Fair and another two hundred young women were known to have disappeared after entering the building and were presumed dead.[54]

Closing tragedies

Mudgett's murders were not the only tragedies that occurred as the fair was winding down. In June 1893 a case of smallpox was diagnosed in Chicago. It likely originated from an unvaccinated European or immigrant visiting the fair. Almost twenty-eight million people came to see the World's

Fair over a period of 179 days. Most of the visitors stayed in overcrowded hotels and boarding houses. By the end of the fair, two people were dead and thirty-five more were diagnosed with smallpox.[55]

Early in the afternoon of July 10, the six-story Cold Storage building, which housed refrigeration units, perishable food, and an ice skating rink caught on fire. Sparks from the two-hundred-foot-tall iron chimney ignited the surrounding wooden tower. Firefighters from the World's Columbian Exposition Fire Department and the Chicago Fire Department quickly responded.[56]

Twenty firemen climbed to the top of the tower with hoses to douse the fire. As they reached the top, the tower collapsed in an explosion of flames. Fourteen firefighters and three civilians were killed. Some were trapped in the burning building and others fell to their death. It was estimated that about fifty thousand visitors witnessed the fire. The fire continued to smolder long afterward and ultimately took twenty-one fire engine companies to put it out. By July 1894 most of the other wooden buildings at the fairgrounds had burned to the ground.[57]

Two days before the extravagant closing ceremony of the World's Fair, Chicago's beloved mayor, Carter Harrison, Sr., was murdered. An Irish-born newspaper distributor, Patrick Eugene Prendergast, assassinated him. Although it was never promised, Prendergast assumed that his political support of Harrison during his second mayoral election campaign would result in his appointment as the chief legal officer for Chicago.[58]

By October 28 someone else was offered the position. Prendergast went to Mayor Harrison's home and shot him three times with a .38-caliber revolver as he was walking out from his bedroom. Prendergast was arrested thirty minutes later. With the city of Chicago in mourning, the closing ceremonies were canceled and a public memorial service was held for the assassinated mayor.[59]

Despite the dark ending to the World's Columbian Exposition, it was considered a tremendous success. In addition to the anthropology and archaeology exhibitions, the fair brought in world famous artists, musicians, developed new foods, drinks, and a variety of electrical inventions that would forever change American households. President Benjamin Harrison called the fair "stupendous" and "triumphant." Author John Ingalls said it was "inspirational" and "prophetic." Thomas Alva Edison spent a week at the fair and called it "marvelous."[60]

Accolades

On April 25, 1892, the Fifty-Second Congress approved an act, which appropriated money to coin five million silver "Columbian" souvenir half-dollars, struck in commemoration of the World's Columbian Exposition. The act also provided funding for the minting of fifty thousand bronze medals and fifty thousand vellum impressions for diplomas to be delivered to the World's Columbian Commission. Artists at the U.S. Mint, Augustus Saint-Gaudens and Charles E. Barber, designed the bronze medals. The medals were struck by Scovill Manufacturing Company in Waterbury, Connecticut, during 1895–96 fiscal year.[61]

Charles received a commemorative half dollar as well as a bronze medal and diploma from Congress for his contributions to the World's Columbian Exposition. The medal he received portrays Christopher Columbus stepping ashore with three of his men behind him on the obverse.

Charles's diploma read,

The United States of America

By act of their congress have authorized the World's Columbian Commission at the international exhibition held in the city of Chicago, state of Illinois, in the year 1893, to decree a medal for specific merit, which is set forth below over the name of an individual judge acting as an examiner, upon the finding of a board of international judges, to

C. L. Metz, Collector,
Madisonville, Ohio.

Exhibit Award

For a model of Fork [*sic*] Hill Mound and of Clark's Earthworks, which is of scientific value. For a model of the Hopewell Group, which presents a comprehensive view of the group and is well labeled.

W. F. Terry,
President Departmental Committee

Alice Palmer Henderson
Individual Judge

George R. Davis
Director General

F. W. Putnam
President, World's Columbian Commission,

Jno. T. Dickinson, John Boyd Thacher,
Secretary, World's Columbian Commission, Chairman Executive Committee of Awards

(Bronze Medal)[62]

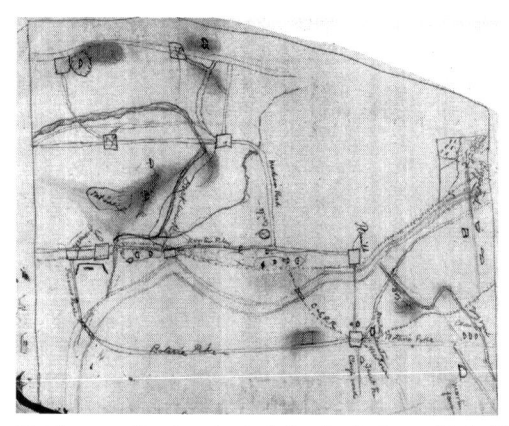

8.1. Charles Louis Metz's map of archaeological sites in the lower Little Miami River valley, ca. 1891.

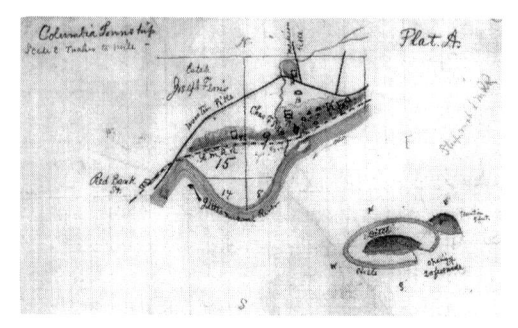

8.2. Charles Louis Metz's map of archaeological sites in the lower Little Miami River valley with a detailed illustration of the burial mounds and an earthen enclosure on the northwest side of the intersection of Plainville Road and U.S. 50, ca. 1891.

8.3. World's Columbian Exposition, Rain in the Face, ticket, ca. 1893.

8.4. Charles Louis Metz's Ohio Archaeology exhibition inside the Anthropology Building, World's Columbian Exposition, Chicago, Illinois, ca. 1893.

8.5. Front of Charles Louis Metz's World's Columbian Exposition bronze medal awarded in 1895.

8.6. Back of Charles Louis Metz's World's Columbian Exposition bronze medal awarded in 1895.

8.7. Front of the Metz family home and medical office,
6111 Madison Road, Madisonville, Hamilton County, Ohio.

CHAPTER 9

The Phebe Ferris Will

CHARLES AND MOLLY began 1895 with the birth of Margaret Elizabeth born on February 27. They were now a family of eight—Anna Teresa, age, twenty-four; Clara Isabel, age eighteen; Charles Wilbur, age fourteen; Beatrice Amelia, age eleven; Ethel Helen, age nine; Julia Marie, age six; and the baby, Margaret Elizabeth.

Indians on display

Charles's passion for studying American Indian culture continued to spread throughout the greater Cincinnati area. After the World's Columbian Exposition, Cincinnatians craved for more opportunities to interact with American Indians. In 1895 a group of Cree from Havre, Montana, were abandoned by a Wild West show in Bellevue, Kentucky. The Cincinnati Zoological Society seized the opportunity and hired the Cree for two months. The zoo's idea was to display "wild people" among the "wild animals."[1]

The Cincinnati Zoological Society made so much money from their living exhibition of American Indians that their manager, William S. Heck, wrote Thomas Smith, acting commissioner of the Bureau of Indian Affairs (BIA), that he wanted to obtain the services of one hundred Lakota from the Pine Ridge and Rosebud reservations. Heck believed that displaying veterans of the Indian Wars at the zoo would be highly profitable. With the assistance of the BIA, the zoo secured the services of eighty-nine Sicangu (Húŋkpapha) Lakota from the Rosebud Reservation.[2]

The Lakota arrived in Cincinnati on Saturday June 20, 1896, and set up their tepees in the grassy areas of the zoo. The Lakota were not prepared for the humid summers of Cincinnati or the German cuisine. While they enjoyed the sauerkraut, they preferred fruit, vegetables, and lean cuts of beef rather than the pork sausage and potatoes that the zoo served them. In addition to posing for photographs, the Lakota performed dances, exhibited horseback riding, and participated in historical reenactments of the battle of Little Big Horn and the massacre at Wounded Knee twice a day, at 3:00 p.m. and again at 8:30 p.m. in the zoo's arena. The Ohio National Guard played the role of the Seventh Cavalry. The evening performances included a display of fireworks.[3]

While in Cincinnati the Lakota were befriended by celebrated Cincinnati artists Henry François Farny and Joseph Henry Sharp. They both were portrait artists who focused on American Indian culture. Farny, like his father, was politically active and an outspoken Republican. He encouraged the Lakota to assist the McKinley Club in their grand opening of the Republican presidential campaign. Farny talked them into parading through town in full regalia, some on horseback and others on foot, wearing McKinley campaign buttons. As they went past the Metz home, Charles called all of the children in the house to come to the window and watch the parade.[4]

At the time of the parade, Charles was under severe financial stress. He was two thousand dollars behind on his mortgage and loans from Putnam. Charles no longer had a supplementary income from the World's Columbian Exposition. To make matters worse, the country was still in the economic depression following the Panic of 1893. While he knew his dear friend would understand, the banks, which were recovering from near failure, would not.

On August 5, 1896, Charles wrote a desperate letter to Putnam.

> I am just working day and night to save my home and family. I am trying to earn every dollar that I can and fortunately I have been

very much in demand—if collectors were in proportion to the amount that I am obliged to charge—all would be well, but you know there is no money in the West among the people (see appendix B).

Shawnee and the Ferris Cemetery

Listening to tribal representatives speak at the World's Columbian Exposition and, more recently, the Lakota at the Cincinnati Zoo, inspired Charles to continue his research on the tribal identity of the people buried in the Ferris Cemetery. He was convinced that they were the direct lineal ancestors of Algonquian-speaking people such as the Delaware, Miami, Ojibwa, and Shawnee. Charles believed that the Shawnee were the most likely candidates because they had used the site as a war camp as recently as 1810. He had found a European lathe-turned bone flintlock awl and vent pick and spent honey-colored French pistol and rifle gunflints that they left behind.

In 1810 Isaac Griffin, his friend Paul, and his son were hunting for turkeys on the Miller Brothers' property at the confluence of Duck Creek and the Little Miami River, then known as Turkey Bottom, today Armleder Park. It was less than three kilometers (less than two miles) southwest of their war camp, the Ferris Cemetery. The bottom was covered with mature old growth ash, eastern cottonwood, maple, oak, and sycamore trees towering above a lush spicebush scrub. The Shawnee war party used spicebush as cover and lured the hunting party in with their turkey calls.[5]

Griffin, Paul, and his son split up crossing Duck Creek separately to surround what they believed were turkeys. As the hunters came within rifle range, the Shawnee shot Griffin and Paul in the chest and shouted out victory whoops. Paul's son hid behind a tree keeping the Shawnee war party at bay with his rifle. When they stopped shooting, he made his way to Nelson Station, home of the Nelson brothers, located today at the intersection of Stewart Avenue and Madison Road in Madisonville. Paul's son returned with a group of armed men from Nelson Station to the scene of the ambush and the scalped bodies of Griffin and Paul.[6]

Two of the Nelson brothers built Nelson's Station about two kilometers (a little more than a mile) north of the Ferris Cemetery along with their sister's husband. Nelson Station consisted of two log cabins facing each other and about forty feet apart. The space between the cabins was enclosed by a palisade of young trees and logs, which served as a coral for their livestock. In 1810 the Nelsons were considered the wealthiest family in the county being the owners of several head of horses and two cows.[7]

Assuming that the Shawnee war party had left the area, the Nelson brothers took their horses to a nearby corralled pasture, located today at the intersection of Madison Road and Blaesi Street in Madisonville. As the Nelsons headed back to their cabins, the Shawnee war party stole away with most of the horses. Once the Nelson brothers realized their horses were being stolen, they turned around and pursued the Shawnee up the hill overlooking the pasture. They were able to overtake one of the Shawnee who was riding a lame horse. They killed and buried him at the crest of the hill. Ever since that incident, the hilltop has been known as Indian Hill. The surviving Shawnee war party then attacked the Christian Waldschmidt home on the Little Miami River, today known as Camp Dennison, before moving on.[8]

Aside from local history, an invaluable resource was made available to Charles in 1896. The Burrows Brother Publishing Company of Cleveland, Ohio, translated the seventy-three volumes of the *Jesuit Relations* from French to English. They provided a firsthand account of American Indians living in the Ohio River valley as far back as 1611. The *Jesuit Relations* discussed Shawnee customs, dreams, foods, games, inheritance, language, livelihood, medicines, mythology, religions, and warfare. Indeed, they recorded all of the details of Shawnee life.

The Jesuits began to focus on the Shawnee in the Little Miami area in 1648. The Jesuits called them Ouchaouanag. In 1673 the Jesuit priest Jacques Marquette reported that the Chaouanons (i.e., Shawnee), were living in great numbers in the Ohio River valley. He reported "as many as 23 villages" in one district "and 15 in another quite near one another." Marquette also noted that they were participating in long-distance trade with the Spanish in Florida. This fact was significant because Charles had discovered Spanish trade goods at the Ferris Cemetery.

In addition to the *Jesuit Relations*, Charles had access to the diaries of David Zeisberger, a Moravian missionary who lived with the Shawnee between 1781 and 1810. He described the Shawnee as culturally similar to their northern Iroquoian-speaking Huron neighbors. The similarity is not surprising given that both tribes were in alliance with the French.

The passing of Phebe Ferris

Charles and Phebe Ferris had been close personal friends since 1871. Charles was also her personal physician. They remained close friends until her passing at the age of seventy. Without Phebe, none of the archaeological research at the Ferris Cemetery site would ever have been possible.[9]

In the last few months of her life, Phebe Ferris realized that her health was failing and she would likely never recover. Phebe wanted to make sure that her lifelong pursuits and family heritage would be forever preserved. In particular, Phebe wanted the Ferris Cemetery site and surrounding twenty-five acres of mature old growth forest to become a public park. She also wanted to turn her grand family home into the Joseph Ferris Memorial Library named after her father. She wanted the library to be free, open to the public, and serve as a lasting monument to her life's work. Phebe wanted the library to contain her personal books, journals, photographs, and artifacts, which had been collected from the Madisonville site and other sites in the lower Little Miami River valley. At the suggestion of Charles, one wing would serve as a "Free Library of Reference" a home for students studying anthropology and the "kindred sciences."[10]

The winter of 1896 had been particularly cold and damp. In December Phebe developed a severe sore throat, which Charles diagnosed as tonsillitis. Today tonsillitis is routinely and successfully treated with antibiotics. However, penicillin, the first antibiotic derived from penicillium fungi, was not discovered until 1928. It was not purified and mass-produced until the advent of World War II, and not available for civilians until 1946. In the nineteenth century, tonsillitis was deadly. It had taken the life of the first president of the United States, George Washington.[11]

By December 18, 1896, Phebe had grown weak from the illness and she feared death was near. Phebe made a phone call to the office of Harmon, Colston, Goldsmith, and Hoadly requesting an attorney come to her residence to formalize her last will and testament and to make her close friend, Edward Colston the executor. Attorney Goldsmith came to Phebe's home and drew up the will.[12]

It was difficult for Phebe to swallow solid food, which contributed to her weakening state. Since Phebe's initial diagnosis of tonsillitis, Charles prescribed malted milk as a nutritional supplement. Malted milk had been routinely prescribed to infants and the sick since its initial formulation of wheat and malt in 1887.

On December 19, 1896, Charles and a number of women were attending to Phebe in her room upstairs. She got up and about and headed downstairs to mix a malted milk. One of her attendants offered to fix the drink, but Charles said, "he would attend to the matter himself."[13]

By December 19, 1896, Phebe's epiglottis, the flap of tissue at the base of the tongue, had become infected, inflamed, and swollen to the point that it nearly closed her windpipe. There wasn't enough room for the food supplement to pass by her epiglottis. She died within ten minutes of drinking the malted milk. Phebe most likely suffocated to death. Her dearest friend and physician of almost thirty years, Charles, assisted the family with the funeral arrangements.[14]

Phebe's Last Will and Testament

On December 29, 1896, the last will and testament of Phebe Ferris was submitted to court for probate and record. Howard Ferris, a relative of Phebe's served as the probate judge. Phebe bequeathed her residence to Charles as well as the three acres of the surrounding land including the bottomland immediately below the Ferris Cemetery site known today as Mariemont Gardens and the Lower 80. Rather than for personal gain, the will instructed Charles to use the property to create a corporation and trust to maintain the Joseph Ferris Memorial Library.[15]

On January 11, 1897, Professor Putnam received a letter from attorney Edward Colston stating that Phebe Ferris had died and he was named and appointed the executor of her will. He pointed out "item 4" in the will, which bequeathed to the Peabody Museum of American Archaeology and Ethnology "the Ancient Cemetery to be by said museum kept for scientific purposes for the preservation of the remains and relics of said cemetery."[16]

Charles sent a letter to Putnam in January 1897 stating that taxes on the land would be due in June. He suggested that trees recently "blown down in a gale" could be sold to pay the taxes. Charles also thought that someone should be appointed to watch over the Ferris Cemetery site to make sure that the ground was not disturbed or the timber cut down. He offered to serve in that capacity.[17]

In January Putnam was staying at the Endicott Hotel on Eighty-first

Street and Columbus Avenue in New York. At the time, the seven-story Pompeian brick and terra-cotta hotel had steam heating, electrical lighting, elaborate marble tile and onyx wainscoting, and an upscale restaurant, the Calle Ocho. Not surprisingly, it hosted members of the most elite social class and the Republican Party of New York.

On January 27, 1897, Putnam replied to Charles's letter from the hotel.

> I had a copy made of the part of your letter relating to the bequest (the Ferris bequest). I sent all to President Elliott but just too late for the last meeting of the Corporation. He will bring it up at the next meeting and then action will be taken. Now that the museum is part of the university the Corporation will act in all property matters. In the meantime, I know you will have a fatherly eye on the place and keep off all vandals. There is no doubt but that your suggestions will be followed when the Corporation acts in the Spring (see appendix B).

Upon his return to Harvard, Putnam alerted the president of Harvard College about Phebe Ferris's will. The college president arranged to hold a meeting with the fellows of Harvard College on May 10, 1897, to discuss the gift. The fellows voted unanimously to accept the tract of land containing the Ferris Cemetery site. Their next step was to survey the land and resume archaeological excavations at the site.[18]

On July 3 Putnam sent a letter to Charles and enclosed twelve twenty-five-dollar checks for a year of archaeological fieldwork. Charles had worked so well with his Harvard students that Putnam invited him to direct the excavation of an archaeological site in New Boston, Scioto County, Ohio, near the Scioto-Ohio River confluence. Instead, Charles suggested that he direct the Harvard students' excavation of the Ferris Cemetery. Putnam agreed.[19]

Charles wrote Putnam on July 27 to let him know that the Harvard students had arrived and excavations had resumed at the site. He noted that he hired six additional men to help the students at a daily salary of $1.25. Charles also explained that excavation of the burial mounds at the Turner site had not been completed and it would be keen if student workers could be sent to help finish excavations.[20]

Charles's letter referred to his excavation of the Turner site with Putnam's student, M. H. Saville, between 1889 and 1890. With Charles's supervision, Saville excavated a small group of graves and pit features on the east side of Mount Carmel Road. He exposed the graves of nine individuals, from children to mature adults, some were partially cremated and others were completely cremated. Grave goods included large conch shell vessels, shell beads, freshwater mussel spoons, large sheets of mica, ceramic vessels, canine teeth, copper wristbands, copper ear-spools, bone awls, and flake-stone knives with antler handles.

On July 27 Putnam sent a small group of his students including Ingersoll Bowditch, R. B. Dixon, and J. R. Swanton to help Charles excavate the Ferris Cemetery. Bowditch made a transit survey of the land, which had been given to Harvard. He also made a map of the gridded excavation. Following Charles's direction, the Harvard students excavated within the grid and photo-documented all of the burials and archaeological features. While they screened the excavated sediments, a large mesh was used and smaller artifacts fell through the screen and were not recovered.

On August 4 Charles wrote another letter to Putnam about the slow progress of work at the Ferris Cemetery site and his concerns that they may lose access to the site because of pending litigations.

> We want to do as much as we can before a possible injunction might be served on us—we want to carry this trench 40 feet wide clear away cross the level to the foot (see appendix B).

The excavations consisted of four trenches across the site, which extended into the dark forest topsoil and underlying hard glacial yellow clay and sand. The dig continued through October 20, 1897, and exposed an unprecedented number of archaeological features and artifacts. Two hundred and thirty human skeletons were removed from burial features, the contents of 177 cache pits were collected, 13 hearth features were uncovered, and 42 complete earthenware vessels were found.

Contesting the will

While excavations were ongoing at the Ferris Cemetery site, Phebe's will was being contested. On July 9, 1897, a petition was filed in the Court of Common Pleas, Hamilton County, Ohio, by attorneys Swing, Cushing, and Morse on behalf of plaintiff John Ferris Jewett to set aside Phebe's last will and testament. John Ferris Jewett was Phebe's wealthy and estranged nephew from California. The Ferris family was both shocked and angered by his challenge. They could not understand why Jewett was contesting the will. Could he really be that greedy? Not only were his children direct beneficiaries of the will so were the children of Uri Jewett, and they were "without wealth."[21]

Despite his disaffected and dysfunctional relationship with Phebe, Jewett spoke as if he had full knowledge of his aunt's life history, final wishes, and mental state. He made bold and malicious allegations about Phebe, not the least of which was the question of her sanity. Even the newspapers of the day had labeled Phebe an "eccentric and unmarried" woman.

Today, a bright, independent woman who dedicated her life to the study of the natural sciences would be considered a good citizen and a great role model. In the late nineteenth century, however, women had almost no political rights, including the right to vote. Even though there were numerous colleges for women, the popular opinion was that they were not supposed to be educated as they were excluded from many colleges. Furthermore, women were supposed to be married. These were the androcentric social norms Jewett and his attorneys were using to question Phebe's state of mind.[22]

Assuming all was going to be okay in the end, Charles wrote Putnam about his improving health and financial problems on February 22, 1898. He explained that "I am just recovering from an attack of La Grippe, which was so as to confine me to my bed for 8 days. Things are getting better with me soon," (see appendix B).

Accusations of murder

There were lingering legal issues related to Phebe's will and they were about to get a lot worse. Judge Wright and the jury of the Court of Common Pleas in Hamilton County, Ohio, met initially on October 20, 1898, to hear Jewett's contest of Phebe's will. The courtroom was filled with people as the case had been well advertised in the two major newspapers of the time, the *Cincinnati Enquirer* and the *Cincinnati Post*. Jewett's attorney's opening statement was described as "sensational."[23]

Jewett's attorneys implied that Charles's behavior was highly suspicious and he was somehow involved in Phebe's death. They posed a malicious question to the jury, How could Phebe Ferris be diagnosed by

Charles with tonsillitis one day, the next day she draws her last will and testament naming him as a primary beneficiary, and the day after that she dies from drinking a malted milk that he mixed? Their implication was that Charles had poisoned the malted milk. Charles was Phebe's attending physician, he had knowledge of chemistry, and he was going to receive a fortune in inheritance. In other words, he had means, motive, and opportunity.[24]

Jewett's attorneys were trying to imply that Charles had manipulated a sick and weak-minded elderly woman out of her money and then he poisoned her. They called on a witness who testified that Phebe took one drink, threw her head back in a jerk, and died. Jewett's attorneys also told the jury that Charles had made it difficult for anyone to gain access to Phebe's home and the room, which contained her body.[25]

Although the word "murder" was never used, Jewett's attorneys used the fact that Charles also arranged the funeral to suggest that he covered up the crime. Charles wrote Putnam that he had to suffer through the accusations that he exerted "undue influence" on "Phebe Ferris" in her bequeathing her farm to the Peabody Museum.[26]

Questions of Phebe's sanity

The defense called on Judge Harmon to testify. He stated "Miss Ferris was a strong, intellectual woman and was of sound mind to her death." Judge Harmon further stated that Charles "was her nearest friend and lifetime advisor, and he has served her well and faithfully." Unfortunately, Harmon went on to claim that Charles knew nothing of the will until he read about it in the newspapers.[27]

In an attempt to discredit Judge Harmon's testimony and Charles's honesty, Jewett's attorneys countered with a letter from Professor Putnam, which was read to the jury. It stated that Charles had told him about the library "and that he was going to be named one of the trustees." In addition to Putnam's letter, James Ferris testified that he tried to see Phebe before she drew up the will, but Charles and his wife, "refused him, and stated that the invalid was too ill to see callers."[28]

Jewett's attorneys also submitted written depositions, which were read to the jury, stating that the whole notion of leaving money to the public was a "foolish" endeavor. Jewett took the stand, testifying that he never knew of his aunt to care for books or papers of any kind. He implied that Charles had put these notions into her head. Jewett's attorneys went on to assert, "the bequest of 25 acres to Harvard College was an indication of insanity."[29]

Jewett's attorney's attributed Phebe's insanity to "consanguity"—generations of inbreeding. James Ferris testified that both Phebe's parents and grandparents were first cousins. Medical experts were brought in to testify about "the results of wedding alliances of blood relations." Actually, marriage between first cousins was not all that uncommon in that day. Such marriages occurred in sparsely populated areas with limited family mobility and they also served to keep generational wealth within the family.[30]

Professors Morton and Hyde of the University of Cincinnati (UC) also testified on the behalf of Jewett. They told the jury "the plan of establishing a library for scientific research at the Ferris homestead was not practical." What Professors Morton and Hyde were not saying was UC did not have an anthropology program at that time and thus none of their students had a use for a library for archaeological research. While UC established the McMicken College of Arts and Science in 1892, it was not until 1969 that an autonomous anthropology program was created. Neither Morton nor Hyde was an anthropologist nor could they speak for the broader anthropological community, but those facts were obfuscated.[31]

The defense attorneys denied that Phebe was of unsound mind. They summoned the testimony of twenty leading scientists from around the world on behalf of Phebe, Charles, and the Ferris family. Some of the testimony was delivered in person and others by written deposition. Their statements were successfully used to convince Judge Wright and the jury that the Ferris Cemetery site, its contents, and surrounding acres were "priceless to science."[32]

The testimony of the scientists highlighted the fact that Phebe only permitted professional archaeologists to excavate on her property. They also noted that Phebe had traveled around the world visiting professional archaeological excavations and she appreciated their scientific merit. The scientific supporters further testified that a large collection of artifacts from the Madisonville site had been displayed at the World's Columbian Exposition and it was because of the scientific value of the site that Phebe bequeathed the land in trust to Harvard College.[33]

On October 26, 1898, Charles wrote Putnam about the status of the lawsuit.

> The Ferris lawsuit, which has been going on since the 19th of this month and will probably run for a week or two yet, this daily attendance at Court takes much of my time and a great loss financially to me. Yesterday the depositions taken at Boston were read and the comments made by the Plaintiff's attorneys were not of the pleasantness they might have been. They tried to make me out of a very bad man—Ex-Judge Harmon of our side of the case vindicated me however and our side of the case is still on top. The Plaintiff's witnesses have all been coached as to what they were to say— but under Judge Harmon and Mr. Coffy's cross-examination they fell to pieces (see appendix B).

Sustaining Phebe's will

On November 4, 1898, the jury and Judge Wright announced the verdict sustaining Phebe's will. Jewett and his attorney's refused to accept this judgment and quickly filed a motion for a new trial. On November 30, 1898, their motion for a new trial was overruled.[34]

Given that Charles's character was under attack in the dispute over the will, he wrote a lengthy letter to Putnam on November 30, which described in detail his current financial situation and consumption of alcohol.

> As regards my being too often in beer saloons I will say this in defense—I seldom, very seldom drink beer at all—none of our saloons keep good wine—I do not think I would drink any of the whiskey dispersed therein and if the saloon keepers were first put under oath the one in the East End would say the Metz doctor has been in my place twice in six months and then I called him in— another would say I have been in business 4 years and the doctor has been in my place not over 4 times, twice to see my wife professionally and when he came to get the money. Another would say the doctor has been attending my wife and daughter and has been in my place about 12 or 15 times within the last year and a half. Once in a while he would stop at the bar take a cigar, a glass of cider or lemonade. I have not seen him take more than one or two glasses of beer at my place—Dear Prof I do not spend my time in the saloons for I should not find anything congenial there. I might at my own house take a glass of wine (see appendix B).

On December 3, 1898, Jewett and his attorneys filed an appeal, which was then called a bill of exceptions by leave. Professor Putnam wrote Charles on May 11, 1899, that he "had not heard anything about the final result of the contest after the decision in favor of sustaining the will." He also noted that he had been in correspondence with a John Brown Jewett and wanted to know if he was in favor or against the contest of the will.[35]

At this juncture, Putnam was anxious to have archaeological excavations resume at the Ferris Cemetery site. Since the initial announcement of Phebe's will, Putnam wrote that he was trying his "best to get the means for exploring the land in Ohio, which has been bequeathed to the Museum."[36]

While Putnam was waiting on the Court of Appeals of Hamilton County to affirm Phebe's will, Charles attended to his patients and his aging in-laws in Vera Cruz, Ohio. As he had done in the past, Charles helped them with the end of summer harvests and chores. However, the stress of the trial was taking its toll on his health. At 4:30 p.m. on August 24, 1901, Charles wrote a letter to Molly. He explained that "I have been quite sick from Thursday morning at 1 o'clock to this morning," (see appendix A).

Charles wrote another letter to Molly on August 30, 1901, which was uncharacteristically more formally addressed to "Amilia." He was concerned that something had upset her, perhaps his continuing illness?

> I have not received a letter from you yet. How is that? Don't you know how a letter from you would please me if it only said I am well and am having a good time. . . . Write me one of those old fashioned letters that are so dear to me. Just try (see appendix A).

Affirmation

On April 1, 1903, the Court of Appeals of Hamilton County affirmed Phebe's will. An important aspect of the will was the establishment of the Joseph Ferris Memorial Library. Phebe requested that the library be established in her home and be used as "an attractive resort for all persons interested in literature, archaeological and ethnological studies and investigations and bring these educational advantages in near proximity to her friends and neighbors."[37]

It was Charles's responsibility to oversee the Joseph Ferris Memorial

Library. Not only did he need good librarians, he needed people to care for the Ferris home. In 1903 Charles had four adult children—Anna Teresa, age thirty-two; Clara Isabel, age twenty-six; Charles Wilbur, age twenty-two; and Beatrice Amelia, age nineteen. Charles reasoned that the Ferris home had more than enough room for them to live. Additionally, they would make ideal librarians and caretakers of the home. Thus, Charles moved all of his adult children into the Ferris home.

9.1. Lakota on the lawn of the Cincinnati Zoological Gardens, ca. 1896.

9.2. Lakota, Quick Bear, posing for a photo at the Cincinnati Zoological Gardens, ca. 1896.

9.3. Lakota family posing for a photo at the Cincinnati Zoological Gardens, ca. 1896.

9.4. Lakota on the lawn of the Cincinnati Zoological Gardens, ca. 1896.

CHAPTER 10

The Twentieth Century

WITH THE JOSEPH FERRIS MEMORIAL LIBRARY and Phebe Ferris's residence under the control of his eldest children, Charles could finally resume his archaeological fieldwork in the Little Miami River valley. On May 8, 1905, Charles wrote a letter to Putnam about his recent visit to the Turner site. He was appalled how much of the site was being destroyed by sand and gravel mining and "the Cincinnati and Eastern Railroad."

Charles also asked Putnam if he would be interested in exchanging one of his family paintings to cover a portion of the money, which he had borrowed.

> I know it is valuable. Cincinnati has no market for such things. I would take however anything that will cover any debt to you and if possible something over (see appendix B).

The picture Charles referred to in his letter was one of the oil paintings that his parents brought with them from Bavaria. Putnam knew well of its place in the history of the Metz family and refused to accept the painting.

On May 24, 1905, Charles wrote Putnam again lamenting about the degradation of the Turner and Stites Grove sites and other important historical locations in the Little Miami River valley.

> At the Turner site the railroad has made great inroads into the tower terrace—about one third of it is removed. Mr. Turner is willing to allow us to excavate the circle if he is paid for the corn. Of the beautiful circle and mound in the Stites Grove it has vanished. It is sad to see these interesting monuments and landmarks disappearing rapidly . . . every lecturer that has anything to say about the prehistoric mounds of this region is in Eastern Colleges and Universities. They have carried off carloads of objects that rightfully belong to Cincinnati (see appendix B).

Resuming fieldwork

Putnam responded to Charles's letter and sent one of his students, Ernest Volk, to assist with the work at the Turner site. Under Charles's direction, Volk excavated some of the most interesting burial mounds at the Turner site as well as a number of mortuary features. They uncovered an unusual quantity of beautifully colored micro-blade, flake-stone knives manufactured from Flint Ridge chert, beautifully engraved long bone awls and shell disks and beads in the mounds. They also recovered ground stone celts and platform pipes—one of which had two bowls and another was made in the shape of an Upper Ordovician fossil horn coral.[1]

The burial mounds also contained some of the most unusual mortuary features and artifacts ever discovered. One mound had a stone veneer with five mortuary features—two single graves, a cluster of three graves, and what appeared to be a grave in an altar-like structure. The graves encircled a round central feature, which contained four earthenware vessels.[2]

An earthwork located within the Great Circle consisted of a complex of seven adjoining smaller stone-veneered mounds oriented in a northeast direction. Other mounds contained mortuary features, hearths, and more than one hundred postholes that predated the construction of the mounds. The most complex of stone-covered mounds contained hearths, crematory basins, cache pits, intrusive pits with human skeletons and a cache of sixteen human skulls, and what appeared to be a circular series of large pits, "tunnels," and postholes.[3]

The tunnels and postholes were likely the remains of a massive wooden structure. When the larger timbers decomposed, they left spaces behind what appeared to be tunnels and pits in the carbonate-rich soil, which was described as "concrete." There were much larger versions of what geologists call root casts.[4]

The artifacts from the mound were equally spectacular. They included meteorites and large masses of copper. The copper was pounded into adzes, bracelets, and celts. Copper was also pounded and cut into sheets used to make elaborate artwork, breastplates, buttons, pendants, and rolled and twisted into beads and ear-spools. Some of the copper artifacts, including tinkling cones, ear-spools, bracelets, and a panpipe, also known as a pan-flute, were covered with thin layers of native silver and meteoric iron.[5]

In addition to earthenware vessels, ceramic earrings and highly detailed human figurines were found. The figurines depicted clothing, footwear, hairstyles, and jewelry. The figurines were of adult men and women seated in different positions and others standing with different postures.[6]

The discovery of a panpipe at the Turner site was especially significant, as they had been found on contemporary Incan sites in the Andes Mountains. Interestingly, it was the same area where tobacco originated. Charles wondered whether or not the musical instrument had diffused from the Andes region of Argentina and Bolivia to the Little Miami River valley, or was it yet another example of independent invention.[7]

Charles also found large flaked-stone spear points manufactured from exotic cherts and *obsidian* (volcanic glass) that were cached along with effigy spear points carved from perforated *micaceous schist*. Caches of more common objects were also found including deer *astragali* (ankle bones), upper Ordovician invertebrate fossils, shell beads, and perforated bear canines. Massive quantities of ground and perforated shell beads were found cached in a mound including those from ground and perforated *Marginella* and *Leptoxis* shells.[8]

Marginella is a small snail, which lives in the temperate areas of the Atlantic Ocean. Leptoxis, on the other hand, is a small freshwater snail, which was at one time abundant on the rocky bottom of the unpolluted Little Miami River.[9]

Algonquian connections

Of particular interest was the discovery of artifacts known to be associated with Algonquian cultures at the Turner site. There were underwater panthers and horned serpents, *Mishipeshu* and *Mishibijiw*—one engraved on a smooth stone, one carved from mica and covered in red ocher, and another extravagantly carved from red slate. The color of red is significant because it is associated with the setting southwestern sun, the direction that the horned serpent faces. There was also a large number of copper tinkling cones identical to those sewn onto the dresses of Algonquian women who perform the jingle dance.[10]

A cache of hammered gold nuggets and perforated freshwater pearls were found in an altar-like feature in the center of the mound. There were large sheets of mica cut into circles, donut shaped disks, zoomorphic Algonquian clan figures such as bears, birds, snakes, and two were cut into the profiles of human heads. Many of the cut mica figures were covered in red ocher. In addition to cut mica, a perforated bone pendant carved from a human cranium was incised with the figure of a *Manitou*—the spiritual life force of Algonquian-speaking people. It included elements of a human head, two paws with four claws, a Carolina parakeet head, stylized feathers, and a tail.[11]

Charles and Volk also salvaged a mound, which was about to be lost due to erosion along the Little Miami River. It was covered in stream-rounded, egg-sized, bluish basalt cobbles. A cache of twenty-five double-perforated, reel-shaped ground stones were found in the center of the mound. They were manufactured from the mineral aragonite, which had been mined from a large stalagmite known as the Pillar of the Constitution in the Senate Chamber of Wyandotte Cave, Crawford County, Indiana.[12]

Traditional Algonquians believe that the Spirit of the North has a heart of ice. At the spring or "goose moon," the Spirit of the North goes into Earth Mother and his heart of ice turns to stone. It remains there until the "long moon" of winter. The large stalagmite in Wyandotte Cave looks like a large petrified column of ice. It was likely mined during the warm months of summer when Algonquian people believed they could remove pieces of North Spirit's heart of stone. The reel-shaped gorgets were bull-roarers used to simulate the sound of the winds made by the North Spirit during story telling. They were likely buried in the mound during the goose moon.[13]

The Ferris Cemetery

On September 25, 1905, Charles wrote Putnam another letter about the progress of his archaeological excavation of the Turner site. He also expressed his concerns about the recent looting of the Ferris Cemetery site.

> Our prehistoric cemetery is being torn up by parties of vandals who are hunting for relics. They should be stopped. Would advise you to place someone in charge of the grounds, or hasten the exploration of the grounds (see appendix B).

The response from Harvard was slow coming. On May 28, 1906, Harvard University president Eliot, asked the University Corporation to "appoint Dr. Charles L. Metz custodian of the Ferris Tract." They did not want to make a commitment to Charles because of their concerns about the implications and restrictions associated with Phebe's will. Rather than caring for the land, Harvard decided to sell the land.[14]

Putnam responded to Charles's request for assistance with the excavations of the Ferris Cemetery site by sending two of his students, R. E. Merwin and Irwin Hayden. Under Charles's supervision, they excavated three new trenches between July 6 and November 7, 1907, and two more between April 1 and September 15, 1908. In total, they exposed 176 mortuary features, 247 cache-pits, and 3 hearth features. Merwin carefully mapped all of the features.[15]

While Charles was working at the Ferris cemetery, his son, Charles Wilbur, was busy following in his father and grandfather's footsteps in medicine and military service. Charles Wilbur worked his way through the Cincinnati Medical College by serving in the Ohio National Guard. He graduated in 1907 and immediately accepted the position of assistant surgeon at the Soldiers and Sailors Home at Sandusky, Ohio. After a few years of service he returned home and accepted the position of district physician for the Cincinnati Board of Health.[16]

Archaeology aside, the Metz and Putnam families had grown very close over the years. On Christmas day 1907, the Putnams wrote a letter to Charles's twenty-one-year-old daughter, Ethel Helen Caroline, and included a gift—a butterfly and wing enclosed in a pendant. At the time, Ethel was living in the Ferris house and attending to the archaeology library.

Dear Ethel,

This is a real butterfly mounted on a portion of another butterfly's wing. Look at it under a magnifying glass. We thought you would like to have it as a little token of our remembrance with our best wishes for a Merry Xmas and Happy New Year to you all from your sincere friends

Mrs. and Mr. F. W. Putnam[17]

By 1908 Harvard University had begun to sell portions of the land granted to them by Phebe Ferris. At this time, Putnam was no longer the director of the Peabody Museum of Archaeology and Ethnology. Although he had a courtesy position of honorary curator, Putnam no longer had control of the museum's budget or its land holdings.[18]

In his letter to Charles on July 16, 1909, Putnam wrote that the Harvard University Corporation had refused Charles's request to be the caretaker of the Ferris Cemetery site. Putnam further lamented that he no longer had the money needed to continue work at the Ferris Cemetery site. By this time, timber cutting and sand and gravel mining operations had severely compromised portions of the site. Still, much of it remained unexplored.[19]

Given Charles's concerns, Harvard University sent B. W. Merwin, brother of R. E. Merwin, in 1911 to help define the limits of the Ferris Cemetery site. In addition to excavating new trenches through the site, Charles and Merwin dug trenches along the boundaries of Harvard's property. While the boundary trenches were void of artifacts and features, those dug within the site were quite productive. They exposed 84 mortuary features and 144 cache pits. Of particular importance, they found 23 postholes suggesting that structures were present at the site. They were thought to represent eight communal houses forty to sixty feet in diameter. It is more likely, however, that they were charnel houses—buildings for corpses.[20]

In 1911 the Cincinnati Museum of Natural History published Charles's *A Brief Description of the Turner Group of Prehistoric Earthworks in Anderson Township, Hamilton County, Ohio*. Despite its humble title, the book provided to date the most comprehensive geographic and geologic description of the Turner site earthworks and mounds. Charles's publication included previously undocumented mounds and two circular enclosures, one with a central mound and another with a circular pit. He also illustrated the correct shape and orientation of the elongated enclosure, which had been distorted in previous archaeological publications.

On Saturday, September 14, 1912, the *Times Recorder* of Zanesville, Ohio ran a story on Charles's upcoming publication. Unfortunately, the direction of the story was more about material culture than the people who made them.

OHIOAN UNEARTHS RELICS, THROWING LIGHT ON
LIFE OF PREHISTORIC RACE

MADISONVILLE, O., Sept. 13.—Dr. Charles L. Metz of Madisonville will be much better known to the world in a year or so than he is today. A certain measure of fame will come to him when the Harvard university research committee, of which he is the head, publishes its report sometime in 1913. This committee had for 25 years been excavating in the vicinity for relics that will throw light on the life of the Mound Builders. For a quarter of a century Dr. Metz has been identified with the work and has made some of the richest finds ever made as to the early life in North America of the Mound Builders. Since 1876 he has exhumed 7,000 skeletons and 10,000 earthenware vessels and other utensils of the people. Thousands of skeletons and curious trinkets and articles have been recovered from a single burial ground of the ancients located on the summit of a hill near Madisonville, overlooking the Little Miami river valley.

Harvard's publication of the Ferris Cemetery site report was postponed because of Putnam's failing health. Frederick Ward Putnam died on August 14, 1914, at the age of seventy-five. The Ferris Cemetery report was further delayed with the onset of World War I.

World War I

On June 28, 1914, Gavrilo Princip, a Yugoslav nationalist, assassinated Austrian Archduke Franz Ferdinand in Sarajevo. A month later, Austria and Hungary declared war and invaded Serbia. As Russia came to the aid of Serbia, Germany overtook Belgium and Luxembourg and then headed toward France. Great Britain declared war on Germany and stopped the Germans from reaching Paris. The face off between the two countries became known as the Western Front and resulted in three years of horrific bloody trench warfare. To the east, Germany prevented the Russian army from overtaking Prussia. By 1916 Bulgaria, Italy, the Ottoman Empire, and Romania had joined the fighting.[21]

In 1917 German submarines began destroying ships bound for Great Britain, including those from America. President Woodrow Wilson called on Congress to declare "a war to end all wars" and "make the world safe for democracy." On April 6, 1917, Congress voted to declare war on Austria, Germany, and Hungary. On December 7, 1917, war was declared by the United States.[22]

Although American Indians were not allowed to be citizens of the United States, approximately seventeen thousand enlisted in the military during World War I. At the time, the military was segregated and all American Indians were assigned to the Thirty-sixth Division. Nineteen Choctaw enlisted to serve as America's first code talkers—Albert Billy, Schlicht Billy, Mitchell Bobb, Victor Brown, Ben Carterby, Joseph Davenport, George Davenport, James Edwards, Tobias Frazier, Ben Hampton, Noel Johnson, Otis Leader, Solomon Louis, Peter Maytubby, Jeff Nelson, Joseph Oklahombi, Robert Taylor, Walter Veach, and Calvin Wilson.[23]

The code talkers were extremely successful as the Germans who were listening to American radio communications thought the Choctaw language was gibberish. Because of their distinguished service during World War I, President Calvin Coolidge signed into law on June 2, 1924, Homer P. Snyder's Indian Citizenship Act. It granted full citizenship to all American Indians who served their country during World War I.[24]

Before the war, Cincinnati was proud of its rich German heritage. Following the declaration of war, the loyalty of German-Americans was under scrutiny. Former President Theodore Roosevelt denounced people who identified themselves as German-American insisting that they had to decide whether they were Americans or Germans—they could not be both. Cincinnati's German-American citizens who sided with Germany returned to their homeland to fight against the United States.[25]

People with German surnames were blacklisted, some were beaten in the streets and others were lynched. Many German families responded by Americanizing their surnames. The Justice Department began to arrest and imprison Germans in America as spies. Schools banned the teaching of German and libraries removed books written in German from their shelves including LSSM's Gustav Brühl's *Die Culturvolker Alt-Amerika's*.

Having died on April 16, 1903, Brühl did not live long enough to see the censure of his work.[26]

Like other German-Americans, Charles purchased war bonds to show his loyalty to the United States. He also had a tall flagpole installed on the front lawn of his home next to the street. Charles raised and lowered his oversized American flag every day with great respect and care. He would gather as many children as he could to assist in the ceremony. Anyone who watched could see the love and pride for America in Charles's face as he watched the flag wave in the wind. To ensure that his children and grandchildren were patriotic, he would draw rows and rows of little stick soldiers marching bravely to the defense of their country while telling them his experiences during the Civil War.[27]

As a further example of Charles's loyalty to God, country, and family, he wrote a twenty-one–bullet-point list that he titled "My Aim and Guide."

1. To respect my Country, my profession, and myself.

2. To be honest and fair with my fellowmen, as I would expect them to be honest and square with me.

3. To be a loyal citizen of the United States of America.

4. To speak of it with praise and act always as a trustworthy custodian of it's good name.

5. To be a man whose name carries weight with it wherever it goes.

6. To have my expectations of reward on a solid foundation of service rendered.

7. To be willing to pay the price of success in honest effort.

8. To look upon my work as an opportunity to be seized with joy and made the most of and not as a painful drudgery to be reluctantly endured.

9. To remember that success lies within my own brain, my own ambition, courage, my own determination and myself.

10. To expect difficulties and to force my way through them.

11. To turn hard experiences into capital for future struggles.

12. To believe in my own proposition heart and soul.

13. To carry an air of optimism in the presence of those I meet.

14. To dispel ill temper with cheerfulness, kill doubts with strong convictions and reduce active friction with an agreeable personality.

15. To keep my future un-mortgaged with debts.

16. To save as well as to earn.

17. To cut out expensive amusements until I can afford them.

18. To steer clear of dissipation and guard my health of body and peace of mind as a most precious stock in trade.

19. To take a good grip on the joys of life, to play the game like a man.

20. To fight against nothing so hard as my own weakness and endeavor to grow in strength, a Christian, a gentleman.

21. So I may be courteous to all, faithful to Family and friends; true to my God.[28]

Despite the fact Charles's oldest son, Charles Wilbur, was thirty-seven years old, he was able to enlist in the army. He had remained in the Ohio National Guard and medical doctors were desperately needed on the front lines. On June 23, 1917, Charles Wilbur was commissioned as a first lieutenant in the National Guard Medical Corps. He attended the Medical Officers' Training Corps at Fort Benjamin Harrison in Indiana. On September 12, 1917, Charles Wilbur was promoted to captain in the U.S. Army Medical Corps.[29]

On October 8, 1918, Charles Wilbur was assigned to the Medical Department of the 148th Infantry. He was sent directly to the front lines at Baccarat and the Pannes, in the Meuse-Argonne and the Ypres-Lys campaign at Rechicourt and Avocourt during three months of heavy fighting. Charles Wilbur crossed the Scheldt River in Belgium on November 2, 1918, and provided crucial medical care for soldiers wounded by machine gun fire, mortar shell explosions, and mustard gas.[30]

With Charles Wilbur serving in the army in France, the Cincinnati Board of Health was short of doctors. Charles volunteered to serve as the doctor for the Madisonville Public Grade School and Saint Anthony Parochial School.[31]

Charles's younger son, George Francis, was twenty-six years old and working on John McCafferty's farm when war was declared. He enlisted in the army on June 15, 1917. He, too, was sent to the front lines in France. In May 1918 Charles read that Germany was trying to overrun the front lines at Somme from the direction of Amiens. They had advanced almost forty miles killing about two hundred thousand people and taking some seventy thousand prisoners along the way. The situation was desperate and one of the largest and bloodiest battles of the war seemed inevitable.

On May 25, 1918, Charles wrote a letter to his son George, which he hoped would take his mind off of the impending combat.

> Dear George
>
> How are you and how do you like it by now? Ethel and I have been working in the garden weeding and hoeing and it is beginning to look fine. We have been making guesses on what the things were that came up. Are those Ponderosa tomatoes you planted? They are big enough to set out and the radishes down there are large enough to use.
>
> Hello George Blacky
>
> This is a letter from Blacky (the dog). I had an awful time making him put the o on hello. I am afraid he is a naughty pup. The chickens are still laying and the pigs are fine. Old Cuppy (the cat) heard it thunder and got quite excited, she is out on her chair now. She looks fine and is increasing in size rapidly. She wants to write to you so I will ask her. Fred was down last Sunday. He had such a good time he is coming soon again. I hope you get home for the wedding in the fall.
>
> Hello Geo. How are you? Take care of yourself. I am well. With love Cuppy
>
> Cuppy let me hold her paw with the pencil in it longer than Blacky could so she wrote a longer letter and wagged her tail about it when she finished. I think she knew what she was doing.[32]

Charles thought that letters from George's beloved pets would give him a warm sense of home and help take his mind off the danger and stress of war. The autumn wedding Charles referred to in the letter was going to be between George's sister Ethel Helen Caroline age thirty-two, and Frederick Joseph Berger age twenty-nine. After the wedding, they planned to move into Phebe Ferris's home along with Ethel's sisters Clara Isabel, age forty-one; Julia Marie, age twenty-nine; and Margaret Elizabeth, age twenty-three. Together, they would care for the Ferris estate and serve as librarians.

Ethel Helen was not the only one who had fallen in love and married. Anna Teresa age forty-seven had married Charles's medical partner, Dr.

Arthur Levy Knight, age fifty-two. In 1918 he joined the LSSM. Like Charles, he shared a passion for American Indians. They were both avid members of the Madisonville Round-Table, a group, which met weekly to discuss books, current events, history, philosophy, and science. Charles and Arthur attended every week except when there was a medical emergency.[33]

Although an armistice was agreed upon on November 11, 1918, George Francis's return home was delayed because his lungs were badly damaged from exposure to mustard gas. On March 31, 1919, Charles received a letter from K. E. Eddy of the American Red Cross at the U.S. Army Base Hospital at Camp Sherman, Ohio.

> The above soldier (George Metz) has arrived at this hospital from over-seas and is glad to again be back in the Country we all love so well. Write him as soon and as often as you can. A bright cheerful letter from home will be most welcome to him. An American Red Cross man saw him upon his arrival and you can be sure we will do all we can to add to his comfort. His address is—care U.S.A. Base Hospital, Camp Sherman, Ohio.
>
> Sincerely
> American Red Cross
> Per K. E. Eddy[34]

Charles Wilbur remained in the army a bit longer. After France he was sent to Manila to serve as chief medical officer. He was honorably discharged on April 2, 1919 from the First Regiment Infirmary at Camp Sherman, Ohio. Charles Wilbur returned home with his dress military sword, an army-issued .45-caliber Colt Model 1917 handgun, French francs, and much to the chagrin of his family, an unexploded mortar shell. While the loyalty of German-Americans continued to be scrutinized in the United States, no one dared to question the patriotism of the Metz family. It was beyond reproach.

Golden anniversary

On Tuesday May 4, 1920, Charles and Molly celebrated their fiftieth golden wedding anniversary. It was a beautiful warm sunny day. They began their festivities with a Roman Catholic Mass at Saint Anthony Church in Madisonville. During the Mass, they listened to a full church choir, which included boy sopranos from Saint Anthony Grade School.

Charles and Molly said they sounded like angels singing. Afterward, they went home to have breakfast with their children and grandchildren.[35]

Charles and Molly held a reception in the late afternoon for their friends and family. Many of them had not been seen or heard from for years. Everyone showed up bearing gifts of gold coins. Charles and Molly had so much fun that the celebration extended well into the evening. Despite the enormous size of the Metz home, it barely had room for everyone as well as all the flowers sent from friends and devoted patients.[36]

Each of the guests gave personal testimonials about the Metz family. They deeply touched Charles and Molly. Among the accolades was that of Dr. Frank B. Dyer, superintendent of Cincinnati Public Schools. He had been principal of Madisonville schools during the time Charles worked to build a strong school system in Madisonville.[37]

> To my beloved friend, counselor of my youth and comrade of Auld Lang Sine (days gone by). Just a little reminder of days of Yore when we took counsel together dreamed our dreams and built our air castles.[38]

The children of Saint Anthony School presented the Metzes with a spiritual "Bouquet of Prayers." The Sisters of Charity and teachers at Saint Anthony presented them with a beautifully hand-printed tribute along with a considerable amount of money. One of the tributes came a day late and was accompanied by gold piece and a note "Better late than never."[39]

The LSSM also presented Charles a certificate.

> The Literary Societies of Madisonville to
> Dr. Charles Louis Metz
> World-known Archaeologist
> Who made this region celebrated for Prehistoric Antiquities
> Organizer and Leader of the first
> Literary and Scientific Society of Madisonville,
> Friend of Public Education
> Projector and Promoter of the First High School and Library in Madisonville. A devoted Friend of Man, who professional services have been generously given to alleviate distress in this community for half a century.
>
> Greetings

With acknowledgment of his distinguished services and gratitude
for them and with Congratulations upon the
Golden Anniversary of his Marriage to Amelia Berger.
The Madisonville Monday Club—The Madisonville Round Table
May 4th 1920.[40]

Continuing work with the Peabody Museum

Although Putnam had passed away before the Ferris Cemetery report could be completed, Charles continued his affiliation with the Peabody Museum of Archaeology and Ethnology. Charles C. Willoughby was Putnam's successor. He wanted to bring closure to the Museum's participation in the excavation of archaeological sites in the Little Miami River valley in the form of two final site reports—the Ferris Cemetery and Turner sites. Willoughby asked Charles to help him and Earnest Albert Hooton in this endeavor.

Hooton was a curator of Somatology at the Peabody Museum of Archaeology and Ethnology. Somatology is a subdiscipline of anthropology, which focuses on the human body. Hooton's interest focused on human skeletal remains from the Ferris Cemetery and Turner sites.

Like other anthropologists of the day, Hooton was trying to fit human remains into Darwin's theory of evolution as it was originally published in November 24, 1859, *On the Origin of Species by Means of Natural Selection, or the Preservation of Favored Races in the Struggle for Life*. The title was shortened to *The Origin of Species* in 1872. Unfortunately, many biological and physical anthropologists continued to focus on the failed concept of "favored races."[41]

The sociocultural adaptation of Darwin's theory to anthropology was called Social Darwinism. It theorized that "primitive races" were reduced in number and their cultures engulfed by the "favored races," which continued to grow in strength and power. In this regard, Social Darwinists argued that human society was governed by what Herbert Spencer called the "survival of the fittest." Not surprisingly, Social Darwinism provided an anthropological basis for Adolf Hitler's *Mein Kampf*, the rise of Nazism in Germany, and ultimately the Holocaust.[42]

While Charles and Willoughby wanted to detail and chronicle the role Harvard University played in the archaeology of the Little Miami River valley, Hooton wanted to use the morphological characteristics of the human skeletal remains to define "primitive races" and racial "subtypes." He wanted to show that American Indians were phylogenetically more primitive than the "Caucasian race." Unfortunately, Hooton's contributions did nothing more than reaffirm contemporary racial stereotypes of American Indians.

In 1920 Hooton and Willoughby published the *Indian Village Site and Cemetery near Madisonville, Ohio* as volume 8, number 1 of the Papers of the Peabody Museum of American Archaeology and Ethnology, Harvard University. It was followed two years later by Willoughby and Hooton's *The Turner Group of Earthworks, Hamilton County, Ohio* published as volume 8, number 3 of the Papers of the Peabody Museum of American Archaeology and Ethnology, Harvard University. With the publication of the Turner and Ferris Cemetery site volumes, Harvard felt that they had brought closure to the archaeology of the Little Miami River valley.

The professionalization of Ohio Valley archaeology

At the time Harvard published their Turner site report, the professionalization and modernization of Ohio Valley archaeology was well under way. The formation of the Anthropological Society of Washington (ASW) was the earliest attempt to organize professional archaeologists. On February 7, 1879, Washington D.C. newspapers ran the following ad:

> Many persons interested in American Archaeology have expressed a desire for an organization in this city to promote study and diffuse knowledge upon the subject. All willing to join an archaeological association are requested to attend a meeting at the Smithsonian Institution on Monday evening the 10th inst. at 7 o'clock for a conference upon the subject and the formation of such a Society.[43]

The first official meeting of the ASW was held March 4, 1879. The first professional paper presented at the meeting was "Relic Hunting," read by Frank H. Cushing. This view of archaeology was diametrically opposed to that of Charles who viewed archaeology in terms of science and historic preservation. By 1888 the ASW incorporated the first scientific periodical dedicated to American anthropology—the *American Anthropologist*.

In 1902 the American Anthropological Association (AAA) was created from the ASW. They assumed responsibility for publishing the *American*

Anthropologist. Their mission was to

> promote the science of anthropology, to stimulate and coordinate the efforts of American anthropologists, to foster local and other societies devoted to anthropology, to serve as a bond among American anthropologists and anthropologic[al] organizations present and prospective, and to publish and encourage the publication of matter pertaining to anthropology.[44]

By 1922 professional interest in anthropology had grown in the Ohio Valley and greater Midwestern United States to the point that it justified the creation of a Central Section of the AAA (later known as the Central States Anthropological Association). The Central Section of the AAA provided an annual meeting place for Ohio Valley archaeologists, a forum for papers to be presented, and a place to share gossip about the profession and brag about one's latest findings. The structure of the Central Section followed Franz Boas's model of anthropology—a holistic field, which integrated archaeology with cultural anthropology, linguistics, and physical anthropology.[45]

With this new vision of professional anthropology, the Central Section of the AAA became the gatekeepers of Ohio Valley archaeology. Although they fully acknowledged the enormous role that amateurs played in the development of Ohio Valley archaeology, they did not tolerate "relic hunting" or the total destruction of sites for the sole purpose of acquiring artifacts.

Even though the Central Section of the AAA embraced the most recent methods and theories of archaeology, Warren King Moorehead was still behaving as if it were 1879. He used the Central Section to circulate his paper *Cooperative Collecting: An Opportunity to Add to Your Collection*. On March 3, 1923, at 9:00 a.m., at the second annual meeting of the Central Section, the officers and members passed a resolution, which stated,

> *Whereas* the plan of collecting outlined in this circular appears to the members of the Central Section to be derogatory to the best interests of the science of American archaeology, therefore be it *Resolved* that the Secretary of the Central Section be directed to forward to Mr. Warren K. Moorehead a letter protesting against the plan of collecting as outlined and informing him that members of the Central Section do not feel they can lend it to either their countenance or support. Ralph Linton Secretary[46]

Although Moorehead had published on Charles's archaeological discoveries in the very best light in his 1892 book, *Primitive Man in Ohio*, Charles was outspoken about Moorehead's personal artifact collecting and destruction of burial mounds and earthworks in the Ohio River valley. The Central Section's censure of Moorehead's unprofessional conduct finally vindicated Charles's position on the proper role archaeologists should play in the science of anthropology.

Founding of Mariemont

In 1923 Mary Hopkins Emery provided the funds needed to plan a new utopian community for middle-class families. She named it Mariemont after her estate in Newport, Rhode Island. The newly formed Mariemont Company was seeking title to all of the Ferris property. Harvard wanted to sell the Ferris Cemetery site to the Mariemont Company to help finance the Peabody Museum. The problem was they needed to get a fee simple title.

Phebe Ferris stated in item 4 of her will that

> I give and devise to the Peabody Museum . . . the Ancient Cemetery to be by said Museum kept for scientific purposes for the preservation of the remains and relics of said cemetery.[47]

Item 3 of Phebe's will created a trust fund for the erection, maintenance, and endowment of the Joseph Ferris Memorial Library, a free library of reference, to be located "in my homestead." It was her intent that artifacts recovered from the Ferris Cemetery site would remain in the library.

Following Phebe's death, the Peabody Museum continued to excavate the cemetery site, employing Charles to supervise work. Following her death, the skeletal remains of 487 American Indians were exhumed and a great number of artifacts and associated grave goods were removed. All of this archaeological material was removed to the Peabody Museum. Legally, it was uncertain whether or not the Peabody Museum had the right to remove any of these remains and artifacts and have them transported to the Peabody Museum. Both the U.S. District Court in Cincinnati and the Sixth Circuit Court of Appeals would address this question in a lawsuit brought by Harvard College, the successor to the Peabody Museum.

In order to sell the Ferris Cemetery site to the Mariemont Company, the president and fellows of Harvard College initiated a "quiet title" action in federal court to have its rights under the will clarified. Harvard alleged in the lawsuit that the purposes of Item 4 in the will, which had created a trust were fulfilled because "all the relics and remains . . . [of the Ancient Cemetery] . . . worth removing . . . had been removed."[48]

Therefore, Harvard argued that it, and not the heirs of Phebe Ferris, was entitled to the Ferris Cemetery in "fee simple," meaning the Harvard owned the site absolutely and could sell it. Harvard argued, in the alternative, that it held the title in trust and that the purposes of the trust could be better accomplished by selling the land and using the proceeds for maintaining the artifacts at the Peabody Museum.[49]

Both federal courts disagreed with Harvard, and denied its claim to take over the Ferris property. The courts said that the property belonged to the heirs of Phebe Ferris. The reasoning of the Court of Appeals in its decision of May 16, 1925, strongly indicates that Harvard violated the terms of the trust by removing the artifacts to the Peabody Museum. Charles was unwittingly complicit in this possible "violation." The court stated,

> While the trust here created was for educational purposes and as such is a public charitable trust, yet there is nothing in this will to indicate that the removal of these relics was in fulfillment of the wishes of the testatrix [Phebe Ferris], or to suggest that she contemplated such removal. On the contrary, the plain and positive language of the [will] indicates a wholly different purpose and intent.... It would appear that it was the intention and purpose of the testatrix, not only to make this homestead and Ancient cemetery an attractive resort for all persons interested in literature, archaeological, and ethnological studies and investigation, but to bring these educational advantages in near proximity to her friends and neighbors.[50]

The precise issue before the federal courts was who owned the land. The court decided that Harvard did not; the Ferris heirs did. The court did not decide the issue of whether the trust had been violated by the removal of the artifacts because the parties to the case were contending about the ownership of the land. However, the unmistakable language of the court indicates that Harvard had indeed violated the terms of the trust by removing the artifacts to the Peabody Museum in Cambridge, Massachusetts, and the intent of Phebe Ferris was that they remain "in near proximity to her friends and neighbors."[51]

With the Court of Appeals' decision, Harvard's trust was terminated and the title of the Ferris Cemetery site reverted to Phebe's heirs. Although the Ferris family subsequently sold the land to the newly formed Mariemont Company, it was with the understanding that the Ferris Cemetery site and the surrounding old growth hardwood forest, known as Dogwood Park, would be spared from development in keeping with Phebe's wishes.[52]

An unintentional victim of the Peabody Museum's action was the Joseph Ferris Memorial Library. Frederick Joseph Berger; his wife, Ethel Helen Metz Berger; their son, Frederick Wilbur Berger; Clara Isabel Metz; Julia Marie Metz; and Margaret Elizabeth Metz had been caring for the Ferris home and library for a quarter of a century. However, after Harvard broke the trust of her will, its ownership returned it to the Ferris family.

The Metz family was forced to move out of the Ferris home and into a much smaller house on Lonsdale Street on the other side of Wooster Pike. Arthur Knight arranged for Phebe's books and journals to be moved to the Madisonville Public Library. Charles arranged to have Phebe's artifact collection donated to the Cincinnati Art Museum.

The loss of the Joseph Ferris Memorial Library and the sale of the Ferris Cemetery site to the Mariemont Company were emotionally devastating to Charles. However, he was able to take some professional solace in the most recent archaeological news. On November 20, 1925, Harold J. Cook published in the prestigious journal *Science*, "Definite Evidence of Human Artifacts in the American Pleistocene." Charles's discovery of American Indian–made artifacts in geological deposits that dated to the last Ice Age had been independently verified by a comparable discovery made near Folsom, New Mexico. Although he was not given credit at the time, African-American cowboy and former slave, George McJunkin, discovered this landmark archaeological site in 1908.[53]

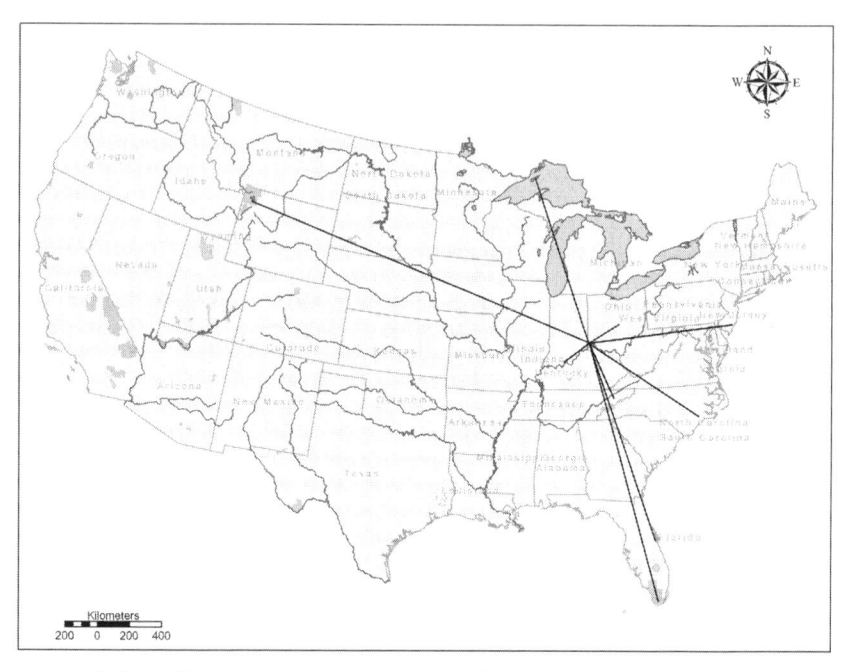

184 American Indian Archaeology of the Little Miami River Valley

10.1 Map illustrating the source areas of artifacts found at the Turner site, Hamilton County, Ohio.

10.2. Amelia (Molly) and Charles Louis Metz.

The Twentieth Century 185

10.3. A butterfly and wing enclosed in a pendant. A gift to twenty-one-year-old Ethel Helen Caroline Metz from Frederick Ward Putnam, December 25, 1907.

186 American Indian Archaeology of the Little Miami River Valley

10.4. Charles Wilbur Metz, first lieutenant, 148th Infantry, U.S. Marine Corps, ca. 1917.

CHAPTER 11

And In The End

On January 1, 1926, Charles's last birthday, over a hundred residents of Madisonville surprised him with a purse of money and a heartfelt tribute of appreciation for his many years of kindnesses to them. Unfortunately, the battle to preserve the Ferris Cemetery site and the Joseph Ferris Memorial Library severely weakened Charles's heart. In the spring of 1926, he suffered a debilitating heart attack.[1]

Charles's heart attack was complicated by congestive heart failure and chronic lung ailments. He no longer had the strength to use the stairs in his multistory home and office. Charles had to be carried from his bed to his office and back again. His brain was just as sharp and active as ever, but it was trapped in a frail and failing body. Despite his physical weakness, Charles was able to continue his archaeological correspondences with Charles E. Willoughby, now director of Harvard's Peabody Museum. He also stayed informed of the most recent archaeological discoveries by reading *National Geographic*, *Science*, and *Scientific American*.

One story in particular captured Charles's attention. On July 14, 1926, Frank Figgins exposed a fragmented flaked-stone spear point in Ice Age clay alongside the ribs of an extinct form of bison in New Mexico. Jesse Figgins, Frank's father, instructed him to ship the sediment block containing the bones and the artifact for to the Denver Museum of Natural History. Harold J. Cook, then curator of paleontology, used the discovery to write "The Antiquity of Man in America: Who Were the Ice Age Americans? Whence Came They?" for the November 1, 1926, issue of *Scientific American*. It was a stark contrast to Aleš Hrdlička's paper, "The Race and Antiquity of the American Indian: There is No Valid Evidence That the Indian Has Long Been in the New World," published just three months earlier in the same magazine.[2]

Hrdlička had been an outspoken critic, not only of Charles's discoveries, but also of everyone who claimed that American Indians were in the Western Hemisphere longer than three thousand years. Hrdlička believed they migrated across the Bering Strait from East Asia at that time. Instead of using archaeological and geological field and laboratory methods to test his theory, he compared human skulls from different geographic areas. In the case of American Indians, he beheaded recently deceased individuals, removed their hair and flesh in the field, and shipped the skulls along with any material possessions they had on them to the American Museum of Natural History. Not only was Hrdlička unethical in his methods, his strongly argued conclusions about American Indians were wrong.

Charles's passing

On a cold, gray Monday, December 20, 1926, Charles closed his eyes and quietly slipped into the past. The next day Molly received a letter from the Catholic Order of Foresters, a fraternal life insurance society.

> Cincinnati, Ohio, Dec. 21, 1926
> To the family of our departed.
> Medical Examiner Dr. Charles L. Metz
> The divine Providence has seen fit to call from our midst, our Doctor Charles L. Metz to his reward, The Immaculate Court. 1504 Catholic Order of Foresters has suffered the loss of their Medical Examiner, The Community a respected citizen, and the Family the loss of a Faithful husband and loving father.
> -Be it resolved
> We as members of the Immaculate Court, 1504 Catholic Order of Foresters, deeply feels the loss of their Medical Examiner and in this hour of the bereavement, We offer to his Widow & Children the sympathy of all of our hearts.[3]

On December 21 his obituary appeared in newspapers across the country, including the *New York Times*.

DR. CHARLES L. METZ,
ARCHAEOLOGIST, DEAD

Made Interesting Discoveries in Prehistoric Mounds of the West
Special to the New York Times

CINCINNATI, OHIO, DEC. 21.—Dr. Charles L. Metz, who died in his home today, was widely known in scientific circles. He had been ill for some time, but despite this and his advanced age, he would have been 80 had he lived until Jan. 1—some of his written reports on archaeological subjects were published as lately as three years ago by the Smithsonian Institution in Washington.

Dr. Metz was said to be the first to find gold buried in prehistoric mounds, and to find, west of the Alleghany Mountains evidences of the existence of man here during the paleolithic age, roughly estimated at 60,000 years ago. He established this fact by finding bone [*sic*, stone] instruments which scientists said must have been chipped by the hand of man.

Published December 22, 1926
New York Times

What the obituaries did not mention was that in more than fifty years of medical practice Charles had delivered 3,357 babies and he had never lost a mother in childbirth. Charles's daughter Margaret wrote a personal obituary of her father, which described her mother's positive influence on him.

> He was a kind and loving father and I loved him very much. My mother should have a place right along side of him, for she was very much a part of him. Her contribution was love and patient understanding, she was far more practical than he but she was not domineering. A devoted and loving wife and mother and I am sure contributed greatly to his life's work just because of his great need for her.[4]

Charles was laid to rest in the Holy Ghost Parish Cemetery in Vera Cruz, Ohio, across the road from the Church of the Holy Ghost where he and Molly were married fifty-six years earlier. A sheaf of red roses was placed on his coffin along with a note from the teachers and students of the Madisonville Public School.

> These flowers bear the love and sympathy of the children. Each child gave a penny.[5]

The sentiments of the students were deeply felt. Charles awarded gold and silver medals to Madisonville Public School students who earned the highest grades. The medals were called "The Metz Medallions" and were greatly prized.[6]

In addition to his beloved family, Charles left behind a large body of anthropological and archaeological work, which is today curated in museums in Cincinnati, Ohio, and around the world, including Harvard University's Peabody Museum, the Field Museum in Chicago, the Smithsonian Institute in Washington, D.C., the British Museum in London, and the National Museum in Berlin, Germany.

Perhaps, more important than the archaeological footprint that Charles left behind were all of the lives that he touched—personally and professionally. Although Charles kept a close and accurate account of how many babies he helped to bring into the world, he was unaware of the untold numbers of people whose lives he affected during his generation and far beyond his death.

In many ways Charles was the quintessential "George Bailey," the principal character in Frank Capra's 1946 film, *It's a Wonderful Life*. Charles positively changed people's lives, inspired countless generations of future archaeologists, and helped change American attitudes about indigenous peoples. While Charles passed away in 1926, his body of scientific work and positive influences continue to live on.

And In The End   191

11.1. Office sign indicating Charles Louis Metz's office hours, ca. 1926.

11.2. Pad of calling cards for C. L. Metz, M.D., Madisonville, Ohio, with office hours, ca. 1926.

Epilogue

The Legacy of Charles Louis Metz

The archaeological contributions of Charles Louis Metz have been historically obfuscated because he lacked the upper class social cachet and academic position of the East Coast anthropologists. While the vast majority of his research has either gone unrecognized or it has been attributed to other scholars in the history of American archaeology, it laid the framework for all subsequent research on the prehistory and history of American Indians in the Ohio River valley.

Charles devoted his academic life to the preservation of sites located in the Little Miami River valley. He knew they were vulnerable to destruction from expanding industries, roadways, sand and gravel mining, and urban sprawl. Additionally, pothunters and private artifact collectors were robbing American Indian graves at an unprecedented rate during the late nineteenth and early twentieth centuries. While Congress passed and President Theodore Roosevelt signed into law the Antiquities Act on June 8, 1906, it was restricted to the protection of American Indian sites, features, and artifacts on federal lands in the western United States. There were no laws during Charles's lifetime which protected archaeological sites in the Little Miami River valley.[1]

James Bennett Griffin

As a graduate student in 1935, James Bennett Griffin discovered Charles's archaeological research. He was especially interested in the pottery that Charles excavated from the Hahn Field, Madisonville, Turpin, and Sand Ridge sites. Griffin used the ceramic artifacts as the basis of his 1937 "The Chronological Position and Ethnological Relationships of the Fort Ancient Aspect" published in *American Antiquity* and his 1943 *The Fort Ancient Aspect: Its Cultural and Chronological Position in Mississippi Valley Archaeology*. Although it was not apparent in his earliest work, Griffin supported Charles's conclusion that the American Indian inhabitants of the Madisonville site were, in fact, Algonquian speakers, and most likely the Shawnee.

New Deal archaeology

Enacted by Congress at the peak of the Great Depression, August 21, 1935, President Franklin Delano Roosevelt signed into law the Historic Sites Act. Aside from organizing federally owned historic sites, monuments, and parks under the auspices of the U.S. Department of the Interior and the National Park Service, it called for the preservation of archaeological sites that were considered to be of national significance. Additionally, a large workforce was made available to assist in preservation efforts through the Works Progress Administration (later known as the Work Projects Administration (WPA), the Civilian Conservation Corps (CCC), and the National Youth Administration (NYA).[2]

In Ohio the WPA operated archaeological projects over a period of eight years in cooperation with state and local governments. Roosevelt's New Deal policy also dictated that the archaeological fieldwork could not allow the discrimination of anyone by "race, creed, or politics."[3]

In order to determine, which archaeological sites were going to be protected, the WPA turned to Charles's groundbreaking archaeological surveys and excavations. Perhaps Charles is best known for his field survey and excavations at the Great Serpent Mound in Adams County, Ohio. Although Dr. S. S. Scoville took credit for discovering the earthwork in the spring of 1892, Ephraim Squier and Edwin Davis, in their 1848 *Ancient Monuments of the Mississippi Valley*, first reported it.[4]

Charles had gone past the Great Serpent Mound as a child many times with his father and he conducted fieldwork there, along with his family, in 1887. WPA workmen carefully reconstructed the earthwork using Charles's field notes and maps. The CCC also used Charles's field notes and maps to assist their work at Fort Ancient in Warren County, Ohio, and Fort Hill in Highland County, Ohio. The CCC and WPA concluded their work on June 30, 1942, with the onset of World War II.[5]

Radiocarbon dating

Perhaps the greatest archaeological challenge Charles faced was addressing the issue of time. "How old is it?" is the single most important question in American archaeology. During Charles's lifetime, dendrochronology and stratigraphic dating offered the only means to determine the age of archaeological sites. Stratigraphic dating only provided a relative means of determining if one archaeological layer or site was older or younger than the other. While dendrochronology provided an age measured within a year's precision, all of the archaeological sites which Charles documented were older than the datable age range for dendrochronology.[6]

During World War II, Willard Frank Libby, a physical chemist, envisioned the radiocarbon dating technique. While he was working on the Manhattan Project at Columbia University, Libby used his spare time to calculate the half-life of radiocarbon, a radioactive isotope of carbon. Libby correctly determined that radiocarbon had a long half-life and by 1946 it had been calculated to about five thousand years. With this figure Libby could determine the age of archaeological sites that were less than forty thousand years old by measuring the amount of radiocarbon in organic artifacts.[7]

By 1947 Libby was using his revolutionary new technique to date artifacts and archaeological sites. In May 1949, during the Fourteenth Annual Meeting of the Society for American Archaeology held at Indiana University, and hosted by Glenn A. Black and Eli Lilly, radiocarbon dates obtained from archaeological sites were announced and later published in the December 23, 1949, issue of *Science*. From that point on, archaeologists had a means to determine the age of American Indian sites in the Little Miami River valley.[8]

Charles knew that different archaeological sites contained artifacts manufactured with different methods and materials. For example, earthenware pottery from the Turner site was made with crushed igneous and metamorphic rocks. Pottery from the Sand Ridge site was made with crushed limestone. Pottery from the Ferris Cemetery, Hahn Field, and Turpin sites was made of crushed shell. Charles believed that these changes in ceramic temper reflected changing technology through time.

With the advent of radiocarbon dating, the archaeological sites, which Charles documented, could finally be dated. His theory of a time depth was indeed, correct. Radiocarbon dating allowed archaeologists to divide sites in the Little Miami River valley into cultural periods based on time and cultural and technological change.

The oldest cultural period was defined as Paleo-Indian, dating to more than 10,000 BCE, a time when bands of American Indians hunted wild game and gathered wild plants. The Archaic cultural period was dated between 8000 BCE and 500 BCE and defined as a period when American Indians domesticated plants, practiced horticulture, and arboriculture, but before the advent of pottery. The Woodland cultural period was dated between 500 BCE and ACE 1000 and defined as a time when American Indians developed and refined earthenware, established long distance procurement routes, and used exotic raw materials. The Fort Ancient cultural period was dated to ACE 1000 to the time of European contact.[9]

In the Little Miami River valley, the Turner site was radiocarbon dated between ACE 50 and ACE 500 and assigned to the Middle Woodland (Hopewell) cultural period. The Sand Ridge site was radiocarbon dated between ACE 430 and ACE 870 and assigned to the Late Woodland (Newtown) cultural period. The Turpin site was radiocarbon dated between ACE 1020 and ACE 1490, and assigned to the early Fort Ancient cultural period. The Hahn Field site was radiocarbon dated from ACE 1430 and ACE 1650 and assigned to the middle Fort Ancient cultural period. The Ferris Cemetery site, renamed the Madisonville site, was radiocarbon dated between ACE 860 and ACE 1890 and assigned to the late Fort Ancient cultural period.[10]

Post–World War II archaeology

Following World War II there was rapid economic growth and development in the Little Miami River valley as well as a population explosion known as the "baby boom." This situation hastened the destruction of archaeological sites at an alarming rate. At the time, Elizabeth R. Kellogg was serving as a librarian for the Cincinnati Museum Association, as well as an art historian at the Art Academy of Cincinnati and the Cincinnati Art Museum. Kellogg explained to Ralph E. Dury, then director of the Cincinnati Museum of Natural History, that the situation was desperate.[11]

Kellogg wanted someone to continue the archaeological fieldwork Charles had initiated in the Little Miami River valley. Because of the lack of time and money in 1886, Charles was unable to investigate the earthen burial mound and the stone mound at the Turpin site. Between 1946 and 1949, Kellogg and her friend, Albert Strietmann, provided the Cincinnati Museum of Natural History with enough money for Charles Oehler to excavate them as well as a portion of the adjacent village site.[12]

Kellogg and her philanthropic friends also provided funding for an archaeological survey of Hamilton County, Ohio. She wanted the money to be used to identify which sites had been destroyed, which ones survived, and determine their scientific integrity. Given that the CMNH did not have a professional archaeologist on staff, Dury turned to Gustav (Gus) Carlson, head of the University of Cincinnati's Department of Sociology and Anthropology, about the possibility of conducting an archaeological survey of Hamilton County.[13]

While Carlson had received a master's degree in anthropology in 1934 and a Ph.D. in anthropology and sociology in 1940, he was not an archaeologist. His doctorate dissertation research was on the cultural complex of numbers gambling. Carlson was also well known for his military service during World War II as chief of the intelligence section of the Office of War Information in Kunming, China. There, he worked closely with Vietnamese translator, Ho Chi Minh.

Carlson did not want to turn down an external funding opportunity. He told Dury that UC's Department of Anthropology and Sociology would, indeed, accept the funds to conduct the archaeological fieldwork.[14]

Carlson used Kellogg's money to hire his son Eric and his best friend, sixteen-year-old S. Frederick (Fred) Starr. Carlson instructed them to use the field notes and maps from Charles's archaeological surveys as a baseline for their work. From 1956 to 1958, Eric Carlson and Fred Starr field checked all of the archaeological sites documented by Charles. Additionally, they interviewed artifact collectors who knew him as well as his surviving associates. Gus Carlson used the field data and interviews they collected to ghost write, *The Archaeology of Hamilton County, Ohio*, a special 1960 issue of the *Journal of the Cincinnati Museum of Natural History* under the name of his son's best friend, S. Frederick Starr.[15]

Starr's book identified the Miami Fort earthwork and surrounding property to have the greatest archaeological potential. The area overlooking the Great Miami–Ohio River confluence contained an abundance of burial mounds, earthworks, and village sites. In addition to Charles, Daniel Drake, William Mills, William Henry Harrison, and Squier and Davis had investigated the archaeology of the area.[16]

In 1960 the Miami Fort Generating Station, a dual-fuel (coal and oil) power generating facility owned the property. With the growth in people and industry, additional transmission-lines and towers would have to be built across what Charles had identified as a significant concentration of archaeological sites. Three civic-minded women from Indian Hill—Martha Rowe, Margo Taft-Tytus, and Elizabeth Hobson—asked James Adams for legal assistance in the formation of a not-for-profit organization that would provide funding to aid in the preservation of the Miami Fort earthwork and other archaeological sites in the Cincinnati area. With the assistance of Mary Heller and Tracy Kropp, the Miami Purchase Association for Historic Preservation (MPAHP) was formed in 1964.[17]

Carlson was asked to serve as a founding trustee of MPAHP and oversee the archaeological fieldwork on the property of the Miami Fort Generating Station. In 1965 Carlson agreed and MPAHP provided him with enough money to hire a full-time archaeologist, Frederick W. Fisher. One of Charles's fervent hopes was that UC would hire an archaeologist to continue his life's work in the Little Miami River valley. Thirty-nine years after his passing, Charles's wish came true.[18]

Between 1965 and 1969, Fisher conducted archaeological surveys and systematic excavations at the Miami Fort earthwork and associated burial mounds and village sites. Ultimately, MPAHP-funded archaeological fieldwork led to the property's acquisition by the Great Parks of Hamilton County and the formation of their first archaeological park—Shawnee Lookout.[19]

National Historic Preservation Act

While Fisher was busy working at the Miami Fort earthwork, President Lyndon Baines Johnson signed into law on October 15, 1966, the National

Historic Preservation Act (NHPA). It established the Advisory Council on Historic Preservation, nationwide State Historic Preservation Offices (SHPO), a National Register of Historic Places (NRHP), and a review process known as Section 106 for evaluating the significance of archaeological sites.[20]

With the passing of the NHPA, two more of Charles's dreams came true: (1) a list of archaeological sites in the Little Miami River valley that were of national significance was going to be compiled, and (2) archaeological sites that were threatened with destruction by federally funded and permitted projects were going to be evaluated to determined if they were of national significance.[21]

By 1969 Carlson was able to use the joint MPAHP-UC project to make a convincing case to the university administration that an autonomous department of anthropology was needed because of the increased interest in and external funding of Ohio Valley archaeology. In addition to creating a new graduate program of anthropology, Carlson was provided with enough money to hire a full-time, tenure-track Ohio Valley archaeologist. He hired Kent D. Vickery, an ABD anthropology graduate student from Indiana University and a mentee of James H. Kellar.[22]

The National Environmental Policy Act

On January 1, 1970, President Richard M. Nixon signed into law the National Environmental Policy Act (NEPA). It covered the management of both archaeological and natural resources. NEPA requires the management of all federal actions on the "human environment." NEPA makes the federal government responsible for the preservation of important archaeological sites, cultural properties, and natural aspects of our national heritage. NEPA requires that an environment of diversity and "variety of individual choice" is supported.[23]

Because of NEPA, archaeologists are needed to prepare either an Environmental Assessment (EA) or an Environmental Impact Statement (EIS) for federally funded projects. In order to prepare EA and EIS in compliance with NEPA, an archaeological survey of the area to be adversely impacted is required. Unlike previous legislation, NEPA connects all "socio-cultural impacts," especially the relationships between past American Indian cultures and their living descendants.[24]

Archaeological and Historic Preservation Act 1974

Charles believed that one of the best ways to preserve archaeological sites imminently destined with destruction was to publicly curate artifacts, field notes, maps, and photographs in a museum. One of his greatest fears was that his lifetime of documenting archaeological sites in the Little Miami River valley would be lost forever.

In 1974 President Richard M. Nixon signed into law the Archaeological and Historic Preservation Act (AHPA). It required all federal agencies to preserve for posterity all archaeological data, including artifacts, field notes, maps, and photographs acquired during federally executed, funded, or licensed projects. The AHPA also greatly increased the number federal agencies, which had to ensure that their archaeological data would be protected.[25]

After the passing of the AHPA, the MPAHP hired Vickery's Ohio Valley archaeology graduate students and instructed them to use Charles's records for the Little Miami River valley to compile an inventory of archaeological sites that were eligible for listing on the NRHP. They successfully nominated the Benham Mound, Burchenal Mound, Conrad Mound, Mathew Mound, Norwood Mound, Odd Fellow's Cemetery Mound, the Perin Village site, and the Turpin site to the NRHP.[26]

MPAHP also used Charles's maps and field notes to define archaeological districts on the NRHP—areas geographically defined with a concentration of significant archaeological sites. The Dunlap site, the Clough Creek and Sand Ridge sites, the Hahn Field site, the Mariemont Embankment and Village sites (also known as the Madisonville site and the Mariemont Earthwork), the Rennert Mound site, the Shawnee Lookout site, the Stateline site, and the Wesley Butler site were successfully added to the NRHP as archaeological districts.[27]

American Indian Religious Freedom Act

On August 11, 1978, President Jimmy Carter signed into law the American Indian Religious Freedom Act (AIRFA). Although American Indians were given the right to citizenship in 1924, they did not have religious freedom. The AIRFA allowed American Indians to practice their traditional religious rights and cultural practices.[28]

AIRFA gave American Indians the right to access archaeological sites they considered sacred. It also prohibited any governmental agencies to interfere with the exercise of religious practices and it required them to provided access to and use of archaeological sites which were considered sacred. As President Carter noted, government agencies have been guilty of denying American Indians access to particular archaeological sites and they interfered with American Indian religious practices and customs. While the law provided American Indians with unrestricted access to archaeological sites, it did not protect them.[29]

Archaeological Resource Protection Act

Aside from sand and gravel mining and urban sprawl, Charles was concerned that grave robbers, looters, and pothunters would eventually destroy all of the archaeological sites in the Little Miami River valley because there were no protective laws. On October 31, 1979, President Carter signed into law the Archaeological Resource Protection Act (ARPA). While it did not prevent picking up an arrowhead opportunistically found on the surface, it did provide federal protection of archaeological sites on public and American Indian lands as well as the removal of archaeological collections.[30]

ARPA prohibited unauthorized excavation, removal, damage, alteration, or defacement of archaeological sites and features. ARPA made it illegal to traffic in American Indian artifacts and to sell, purchase, exchange, transport, receive, or offer to sell, purchase, or exchange any American Indian artifacts removed from public lands or tribal property. ARPA also made it illegal to traffic in interstate or foreign commerce in American Indian artifacts wrongfully acquired under state or local law.[31]

For the first time in American history, a person found guilty of violating ARPA faced a fine up to ten thousand dollars, imprisonment up to one year, or both. If American Indian artifacts and features were damaged in any way and the cost of their restoration and repair exceeded the sum of five hundred dollars, a person could be fined up to twenty thousand dollars, imprisoned up to two years, or both. Unfortunately, the law did not cover violations made prior to October 31, 1979, nor does it provide protection of archaeological sites or American Indian sites on private property.[32]

Native American Graves Protection and Repatriation Act

Until 1990 the United States only provided legal protection to marked graves. Because most American Indian graves were unmarked, they were not protected. None of the treaties with American Indians took into account American Indian religious practices, graves, or burial practices. Because there were differential treatments of American Indian graves and remains, American Indian burial sites had been desecrated. The religious beliefs and practices protected by the First Amendment had been infringed upon.[33]

On November 16, 1990, President George H. W. Bush signed into law the Native American Graves Protection and Repatriation Act (NAGPRA). It requires all federal agencies as well as academic institutions and museums that receive federal funding to return American Indian remains, funerary objects, sacred objects, and objects of cultural patrimony to the lineal descendants, culturally affiliated American Indian tribes, and American Indian organizations. Federal agencies, academic institutions, and museums failing to comply with NAGPRA face civil penalties.[34]

NAGPRA also covers the inadvertent discovery or planned excavation of American Indian graves or sacred objects on federal or tribal lands. NAGPRA also covers the collection of American Indian remains, funerary objects, sacred objects, and objects of cultural patrimony obtained from private property if they are acquired by an academic institution or museum, which receives federal funding.[35]

NAGPRA also makes it illegal to traffic in American Indian remains, funerary objects, sacred objects, and objects of cultural patrimony without right of possession. First offenders of violating NAGPRA may be fined up to one hundred thousand dollars, imprisoned up to a year, or both. Unfortunately, NAGPRA does not apply to private property or state land.[36]

Sacred Lands Act

On July 18, 2002, the Sacred Lands Act (SLA) was introduced to the Republican dominated 107th Congress. The SLA would requires managers of federal lands to allow American Indians to have access to archaeological sites for religious practice. It also would prevent significant damage to land considered sacred to American Indians. SLA would require federal agencies to consult with American Indians before any planned disturbance of sacred sites.[37]

In addition to prohibiting the damage of American Indian sacred lands, SLA would give American Indians the right to petition to have lands containing sacred sites to be designated as unsuitable for development. The SLA would also provide funding for monetary damages, injunctions, or mandamus. It would protect the confidentiality of traditional American cultural practices, religions, or the significance and location of sacred land. The SLA would impose criminal penalties for violations of such confidentiality. While the SLA was introduced in Congress, it has yet to be enacted.[38]

John C. Court

John C. Court was an alumnus of Amherst University and a successful Cincinnati businessman. He had a strong sense of public responsibility having served in the White House on the National Security Council under Dr. Henry Kissinger, the Department of Defense under Robert McNamara, and the U.S. Environmental Protection Agency under President Richard M. Nixon.

After reading Charles's publications about the burial mounds and earthworks of the Little Miami River, John developed a strong passion for Ohio Valley archaeology. Charles's publications convinced him that the archaeological sites in the greater Cincinnati area were fascinating and worthy of international attention. Not surprisingly, John envisioned a future of public education, scientific investigation, and preservation of Cincinnati's earthworks and mounds. To this end, John became a passionate philanthropist actively working with and supporting UC's Department of Anthropology in reestablishing an academic program on Ohio Valley archaeology.

In 2007 John learned that UC had lost their Ohio Valley archaeology position. Through the Court Family Foundation, he provided funding for a new tenure-track position in Ohio Valley archaeology. The senior author, Dr. Kenneth Barnett Tankersley, filled the position. When John learned that UC did not have a proper curatorial facility, laboratory, or classroom for the annual Ohio Valley field school, he provided funding to build the Court Archaeological Research Facility (CARF) at the University of Cincinnati Center for Field Studies.

On March 8, 2009, John passed away at the age of sixty-seven following a long and difficult illness. In his honor, John's widow, Georgia, established the John C. Court Memorial Scholarship. It provides a fifteen thousand dollars stipend and full tuition for a graduate student whose research is focused on past American Indian cultures, with preference given to the mound-building cultures of the Ohio River valley (i.e., Early Woodland, Middle Woodland, and/or Fort Ancient). It was John's dream to ensure that future generations of students and the public learn about the unique archaeological sites documented by Charles.

Because of John's gifts, UC teaches undergraduate and graduate students, as well as the public and K-12 educators and their students about the earthworks and mounds in the Ohio Valley, the people who made them, and why they are an important part of our national heritage. Because of John's gifts, the UC Department of Anthropology is able to offer a successful archaeological field school focused on the prehistoric mound-building cultures of the Ohio River valley.

Recent archaeological discoveries funded by the Court Family Foundation have caught international attention and interdisciplinary teaching methods have attracted the notice of other major academic institutions. The money John donated provides students with the opportunity to engage in Cincinnati-area archaeology through hands-on, in-the-field, and learning-by-doing activities. It gives them a chance to both experience archaeology as a science as well as gain an appreciation for American Indian culture and historic preservation.

CARF acts as a major catalyst for a future long-term programming of Ohio Valley archaeological study at UC. This facility ensures that artifacts from the Cincinnati area are properly curated, preserved, and conserved. Additionally, the facility provides access to Ohio Valley artifacts and field data for visiting scholars as well as the interested public. CARF is a place to educate and enthuse many decades of aspiring Ohio Valley archaeologists. John's generosity continues to have a deep and profound impact on Ohio Valley archaeology.

Current threat

The communities of Mariemont, Newtown, and Anderson Township have worked hard over the years to preserve the archaeological sites that

Charles documented. In addition to the Madisonville site and Mariemont Earthwork, the entire village of Mariemont has been declared a National Historic Landmark District including the South 80 Park (also known as Mariemont Gardens), which includes a recently discovered historic contact Fort Ancient village, known as the Wynema site.[39]

The historic preservation efforts of these communities have left a long corridor of rural land, public parks, and nature preserves in the Little Miami River valley. From the perspective of the Ohio Department of Transportation, this is an ideal setting for the construction of a four-lane highway. Because of the density of archaeological sites on the NRHP and those potentially eligible for nomination to the NRHP, any construction in the Little Miami River valley would be devastating.

Looking into the future

Archaeological sites are nonrenewable. Once they are disturbed, they are gone forever. In order to continue to preserve the archaeological sites documented by Charles, federal, state, and local governments have to enforce the existing historic preservation legislation as well as improve upon it. Thousands of archaeological sites are destroyed every year because they occur on property not covered under federal, state, or local laws. Ultimately, it is the responsibility of the public to preserve the past for the future. After all, we are the stewards of the past.[40]

While a remarkable number of archaeological sites were documented by Charles and those who followed in his footsteps, they likely represent less than 1 percent of those which lie deeply buried beneath the surface of the Little Miami River valley. With the demands associated with increasing human population, there is an urgency to document these archaeological sites. This situation will continue to be complicated by the fact that there are very few professional Ohio Valley archaeologists and very limited funding. Private funding from inspired philanthropists such as John C. Court, Elizabeth Hobson, Elizabeth R. Kellogg, Martha Rowe, and Margo Taft-Tytus will continue to make a lasting difference.[41]

The Village of Mariemont is endeavoring to commemorate the legacy of Charles Louis Metz by seeking to have returned artifacts from the Madisonville site to a museum in Mariemont. Similarly, a number of Algonquian tribes are seeking the repatriation of human skeletal remains, grave goods, and items of cultural patrimony. Presently, the artifacts and human remains are now buried in drawers in the storage rooms of the Peabody Museum of Archaeology and Ethnology at Harvard.

The 1925 Court of Appeals decision has very strong implications for the holdings of these artifacts by Harvard University. If the artifacts were removed in violation of the trust, does Harvard have any right to keep them? With regard to the human skeletal remains, grave goods, and items of cultural patrimony, the recent NAGPRA legislation gives American Indians rights to their return and reburial. These issues must be addressed as Cincinnatians and American Indians knock on the doors of Harvard University that has consigned these artifacts to storage rooms out of public view.

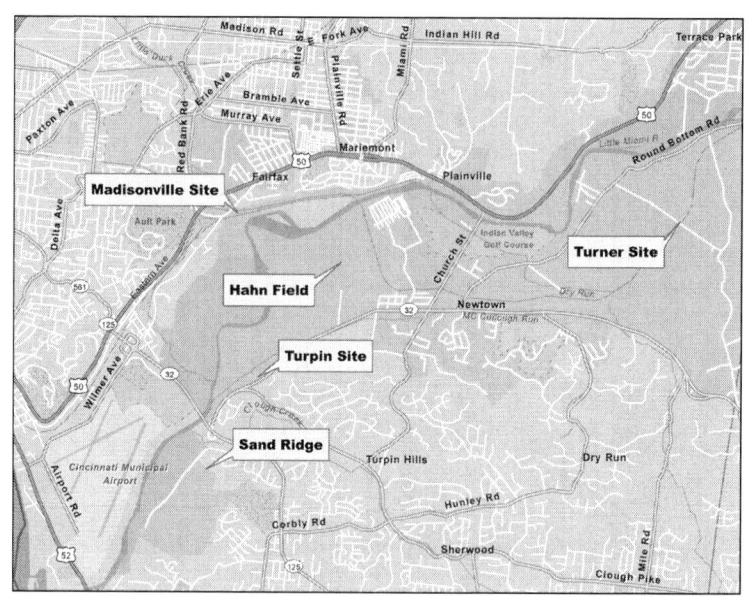

E.1. Location of archaeological sites in the lower Little Miami River valley investigated by Charles Louis Metz.

Appendix A

Family Letters

February 23, 1871,
8:00 am
Beloved Wifey,
So far I have fared all right. Pray to God for me. This morning I feel very sick, have a violent headache and vomiting, but I must bear up as well as I can. I will be home on Saturday and I think I will come home all right.
Your devoted Charley

September 13, 1875
Dear Wifey:
This is the day I am to send the grapes and thought I would send you a few lines in the box. We are getting along well. Business is pretty fair, making over $5.00 a day. I paid Tomahawk what I owed him and Casper also. That I feel lonesome you no doubt know. We are trying to keep everything about right. How do you like your hat? I think it's splendid don't you? In the box you will find a little bouquet for you from our own flowers. I know you will appreciate it. We take dinner and supper regularly at Anna's. They

are all well. How is our little Anna? Is she a good girl? Tell her that Papa says she must be good and not cry any and do all that Mama and Grandma tells her to do. Wifey dear could you not find a little time to write me how you are enjoying yourself and how you are feeling. Peaches and tomatoes I have none yet but will see about tomatoes today. Have had the house scrubbed as you directed. Out front walk has been cleaned up also. There will be a little change about the place until you come back home. I will go to the city next Thursday and I will send you your silk necktie by mail. Look for it Saturday. Wifey stay up as long as you wish. I will send you some money on Wednesday in the mail. Hoping you are well and that you are enjoying yourself I am, as ever,
Your loving, Charlie
P.S. My love to all the folks. Can Nick make arrangements for hay? I think our place will sell soon. Several have gone to see it.

September 19, 1875
My own Darling Wifey,
Your letter of the 15th I received, you cannot imagine how happy it made me to hear from you. Since writing to you last, I have had a terrible time in which I did not get a bit of rest for 60 long hours. Mrs. Y was confined and had a fearful time the baby was born dead, however all are satisfied that I did my duty and all wondered that I could stand it so long without sleep. Our little darling Anna, I hope, is well and when she comes home she will no doubt have much to tell her papa about Brown County. Be a good Boy, you say—yes darling when you come home you will find I have been a good Boy. Please write again and soon to your loving and even
Faithful,
Charley

September 1875
Why don't you write? I will impose a heavy fine on you for not writing, you see when I feel lonesome I could sit down and write twenty pages of fools cap paper full, thinking all the time I am talking to you. If I go over to

Mats I cannot stay long for I feel as if it were wrong for me to be there and to listen to their beerhouse politics is disgusting. But I enjoy myself when Mr. Low comes up and we can talk the whole evening over a bottle of wine. I will close, please write Lovely, what if they do laugh at you it is only us two that are interested.

So thinks Your Charley.

September 19, 1878

My Own Darling Wifey,

Your letter of the 15 I received. You cannot imagine how happy it made me to hear from you. Since writing to you last I have had a terrible time in which I did not get a bit of rest for 60 long hours. Mrs. Yost was confined and had a fearful time. The baby was born dead. However, all are satisfied that I have done my duty and wondered that I could stand it so long without sleep. The grapes I sent up on Monday as I promised but sent them to Danaddelp's. Enclosed please find the sum of money you wrote for. Little Charlie is well and so are all the folks. The little fellow is getting to love me more and more everyday and I love him. Our little darling Anna I hope is well and when she comes home she will, no doubt, have much to tell her Papa about Brown County. Be a good boy, you say. Yes darling when you come home you will find I have been a good boy. Smear cheese is good in Brown County. That is what mothers make. I would eat no other. If we only had some here now. I do wish you would let me know when you are coming and what way. Please write again soon.

Your loving, ever faithful, Charlie.

October 3, 1879

My Own Darling:

You have not been gone long from home but yet I know that you would like to hear from me and how I am getting along. The first night we had a political meeting at Aiken Corner and I turned in at 10 o'clock. Next morning for breakfast I had coffee and bread and two boiled eggs. For dinner coffee and bread and for supper I tried oyster soup but that proved

a failure. I boiled the water and then put in the oysters but it did not taste right and I shared the soup with the chickens. Mr. Lowe came and spent the evening with me until 10 o'clock when I went to bed and slept until 8 o'clock the next morning. I got a beefsteak and fried it and this proved a success. Baked two Irish and one sweet potatoes and I have need of a good 10 o'clock breakfast. On account of my late breakfast I took no dinner and supper on steak and coffee [sic]. Last night I went to bed at 9 o'clock and got up at 5 this morning (Friday). Finished my beefsteak and made new coffee. Then cleaned and fed my horse and then stacked all the dishes. Scoured the rooms and office, dusted and made the bed. I had all this work done by 9 o'clock. This afternoon I am going out collecting. I have not seen anything of Casper since last Tuesday. My horse will go blind in the right eye that was battered up by that shutter [sic]. I am afraid for him. Tomorrow I will go to the exposition with Britten and come out with Mr. Lowe Business is very slack just now. I got a letter from mother asking about her beans that she thought she had left on the chicken house to dry. How is our Annie? Please tell me about her. And Clara, how did she enjoy the trip and you darling, did the bus cause you any pain? Are you having a good time? Please write soon. If the folks should like to have a box of quinces now is the time for them. Did they get the grapes? Give my regards to mother and all the rest. Tell Annie her papa would very much like to see her. Are the girls going to come to the exposition? I will close. My love to all and hoping you are well.
Faithfully yours,
Charlie

October 6, 1879
To: Bug
My Own Wifey:
I packed the bucket this morning and have all of your medicine in it. The big bottle is for mother. She need not be afraid of it. It is good for anything no matter what and like the homeopathic medicine if it does no good, it will do no harm. Annie's medicine is a menic and you give no more than the dose marked on the label. Six drops three times a day. Your

medicine is iron and whiskey. Take it the same as you did before. Now Emma let me hear from you soon and write often say every two days. Do not let Annie eat any fat meat while she is taking this medicine. No pork, ham or bacon. How is dear little Clara? Does she miss her papa? Her papa misses her and Annie very much. And little Robbie, how does he enjoy himself. I suppose well. Charlie I almost forgot him, but I suppose he is okay. My kindest regards to all of the folks.

Dearest wifey write soon.

Ever yours,

Charlie

P.S. If anything should happen or if you or anyone gets sick, telegraph Dr. Metz at Madisonville, to come to Vera Cruz. Again good bye your husband or Mucklee-Muck Charlie

---

October 8, 1879

My Dearest Wifey:

I enclose the amount of money you wrote for. I am well and getting along well. Lonely, of course, but I have so changed my mode of living that I find it very beneficial. Morning—Coffee, bread and butter. Dinner—Coffee, bread and butter. Twice a week beef steak and sometimes oysters. Supper—Milk and oatmeal crackers. I go to bed at 10 o'clock and get up at five or half past five in the morning, do my chores, dress and wait for business. My only visitor this week was Mr. Lowe. Tomorrow I shall go to the exposition for the last time and on next Monday we move our things back to the Odd Fellows Hall and return them to the members. I have many visitors from a distance to see my collection. Mr. Quick, Mr. Shelton, Professor Andres of Columbus and a lady, Mrs. Whetstone and son from Walnut Hills. Britten dug up a nice vase last Saturday evening. Joe Coz drew it. It was shaped like this (Drawing). I drew the horn plow and other implements. Mr. Lowe again got the poorest draw. Hope you got the medicine alright. Why don't you write? I will impose a heavy fine on you for not writing. You see when I feel lonesome I could sit down and write 20 pages of foolscap thinking all the time I am talking to you. If I go over to Mat's I cannot stay long for I feel as if it were wrong for me to be there and listen to their politics is disgusting. But I enjoy myself when Mr. Lowe comes if we can talk to whole evening over a bottle of wine. By the way, mother did not get scared at her bottle, did she? I shall see about quinces tomorrow and send them up. Give my regards to all the folks. Kiss Annie and Clara for me and tell them papa says they must be good girls. You cannot kiss yourself from me so I will credit you with a half of dozen and charge you with them when you return. I am glad you have such nice weather for your visit. Have the boys any relics for me? Get all you can. I will close please write soon. What if they do laugh at you? It is only us two that are interested.

Yours,

Charlie

October 12, 1879

To: Mrs. Bug Metz

(Drawing of his face)

My Darling Bug:

Your very welcome letter I received in yesterday evening's mail. It made me very happy to hear from you, but yet many questions that I asked you in my letter you forgot to answer. I will give you a list of things that you did not write about. First, did you get your medicine? Second, was mother afraid of her bottle? Third, did you kiss Annie and Clara for me? Fourth, how much money did you want? Five, are you any better? Six, how about the flapjacks? Seventh, what do our darlings do and say? Eight, why did you not send me a kiss? My washing came home Friday and I will tell you that if anyone says that they can iron half as nice as my bug and then I say they lie. I did not go to the exposition nor to New Richmond nor anywhere else. I spent this evening with Mr. Lowe and looked over $200.00 engravings and shall go back tomorrow evening and finish up. I captured a little girl for George Lingardner on Thursday night. Have you any skeeters up there? 27 are now singing their sweet music in my ear. I went to church this a.m. to early mass and this afternoon rode over to Red Bank pottery fields with Mr. Lowe and this evening I was at his house. I have refused invitations to dinners as follows: Brennans—2, Vanderburgh—1,

Kirsch—1, Conkling—1, Kratsack—1. Quinces are $2.00 a bushel. Tomatoes two bushels for $.15. I am a poor cook and the consequence is I almost give it up and live on milk and crackers, coffee, butter bread. Four mice have been caught up to date in the closet and I believe the rest have moved away. Tomorrow I will go to the City after our relics and then arrange my collection at home. I will put in $4.00 in this letter and if it is not enough Darling you must write me how much you want. The boys and I may come up this month on a hunt—that is, Brockhaven, Weber and myself. Perhaps Casper will go along. I spoke to him about it today. He came over and took dinner with me. We had fried ham, scrambled eggs, coffee, bread, and butter. Now my dear Caffer I will close the new post-mortems in Vera Cruz will think that I do nothing but write letters [*sic*]. Well I cannot help it and I am writing to my best and dearest friend, my wife, my all, and where is the harm in it? Now if you should desire to stay another week do not come home on my account if only you are well. This is the wish prayer of your own devoted Charlie. My love to all.

Miss Annie and Clara for me.

Appendix B

Archaeological Notes and Letters

Minutes from November 12, 1878 to November 11, 1879

1878	Members		
Nov. 12	H. B. Whetsel	Madisonville O.	12
	S. F. Covington	"	12
	Hon. Joseph Cox	"	12
	Charles F. Low	"	12
	Dr. C. L. Metz	"	12
	E. A. Metz	"	12
	R. O. Collis	"	12
	F. W. Langdon	"	12
Nov. 19	Dr. G. W. Lasher	"	12
	M. L. Rogers	"	12
1879			
Jan. 14	Dr. Alex M. Johnston	"	
Resigned			
Sept. 23	Elect. H.T.C.M.	"	14
	A. A. Hawes	"	
Feb. 25	Joseph Cox Jr.	"	
July 5	J. A. Hosbrook	Madera O.	
5	D. S. Hosbrook	"	

Sept. 23	A. S. Oliver	Madisonville, O.
Dec. 23	A. S. Butterfield Jr.	"
	W. M. Wert	"
	W. N. Peabody	"
	Col. P. P. Lane	"
Sept. 9	A. J. Ferris	Plainville, O.
	C. K. Ferris	"
	C. F. Stites	Columbia, O.
	Dr. R. M. Byrnes	Cincinnati, O.
	Dr. H. H. Hill	"
	Dr. Gustav Brühl	"
	Prof F. W. Putnam	Cambridge, Mass.
Sept. 9	Joseph Ferris	Plainville O.

Corresponding Members

1879 Honorary and Corresponding Members

Sept. 23   Dr. Gustav Brühl

Archaeological notes—March 20, 1879 to November 22, 1879

Archaeology	10
Upcoming & resolutions in regards to the Ferris Cemetery Exploration	21
By-Laws	27
Summary of results of Excavation	150
Election of Affairs for 1878–1879	
Archaeological Notes—Continued	H 31
Minutes of meetings after April 19th	H 60
Newspaper extracts in regard to Excavations	H 160
Archaeological Notes Continued	H 120
List of Regular Members of the Society	148
Honorary	149
Honorary and Corresponding Members	149
Appendix A Prof. Short's North Americans of Antiquity	157

Undated letter from Theodore Brühl,
son of Dr. Gustav Brühl, to Charles Louis Metz
Dear Doctor!
Dr. Brühl sent me to return those bones you had loaned him—He begs pardon for his delay in returning them—it was caused by the death of his son & sickness of his wife, he was so much engaged with his family affairs that he has given no attention to his studies for the last ten weeks. An arti-

cle has appeared about your last contributions to Dr. Virchow in Germany—The corn is now being examined. They are anxiously awaiting the completion of that skeleton of which you has [*sic*] spoken to Dr. Brühl. Please let Dr. Brühl know how it is progressing. Dr. Brühl is very thankful for the loan of the bones.
Yours respectfully
Theodore A. Brühl

Charles Louis Metz's Field Notes
August 30, 1882
Finished last night the exploration of the large mound of the Turner group—the one that we ate our luncheon on with Mr. Putnam last spring. Deep down—14 feet found a bed of ashes of animal remains. Britton was assisting on the day. Low came the next morning found a large sheet of mica and immediately about it a perforated sheet of copper 8½ by 4½ inches, then large quantities of pearl beads, copper scrolls, spools, shell beads, ornaments and an altar. All of this was sent to Cambridge.

August 30, 1882
Letter from Charles Low to Frederick Ward Putnam
An ash pit at the bottom of the mound 14 feet below the top and 6 feet deep containing the usual animal remains and excepting the absence of relics. What does this mean? After finding the mica and pearls the men all dreamed that night of finding gold and silver the next morning and Metz outdid them. He dreamed of big tablets all covered with hieroglyphics. (Don't give me away on this). Next morning at the excavation glittering pearl beads rolled out in great quantities. It was a sight to see the Doctor scooping them up in great double handfuls filling box after box. Everybody was excited over the discovery—the Doctor in his haste and excitement wore off the ends of his fingers to the quick. Altar appeared to be filled with sand and pearls and it was a wonderful sight to see them run down like grain, bright and clear glistening in the light. I noted that in the center where the coals and ashes were thickest and blackest that many of

the teeth and shell beads were calcined as though they had been deposited before the fire was wholly extinguished and the embers were hot. The corner of the altar below the mound were precisely aligned to the true cardinal points of the compass N.E.S.W. Suggests that in displaying the altar that a reduced model be made of it.

Dr. Low

September 9, 1882

Letter from Charles Louis Metz to Frederick Ward Putnam

I have just returned from the Turner Group of Mounds where I have been examining the contents of another altar similar to the one discovered in the big mound varying however in the contents. In this altar I found fragments of seven human images all more or less broken by being exposed to great heat. There is a pottery image of fish or alligator in many fragments wrapped in mica. One find, a bracelet of copper and a handful of small copper beads were found in a circular depression on the top surface of the altar. Very few bone or pearl beads were found. The ashes on the altar contained many animal remains. I scooped up all that was on the altar and will send it on packed in boxes as soon as I have all that is in the mound. I am very much elated over our recent finds and shall keep up the work until all of the mounds are explored in this group. I have secured the exclusive rights to explore all of the mounds about here. In this evenings mail I received a check for $50.00, which made the men happy. I have a good force of five men and horse and wagon and I put the men through 7:00 a.m., one-half hour for noon and they quit work at 5:30 p.m.

Yours respectfully,

Dr. Metz

October 6, 1882

Letter from Charles Louis Metz to Frederick Ward Putnam

I have just returned from the Turner Group of Mounds where I have been all day hard at work trying to take up an altar bodily so as to be enabled to pack it and send it on to the museum. The altar was the sixth in number and also the smallest one yet discovered. It's inside measurement being three feet long and two feet wide. I carefully cut away the earth on the sides and excavated underneath for some distance and then filled up all around with plaster of Paris when this was set I pried up the altars so as to place it on end. My object being to get a good cast of the plaster on the bottom of the mass. Through the neglect of one of my men who removed his level too soon the altar was allowed to slip and the result was numerous fissures across its surface. It still retains its form and barring the fissures and a somewhat broken corner it is as good as new. It weighs probably about 800 lbs. I thought to fill up the fissures with cement thinking it might strengthen the altar so as to be enables to ship it, but I hardly think that I will succeed. I gained considerable experience today and it was not improbable that ere long the Peabody Museum can exhibit a genuine altar from a mound and anyone who might doubt the reality of the thing, would only have to see it and be convinced. Ever since I received your last letter I have been planning how to take up an altar and send it to you. I am working in the fifth mound of the Turner group. It being the small one southeast of the large mound and the altar I have been working on today is from this mound. This rough sketch resembles the altar somewhat. The last four altars contained no relics. In our trench this last mound we found a skeleton it being but 8 inches below the surface. Hoping to hear from you soon. Sketch of an "altar" showing a coffin-like box included.

November 18, 1882
Letter from Charles Louis Metz to Frederick Ward Putnam
Work began on this mound on November 6. There is a stonewall that was included in the mound. In the mound on a fine stratum of sand there was an adult skeleton with a head placed to the northwest. The skeleton was in a doubled up position. The bones were much decayed and the skull in fragments. No relics were found with these remains. On the other side of the wall inside the mound another adult skeleton was found in the horizontal position with the heard to the northwest. On the southwest side of the mound another skeleton was located in the horizontal position with the

head pointed northward and a fourth skeleton was located which measured 5'6" in length evidently a male and in each hand a copper spool or "boss" was found. A female was found and she was 5 feet in length and at the left-hand was a copper spool and at intervals along the right arm several shell beads were found. At the pelvis there was a fragment of a copper spool and at the head about seven inches distant from it was a large marine shell. "The finding of the two skeletons outside the wall induced me to have all the earth excavated that formed the mound outside the wall." Skeleton No. 5 was found in a doubled up position on the southwest side and it was an adult much decayed. Skeleton No. 6 was found 8 feet southeast from No. 5 and was an adult in the doubled up position, skull to the east and at a depth of 3 feet from the surface of the mound. Skeleton No. 7 was found in a horizontal position head to the northeast, adult length 5'6". There was a quantity of shell beads at the neck and shoulder. Skeleton No. 8, an adult buried in a doubled up position 3 feet distant from No. 7. All of the bones of this skeleton were in fragments. Skeleton No. 9, adult in a horizontal position, length 5'4". A plate of mica was found at the neck and right shoulder. At the northeast side of the mound at three different points portions of human skeletons were found. At one place a right femur and a portion of the pelvis was found. With all of the skeletons in a horizontal position relics were found and great care seems to have been taken in their internment. Being placed either on a bed of sand, gravel or flat stones. While those that were interred in the doubled up position no relics were found with them nor were they're any evidence of care being taken in their burial. The bones also were more broken and all of the skulls and fragments of those buried in the horizontal. We were able to secure two fair skulls. We failed to discover a single fragment of pottery nor a flint chip in the entire mound. On the slopes of this mound are found several stumps of trees. One an oak measures 12 feet in circumference, another 10½ feet. Respectfully submitted,
Charles Metz

November, 1882
Letter from Charles Louis Metz to Frederick Ward Putnam

Having completed the exploration of the Whittlesey mound we commenced work on a small mound about 60 feet southwest from the above. We carried a trench 15 feet wide directly through the mound at a depth of 2 feet. We found a pavement of flat river stones. This pavement was circular in form and had a diameter of 15 feet. It rested on a layer of sand 8 inches deep. Before the sand the clay was homogeneous. We excavated down three feet. An ash pit was found of a depth of 27 inches, width at the top was 6 feet, and width at the bottom was 16 inches. In it we found animal remains, fragments of pottery, mica and charcoal. Nothing further of note was discovered.

November 26, 1882

Letter from Charles Louis Metz to Frederick Ward Putnam

Dear Sir:

On last evening the work of the exploration of the Turner group of mounds was completed. They numbered 13 in all. Of these six were altar mounds. I've had the group surveyed and all the mounds correctly located on a chart, which is now nearly ready to send on. Tomorrow I will pack up the material obtained from the group and forward it per freight. The weather still keeps very fine. Early this morning we had a light snow but it has gone off before noon and it is now clearing weather. I would like to work up another interesting group of mounds on the lands of Mr. Samuel Edwards and about one mile west of the Turner group. This is located on land that is annually cultivated and in consequence permission to explore would be granted only at a season of the year in which the land was not being cultivated. Another mound that I am very anxious to explore is the one in the great work near Milford on the Little Miami River about two miles distant from the Turner group. The mound in question is situated on the edge of a steep bank that was probably on ancient bank of the East Fork and the Little Miami River. I would refer you to Squire and Davis Plate XXXIV. It is these however as being some distance from the edge of the bank. It is however, just on the edge. Two days work would finish the exploration. The time of the men since last reported is as follows:

From November 4 to date, November 26:

Mr. Britton	17 days	$21.25
C. Zingale	17 days	$21.25
Tom Jackson	16 days	$21.00
Frank Kniff	16 days	$20.00
Wagon	17 days	$34.00
	Total	$116.50

The report of the work in the Whittlesey mound I have forwarded as also the relics obtained from that mound which were sent by express yesterday morning.

Respectfully yours,

Charles Metz

On February 21, 1883

Letter from Charles Louis Metz to Frederick Ward Putnam

The Mound No. 2, Group C of my chart of Anderson Township has been explored. The work being completed yesterday evening. Five skeletons were discovered yesterday evening. Five skeletons were discovered proving it to have been a burial ground. The mound was about four feet high, oblong in shape, its diameter measuring in the direction of its greatest length 50 feet.

March 3, 1883

Letter from Charles Louis Metz to Frederick Ward Putnam

Professor Putnam:

The exploration of Mound No. 22, Group C on Mr. Samuel Edwards farm was completed this evening. The mound proved to be a burial mound. It showed a perpendicular height of 14 feet above the natural surface of the plain in the center of the mound. A stone axe was found and a stone implement which was about 3 inches in length.

March 8, 1883

Letter from Charles Louis Metz to Frederick Ward Putnam

When he was engaged in the exploration of the large Edwards mound Mr. Edwards called his attention to another mound on a higher position near the little Miami River. The mound was located about 100 yards from the River Bank. On the higher portion of the plain which has an elevation about 25 feet above the low water mark of the river and is not subject to inundation. The mound appeared about 2½ feet high, 100 feet in diameter and measured 120 feet in length east and west. Mr. Edwards informed me that 60 years ago the mound was between 8 and 9 feet high and was covered with a forest and also occupied all of the surrounding plain. Mr. Edwards explained that in clearing the land he removed about 4 feet of the earth from the top when he encountered stones and human remains. For 50 years he has cultivated the mound annually and during that period has removed quantities of stone from it besides plowing up many skeletons and other cones, however finding no relics. On March 8 we began the exploration of the mound by making an excavation 15 feet wide at the edge of the mound on the northeast side at a depth of 8 inches. A layer of stone was found which extended upward conforming to the slope of the sides of the mound. The stones were all of all sizes from those not larger than a man's hand to those, which can hardly be lifted. The larger stones were the hill limestone and were brought from the hills three-quarters of a mile distant while the smaller were flat and water worn and were evidently taken from the river. The men were instructed to completely uncover the stone all around the base of the mound. After this was done a trench 25 feet wide was begun on the northeast side and carried through the center of the mound. About 2 feet from the edge of the mound a skeleton was discovered. No. 1 in the horizontal position, head to north, length 6 feet. A few fragments of pottery accompanied the remains. No. 2 was laying with its feet resting at the right side of the preceding skeleton in a horizontal position with the head to the south. Hands folded over pelvis, a few fragments of pottery, and two bear teeth. Other skeletons were found. One was 6 feet long. Another was 5'8". A child lay alongside No. 6. The age was probably three years. Another 5'6" burial and a bone awl were found near it. Another 6-foot adult was found. A turtle shell was found placed on its chest. A land turtle, that is. Skeleton No. 37 was 6'2". This male had shell ornaments and arrow points nearby. No. 39 had a spearhead and a stone ornament near it and near another Skeleton No. 63 there were remains of a young bear or dog and by another one flint. On the south side of the mound was a space 10 feet wide and 12 feet long where a fire had been kept up for some length of time as the earth was burned red to a depth of two or three inches. In this space almost all the animal remains and fragments of pottery sent you were obtained. Here was also found a considerable quantity of burned shells. The plain between this mound and the river gives evidence that it had at one time probably occupied by a village. Many fragments of flint, pottery, broken potstones, arrowheads, Celts are ploughed up. Also animal remains are plowed up. The big mound above Newtown No. 7 is due south from this one and about three quarters of a mile distant. In all there were 71 skeletons found in this mound.

March 16, 1883
Letter from Charles Louis Metz to Frederick Ward Putnam
Dear Professor:
The mass of iron last sent you are from altar in Mound No. 4 without a doubt (Marlow is working with Metz at this Mound). In the mound near the riverbank we had discovered up to the present time 35 skeletons. I will lease the field in a few minutes and will write you on Sunday the results of our work for these two days. I would suggest that the museum purchase the collection of Mr. H.B. Whetsel of this place. This all from the cemetery and has the copper cross ornament. If the museum would purchase them they would have all of the ornaments of that kind in the U.S. I think $40.00 would buy all he has and is well worth that amount.

April 2, 1883
Letter from Charles Louis Metz to Frederick Ward Putnam
Yours of the ninth instance received enclosing check for $188.02. I have seen Mr. Low and he told me that all he has was a few fragments of burned earth from the altars. I cannot think that it is possible that it is anything else. When I saw that slip I was under the impression that you had sent

him some of the duplicates from the altars to present to the Society of Natural History and I felt piqued for I thought that they did not deserve a thing. I am going to the City today and I will see all that Mr. Low left then. The men begin a new mound yesterday it being the larger of one of the small mounds.

April 6, 1883
Letter from Charles Louis Metz to Frederick Ward Putnam
Dear Professor Putnam:
I forwarded the relics obtained from the mound last explored by express today. My report goes in tomorrow's mail. I also sent my expenses. Mr. Turner refuses to allow me to go into Mound No. 4 until his crop is gathered in the fall. I had been to his house once before but the old gentlemen was not in and his son said that he thought there would be no objection but Mr. Turner desires me to wait until fall. Too bad. In today's paper I noticed in the *Madisonville News* that Mr. Low had made a donation to the Natural History Society of Cincinnati of relics from the altars of mound in the Little Miami River. I enclose the slip. Did you feel offended for I do not think that they deserve any? I think the best recreation you can take, and I would recommend it, is to come west and we will explore mound together. I am to go at some this coming week and I expect them to be of great interest. I visited the "Hahn Field" on last Tuesday. It is being plowed up. I found a portion of a ground bone scraper and solid cylinder bean I am very anxious to get as much work done as possible and get as many to explore as I can so to keep a working party out that has recently organized. Included is a notice from the Madisonville paper that reads "Auditor Charles F. Low of the Baltimore and Ohio Railroad our worthy fellow townsmen has made a fine donation of altar relics from the Indian mounds near here to the Natural History Society."

April 15, 1883
Letter from Charles Louis Metz to Frederick Ward Putnam

I would be greatly pleased to have you visit me as I am right in the work and my professional services are not in great demand during this and next month. I am at the mound everyday and keep things going. Am anxious to complete the exploration of the Miami Valley from the Turner Group to the mouth of the river by fall if possible. I shall take some men and go to the mound located in the great work above Milford and explore it soon.

May 2, 1883
Letter from Charles Louis Metz to Frederick Ward Putnam
Mound No. 3, Group C located on the same plane as No. 4 and distant about 200 feet to the east from it was explored by taking a trench 17 feet wide, gradually widening it at the center. It measured 30 feet in diameter. The mound was 2'9" in height.

May 5, 1883
Letter from Charles Louis Metz to Frederick Ward Putnam
Today we begin work on Mound No. 1, Group C and in a short time ten skeletons were found. I shall be at this mound several hours every day as I think it is an important one. I learned recently that a man had found a copper hammer in the Ferris Woods. I went to the gentlemen's house and he showed me a squared mass of pure copper weighting nearly two pounds with a perforation through it. He told me that when he found it was encrusted with sand and gravel and was of a green color. To me it looks very much like it was of European manufacture so I do not doubt at all that the man found the hammer just where he said found it but I doubt very much that it was made by the Indians or their ancestors. The ends of the hammer are much battered and the whole mass seems to have been subjected to great use. Work on Mound No. 2, Group C was completed today. This mound was 3'10" in height, 25 feet in diameter. It was of oblong shape. Its longest diameter being north south 200 feet south of No. 3 mound of the same group. Two skeletons were discovered.

May 9, 1883

Letter from Charles Louis Metz to Frederick Ward Putnam

The exploration of Mound No. 4, Group C, Anderson Township, was completed on the 30th of April. This mound had an elevation of 10½ feet diameter east and west 86 feet. 21 skeletons were found and some copper ornaments and *unio* shells were also found. We began the exploration of the two mounds designated C and D on the accompanying plat of the ancient earthwork near Milford, Clermont County, Ohio. Mound D is located on the edge of a steep bluff bank and distant about 200 feet from the southwest side of the circular embankment of the great work. It was five and a half feet high and had a diameter at the base of 45 feet. A small portion of the base of the mound had been cut away during the construction of a roadway along its northern side. In the mound a grave was discovered eight feet long two feet wide in which a few fragments of a human skeleton together with a spearhead and several flint chips were found. A second grave was discovered in which the skeleton lay with head to the north was in a better state of preservation than the first. A fine stone ornament or gorget and also a stone celt were found in this grave. Mound C was three and a half feet in height with a diameter east and west of 35 feet. In this mound there was found a rough stone celt and five spearheads flint arranged in the heap at the bottom. The remainder of the depression was filled with fine sand. Two other badly decayed skeletons were located in this mound.

May 18, 1883

Letter from Charles Louis Metz to Frederick Ward Putnam

After finding what we did in the Turner altar mounds, I feel greatly disappointed in the mounds that I am now working. The results are meager but there is no telling what tomorrow may bring forth. Today I forwarded by express a small box No. 7. It contains all that I found in the way of relics. In mound six recently explored among that sent today you will find a few fragments of pottery. Would you advise me to go on and clear up the smaller mounds. Thirteen mounds yet remain between here and the Ohio

River. The largest outside of No. 7 is 15 feet in height, the Jewett mound. On last Tuesday I met Reverend Mr. Easton, the gentlemen that wrote you in regard to the altar mounds in the Great Miami Valley. The gentleman is coming out to visit me during the coming week. I dare say a little trip out here at the present time would be the best tonic I could prescribe for your overworked condition. Can't you try it? There is not enough of the material obtained from Mound No. 1 to warrant sending. In regard to Mr. Wetzcl's collection from the Ferris ancient cemetery I have asked him to give me a list of what he has and shall send it to you with prices for which it can be purchased and you can then better judge if you will purchase it or not.

June 6, 1883
Letter from Charles Louis Metz to Frederick Ward Putnam
Yesterday I called at Mr. Whetsel's to see what he had in the way of relics from the old cemetery. He has eight vases, more or less perfect. Four fine axes and celts. Several find spearheads, one copper "cross", one long copper bead, one unfinished pipe, three fragments of pipes, several fine Elkhorn relics, a good lot of the Venice bone and horn implements. I think that the whole collection is very cheap at the price he offered for it—$50.00. There are numerous little odds and ends that would be of interest to you that Mr. Whetsel calls trash. Yesterday we found only a decayed skeleton at the head of which we discovered 15 copper beads and numerous pieces of mica. Several have the buckskin thong upon which they are strung yet remaining in them. The beads are like those figured in your 15th report of the museum, page 95.

June 23, 1883
Letter from Charles Louis Metz to Frederick Ward Putnam
The mound recently explored near Camden had proved to be the most peculiar in regard to its construction of any yet fallen under my notice. I have sent on the report and diagram of the mound and you will notice in them the peculiar points of the mound. In looking over some small copper

ornaments that fell to my allotment from the Ferris Cemetery I dropped from my hands one of two ornaments found with a skeleton of a child. They were probably ear pendants. In coming in contact with the floor it was crushed. On picking up the fragments I found that the core of the pendant was of wood and the copper was hammered around it completely enveloping the wood. Will you be enabled to visit us this fall?
Yours truly,
Charles Metz

June 25, 1883
Letter from Charles Louis Metz to Frederick Ward Putnam
The enclosed newspaper slip cut from today's *Commercial [Gazette]* announces the death of Mr. James Couden, the proprietor of Ft. Ancient. Now would be the proper time to take steps to secure the ancient earthwork as it will undoubtedly be divided and sold in lots or parcels and before this is done a proposition might be secured from the heirs. Write Mr. Low or myself what you think best to be done.

July 2, 1883
Letter from Charles Louis Metz to Frederick Ward Putnam
Mr. Low has a proposition from the Administrator of the Couden Estate in writing and binding on the heirs for Ft. Ancient. He would not tell me what it was only that it was about $5,000.00 less than the first proposition he received from the heirs. I sent a box containing the relics from the mounds and from the Sand Ridge by express. Among the relics from the Sand Ridge are two small fishhooks. A detailed report of our work at the Sand Ridge will be sent on Monday. Of the human remains from the Sand Ridge many are well dressed and we have secured an almost entire skeleton. Several of the crania are very good. I am working with but four men and I do hope that something of great interest will run up soon.

July 20, 1883

Letter from Charles Louis Metz to Frederick Ward Putnam

Having received permission from the owners of the "Sand Ridge" to explore a small portion of ancient burial place designated number found on my chart of Anderson Township. This place resembles the Ferris Ancient Cemetery very much. Differing from it, however in that there are no ashpits and the burials are three feet deep. I have most necessary work at present. Hoping to hear from you soon.

July 22, 1883

Letter from Charles Louis Metz to Frederick Ward Putnam

I have received the enclosed letter this a.m. I met the gentlemen here last summer. He is an attorney-at-law residing at Hillsboro, Ohio and at present engaged in a work he calls "Shepards Popular History of Ohio" and he is very anxious to mention the explorations that we are carrying on. I have made him no promises. What do you think of it?

August 15, 1883

Letter from Charles Louis Metz to Frederick Ward Putnam

On the 13th of this month we began the exploration of a mound in the Stites Grove one mile from this village. Our first day's work brought to light two stone pestles, one fragment of a vase and a slate stone ornament, and several rough flints. The second day we found traces of two skeletons, fragments of a dish, a stone pipe, several rough flints and warped stones. It is raining today. Tomorrow we continue the exploration and I hope with good results. The photographs you sent me create great surprise and wonder to everyone that I exhibit them to. With your permission I would like to take them to the Society of Natural History meeting and exhibit them to the members. If you think it not advisable to do so write me. I will pay my dues for the past two meetings when you arrive here. I do wish to be continued on the list of members. Hoping to hear from you soon.

October 22, 1883

Letter from Charles Louis Metz to Frederick Ward Putnam

We have made very interesting discoveries in the unexplored portion of the Turner Mound No. 3 consisting of an extensive hearth beneath which were six furnaces or ovens in which probably cremation of human remains may have taken place. Many evidences indicate that such may have been the case. Several ash pits have been discovered containing a few relics and animal remains are very much like our old pits in the Ferris woods. I will send you what notes I have and I dare say you will be interested as we are making a discovery that will bring out many new ideas. I am sorry that you are not here or to see what we have. Will write you more in detail soon.

October 29, 1883

Letter from Charles Louis Metz to Frederick Ward Putnam

I forward today a report of the work done on the Turner Mound up to date. The discovery of the ashes or ovens is I think of great interest as they are also the peculiar pits with the flues or chimneys. The ashes found in the flues are carefully preserved and may on analysis give some light on the use for which the arches were constructed. Again the covered pits, two very large ones, I uncovered on Saturday last and have had them explored to a depth of over six feet and I think they go considerably deeper. Considerable ashes were taken out containing numerous fragments of bones. These ashes are all being saved. Bits of mica and a few animal bones are found in them. Our men call those covered pits cisterns. The covers are of pure clay showing little or any traces of being exposed to fire and seem to have been built after the purpose for which the pit was constructed had been accomplished.

November 9, 1883

Letter from Charles Louis Metz to Frederick Ward Putnam

As everything of interest in this mound has been discovered beneath the layer of gravel or concrete then men are allowed to dig down to it when I am not with them but on no account to disturb it until I am with them. Tomorrow's Saturday I put in the whole day at the mound taking up a section of the concrete and seeing what may be under it. Could you only be with me and see for yourself the wonderful puts, flues, and ovens. I am inclined to suppose that the ovens or arches were crematories but whether they burned human or animals remains that will be a question to decide. Something maybe learned from the ashes and bits of bone that were found in them. In the pits directly in front of the arches coarse charcoal and ashes are found in abundance. The bottom of these pits being burned red and hard. Also the sides. Was this heat from these pits conducted through the arches? And in what manner? These are questions that I want to solve by further careful exploration. I am greatly please to learn that you will be with us in January next and if I could only save some of our good things until then so you could see for yourself. But this cannot be for anything we would leave uncovered over a Sunday would be destroyed by a plagued set of fellows that we are compelled to constantly to guard against. While we were uncovering the great hearth I kept a man on guard during two Sundays and he had his hands full to keep off the crowds of farmers and others that would have like to have town up the hearth to see what was under it. You may rest assured that the work will be done carefully and that I will note everything myself and make the explorations. The weather is delightful, warm and spring like. The violets and other early spring flowers are out in bloom.

November 11, 1883

Letter from Charles Louis Metz to Frederick Ward Putnam

Box No. 16 was sent yesterday containing the rough material collected from the altar mound 3 up to the present time. The most interesting of which, may prove to be the ashes taken from the floors of the different arches. I am very sorry that we have nothing in the way of relics to send you but we may make a find soon. The next box will contain material from the Sand Ridge sites and Edwards' mounds and also the boxes you packed when you were here.

November 18, 1883
Letter from Charles Louis Metz to Frederick Ward Putnam
The event of the past week was the peculiar recess discovered in the wall on the east side of the Turner mound containing the relics sent you by express last Saturday a.m. the charred bones I conclude from a hasty examination to be human remains. Do you not think so yourself? I did not remove all of the dirt from the large shell as I found it contained some of the charred remains. Is not the carved bone a wonderful relic? Britten says we not have the whale and we will dig further for Jonah. What a wonderful mound this is and what may we yet discover? Pick and shovel time and patience will reveal all. Could you only be here when we make a find and see things as we see them in the position they were left by their builders?

November 20, 1883
Letter from Charles Louis Metz to Frederick Ward Putnam
Dear Professor Putnam:
Enclosed please find note for $500.00. I cannot express the gratitude and thankfulness that I feel towards you. I should not have troubled you had it not been extremely necessary but by your aid I am over the (crisis) and all okay.

Thanking you many times with all my heart I am,
Sincerely yours,
Charles Metz

December 2, 1883
Letter from Charles Louis Metz to Frederick Ward Putnam
From indications I think we are again on the eve of making another discovery. Yesterday's excavations revealed a scatter of charcoal and ashes from which I have taken numerous pieces of burned human bones. Altar mound 3 is apparently composed of from six to eight small mounds. These

small mounds were eventually covered over forming one large tumulus.

January 20, 1884
Letter from Charles Louis Metz to Frederick Ward Putnam
It pains me very much to learn of your illness but I sincerely hope that by the time this reaches you that you are convalescent. The cold blizzard has put a stop to the work at the mounds at present. Britten has proposed that if he were paid $1.50 per day he would keep all of the tools in repair and sharpened. I think this would be to our advantage and if you approve of the advance to Britten please notify me in your answer to this letter. On last Thursday I visited Remington and took Britten with me. We succeeded in locating five stone graves. These graves I will keep until you are able to come out here during the spring. Mr. Turner's son (John) was to see me yesterday in regard to leveling the mounds and excavations we made to their farm. They are anxious to begin the work, which will take them at least two months. You will remember that they agreed to do the work and give a full release for $125.00. Martin Noon is again anxious to work for us and says if we take him he will never leave us again. He wants, however $1.50 per day. He is always worth two men in the amount of work he does. Should you think best to put him on I will take him. When we get into the sand field we will want about six men so we will be limited to one season and we had best make the most of it while we have the chance to do so.

April 22, 1884
Letter from Charles Louis Metz to Frederick Ward Putnam
I have uncovered the encircling walls of the group and shall make a sketch with accurate measurements and send it to you. (Drawing of mound, which I will copy). The above may give you an idea how the wall extends around the group. This you must see yourself and get a correct idea of it. Do be here by the 10th of May and make arrangements to stay a month for I am certain you will make remarkable discoveries. The fates have used me very roughly during down the last three weeks. I have been broken down

considerably myself by continued exposure to the weather and loss of sleep. I've brought my poor mother from Springfield who is suffering with a cancer of the wound and cannot live longer than a month or two from now. My mother-in-law came to visit my mother last Wednesday a week ago on Friday. She was taken very ill and died at my house on Sunday evening the 13th. So the trouble with my men, of my wife's mother following each other so rapidly is what I mean by saying the fates have been using me roughly.

July 25, 1884
Letter from Charles Louis Metz to Frederick Ward Putnam
Dear Professor Putnam:
Your letter of the 22nd was received today. I never signed any paper or authorized any person whatever to sign my name to anything and should the S.I. people have my name signed to any circular or paper in regard to the matter in question it is a *fraud*. The gentlemen from Ohio is possibly Judge Cox for he was at Washington and had seen the S.I. people just two weeks before the circular was printed for he told Mr. Low about his visit to the S.I. of speaking about our work in the Turner Mounds and I suppose that he put one of the high priests into one of the covered pits. The Judge is the only man that I feel anxious about for he may act as an escort. No one can go to the mounds. Britten's orders are to let no one come to them unless he has a note from me in German writing. I did write to Professor Baird in regard to my collection that it was for sale and told him what I had in it and also told him that there were only two collections of similar bones and horn implements from the same locality and they were in the Peabody Museum and the other in the Society of Natural History of Cincinnati. There is no other man by the name of Metz that is engaged in archaeology in this part of the state. I know them all here. I have just returned from No. 4 mound. Work is progressing. Four hooded or covered pits have been found, no flues as yet. Hearths and fireplaces are numerous. But this mound is going to be a big thing from all indications. I do wish you were here. The Sand Ridge man won't lease but I have his promise that

we can go in and explore it and that he will not grant the privilege to any other person. The four acres brought him in nearly $800.00 this year and it's the cream of the 1,000-acre tract. Turpin will allow us to explore and he will see the party owning it this week. Should the S.I. man come here and desire to see the Turner mounds how shall I get out of taking him there? I could escort him to the Stites Grove and show him some works already dug over but the Sand Ridge he must not see. I will close in haste.
Yours (Only), C.L. Metz
[Note: S.I. means Smithsonian Institute]

August 2, 1884
Letter from Charles Louis Metz to Frederick Ward Putnam
I am making my arrangements to take a trip up to East Fork of the Little Miami River. The purpose is to secure the right to explore for the museum what earthworks and mounds that may be found along that stream. Colonel Jewett, a civil engineer, desires to accompany me and I may get him to make surveys of all we may find of interest. I have a Mr. Bell, an intelligent and well-known farmer, engaged in securing several groups of mounds on the Millcreek Valley in Sycamore Township and not very far from the mound we explored on the Gould farm. Professor Francis has not made his appearance as yet. I received four numbers of the Antiquarian this a.m. with your compliments. Thanks.

August 7, 1884
Letter from Charles Louis Metz to Frederick Ward Putnam
Yours of the fourth received enclosing check for $300.00 I shall be careful not to expend a cent unless it is absolutely necessary for I am anxious to see the Little Miami Valley explored and by the Peabody Museum. I would like to save my collection for the Peabody but I need the money and should Thomas give me my price I will sell to him only I do hate to see them get things that come from the places in which we are so much interested namely the Ferris Woods, the Sand Ridge, and Hahn Field that I

would sell to the Peabody Museum on monthly or quarterly installments. In the mound we are finding small covered pits that is they are of some depth as the other but very narrow.

August 10, 1884
Letter from Charles Louis Metz to Frederick Ward Putnam
Professor Thomas arrived here last evening and stopped over one hour and then went on to the City where he is stopping at the Burnet House. He should have remained here but our hotel did not suit him. He returned here Monday and Tuesday. He is a sharp old coon and I think means us no good. He said he would not interfere with us in any way and then with the next breath tells me that he is going to open a mound at Foster's Crossing, which is about 15 miles above here on the Little Miami River about 8 miles this way from Ft. Ancient. I shall keep him in tow as long as he is about here and today will look up my fences and see that all is safe. The old coon told me that he was going to organize exploring parties and put men in charge of them to whom he would pay a good salary. Notice the recommendation for membership for the AAAS. Will you please sign it? He is a good man, an old Quaker of most excellent family. He has occupied numerous offices of trust in this county and is okay in every way. He has sent me the $8.00, which I will apply to next month's AAAS.

August 18, 1884
Letter from Charles Louis Metz to Frederick Ward Putnam
Box containing the photographs and copy of the reports received many thanks. Professor Thomas has not turned up as he promised and I haven't seen anything of him since he was here on Saturday evening. On inquiry I cannot learn of his whereabouts. He is somewhere in Ohio and that is all I know. Work at the mound is progressing and will reach the old altars about the latter part of this week. A few copper ornaments have been found and also one of the small button-like copper ornaments. Many perforated teeth have been found in the black soil beneath the hearth. My family all has the whooping cough and I am suffering greatly from the dry hot weather. Oh

for a good rain and cooler atmosphere. In the last evening's mail I received five numbers of *Science* for which I am indebted to you. I have seen young Turner today and have him his photo. After gazing at it for some time he said, "it is a mighty good picture of the mule."

August 24, 1884
Letter from Charles Louis Metz to Frederick Ward Putnam
We have now reached within six feet from the center of Mound 4 and whatever of interest will be found within the next week two's diggings. Can I leave to go to Philadelphia just at the time when I should be at the Mound everyday? Whatever fragments of the stone dishes or figurines that will be found will turn up now and the men must be kept spurred up and watched closely. Should I stop the work until I would return the men would certainly seek other work and would lose the best set of hands I've ever had working for us. I was up to the mound yesterday until 4 o'clock p.m. After I left there the men discovered a skeleton probably an intrusive burial. I must go up tomorrow morning and ascertain the facts in regard to it. Professor Thomas has kept remarkably quit since he has been in Ohio. I cannot learn anything of his whereabouts nor do the Cincinnati men know of him. I sent you a copy of the *Christian Advocate* containing an account of Judge Cox's letter at Acton Camp Meeting Grounds. Did you receive it? My chances to be present at the Philadelphia meeting are growing slim and slimmer. I am not well. My family is sick and I shall have to forego the pleasure of seeing you again until you again come to Madisonville.

September 9, 1884
Philadelphia, PA
Letter from Frederick Ward Putnam to Charles Louis Metz
It is hereby agreed between Dr. Charles L. Metz of Madisonville, Ohio on the one part and F. W. Putnam curator of the Peabody Museum of American Archaeology and Ethnology, Cambridge Mass on the other part, that Dr. Charles L. Metz shall give to the Peabody Museum all the specimens of archaeology and ethnology now in his possession, and all that may come

into his possession during the continued of the joint explorations in Ohio by himself and F. W. Putnam. And that F. W. Putnam, a curator of the Peabody Museum, shall allow twenty-five dollars ($25.00) on each monthly bill, from August 1, 1884, an account of the explorations in Ohio to Dr. C. L. Metz for his services as agent of the Museum, so long as this joint explorations in Ohio are continued as above stated. It being further agreed on this part of F. W. Putnam as Curator of the Peabody Museum, not in case the joint explorations are discontinued from any cause now unforeseen, not the fragments of twenty-five dollars a month shall be continued to Dr. Charles L. Metz, the sum of all the fragments made under this agreement shall have amounted to twelve hundred dollars ($1200)
F. W. Putnam (Signed)
Curator Peabody Museum
Am. Arch. And Eth.
Cambridge, Mass.
C. L. Metz M. D.
Madisonville, Ohio

October 12, 1884
Letter from Charles Louis Metz to Frederick Ward Putnam
I arrived home at 3 o'clock this a.m. the train having broken down and delayed us eight hours. I found all well at home and also the letter from Professor Holmes of which the following is a copy.

Dear Dr. Metz,
Dear Sir: The matter of arranging for the purchase of collections by the Bureau of Ethnology has been left entirely to me. I have several collections in view which if purchased at all must be paid for with the funds appropriated for the New Orleans Exposition, arrangements must therefore be made within the next month. I wish you to prepare for me a short list to present to the Director indicating the classes of objects and the approximate number of each.
Yours Truly,
William H. Holmes

November 13, 1884
Letter from Charles Louis Metz to Frederick Ward Putnam
My Dear Professor Putnam:
Some time ago I mentioned my financial troubles in regard to two of my relatives and regarding the property I occupy. I now see my own way clear if I could get either $400.00 or $500.00. With this sum I could wipe them both out and forever put an end to my troubles. One of them desire to purchase a lot and the other desires to furnish his house and they want to money forthwith and I am not now ready to comply with their demands. Could by sending you a note for $400.00 or $500.00 payable in one year possibly send the money? After January I could pay off the part of the expenses of the note each month so as to pay all of the amount before the note came do. Should you be enables to assist me in such an arrangement will you please telegraph me at my expense at once?

December 11, 1884
Letter from Charles Louis Metz to Frederick Ward Putnam
Since the time that we have completed the Turner exploration we have explored the Broadwell mound, which gave us little satisfaction. The schoolteacher's Mr. Durham's mound proved quite interesting. In it there had been a long and continued fire, several post holes, a lot of pottery and fragments and the most interesting find a fossil elephant's tooth (not a mastodon's). We are now working on Mr. Hahn's place and two mounds that adjoin each other and I think are just without the gateway of a large enclosure. This enclosure I have not as yet had time to trace out but will do so the next time I go over to the diggings.

December 12, 1884
Letter from Charles Louis Metz to Frederick Ward Putnam
We are now working in the Broadwell mound but up to this time have discovered nothing more than a small burn space. If it does not pan out bet-

ter today we will go and work on the school teacher Mr. Durham's mound. My health has been greatly improved since my troubles have been removed. I feel stronger than I have for some time past. I shall send all notes in from the Turner group and all material that we have obtained since sending the last two boxes.

December 31, 1884
Letter from Charles Louis Metz to Frederick Ward Putnam
Your letter enclosing check came duly to hand. I was pained to learn of the illness of your daughter and sincerely hope that the patient is convalescing. My little people have fared very well so far. There is but little illness among the people at the present time. Today the weather was very warm with frequent showers of rain. The temperature is running up to 72. Had it not been for the rain we would have finished the smaller mound on the Hahn Farm and will begin tomorrow on the larger one. Another week may find us in the Sand Field (i.e., the Sand Ridge site) and then the results may be of more interest. I enclose the amount due the men from December. From this bill you may deduct and place to my credit $56.50. Did you receive the three boxes I have sent on since my collection was shipped?

January 31, 1885
Letter from Charles Louis Metz to Frederick Ward Putnam
Dear Professor Putnam:
Your letter enclosing the one from McCalls duly received. I am happy at the welcome intelligence you are able to be about again. The bad weather of the last week has suspended operations in the mound for the present. I allowed Britten one-half day extra as he was with me at Remington lately searching for stone graves about which I wrote you.

March 2, 1885
Letter from Charles Louis Metz to Frederick Ward Putnam
Your postal card announcing the finding of the missing notes duly

received. I am glad. I will now forward you the notes from mounds Nos. 4, 5, 6 and 8 east of the Turner Group. It has been thawing for four days past. The snow is gone but it is very muddy and soft and on account of this will delay work for a day or two yet. Mr. Turpin has sent me permission to work in the Hahn Field, which is an ancient cemetery. Many skeletons are being plowed up from there. Could you spare me a few copies of the last report as Mr. Hahn and Mr. Turpin and several others want them. Hoping that you will be able to remain a considerable time in Ohio when you again come out for I have many interesting places that you should look after that may prove of great interest. My family are all well.
I am yours faithfully,
C. L. Metz

March 7, 1885
Letter from Charles Louis Metz to Frederick Ward Putnam
I have found another small mound near the Marriott mound back of the Whittesey work and it should be explored had we but the means to do it with. I forward with this mail a book that is a literary curiosity *The Book of Algoonah*. You have heard of it no doubt. The author lives here at Madisonville. He seems to be very intelligent yet he talks queer and claims that the book is a spiritual revelation or something of that sort.

March 8, 1885
Letter from Charles Louis Metz to Frederick Ward Putnam
We have resumed work in the Hahn mounds and have put in four days during the past week with six men. According to your instructions somewhat I have suspended two men and will continue with four until the mounds that we are working are completed when I will lay them all off and await your further orders. The men I dispatched are Chris Marbach and George Hamilton and I'm keeping Britten, Noon, Ryan and Kneiff at work at this mound. The interesting places to work in during the spring are the Sand Field, the Turpin Mound and the Hahn field. I sent you the notes

of the Mound 4 of the Turner group. Did you receive them? I am very confident that we will make a big find in the Turpin mound when we begin there.

March 18, 1885

Note from Charles Louis Metz to Frederick Ward Putnam

The exploration of the Hahn mound was completed yesterday. The results were very meager. In the Hahn field two skeletons were found in a small excavation.

March 29, 1885

Letter from Charles Louis Metz to Frederick Ward Putnam

Yours of the 25th instance received yesterday evening. I am sorry that we cannot carry out our explorations with the full force. I have today notified the men and let them all go but Britten, Ryan, and Noon and have dispensed with the wagon also. We begin work on April 1 in the Hahn Field with three men to whom I will have to pay $1.50 a day. I shall try and pay as much as possible of this amount each month but I will not be enabled to carry it all. Tomorrow I will send the wagon out to bring in the tools, plank, and wheelbarrows belong to us and store them in my barn. I expect rich finds in the Hahn Field and am anxious to see the work begin. When can we expect to see the 18th annual report of the museum?

April 2, 1885

Letter from Charles Louis Metz to Frederick Ward Putnam

The first day's work in the Hahn Field with three men has already developed a very promising and interesting exploration. Ash pits are exactly similar to the ones in the Ferris Woods with burials over them. Animal remains are very abundant. Several good relics have been obtained. You may deduct $50.00 and place to the credit of my notes. Hoping all is well.

April 3, 1885

Letter from Charles Louis Metz to Frederick Ward Putnam

The results in the Hahn Field yesterday was two ash pits and two skeletons discovered. Over the skull of one was an inverted vessel. This was unfortunately broken by a pick stroke. I have done way with the picks as the ground is easily worked without their use. Fragments of the grooved bone and several perforated unio shells were found in the ash pits. Three fragments of pipes were also found. We have almost a cartload of animal remains of which we will preserve the best specimens to send on. This place is precisely like the Ferris Woods and is about three-fourths of a mile due south from the same. Of the skeletons I shall secure only the skulls, arm and leg bones and such pelvic bones as we can get entire specimens. We keep a sharp lookout for bones exhibiting masks of disease or injury. I do expect a good return from this place and am anxious to see my expectations realized. I want to find copper, meteoric iron and everything else of interest to you and for the museum. Mr. Finch has sent me down a sample jug of the last year's vintage of Ives. I am now drinking first to you and yours and the success of the museum. Second I shall send word to Mr. Finch to fill a keg to send on to you. I was away during last night on a very interesting "labor" a twin case where one of the pair of female was a "monster." No bone above the orbital plates in front parietal bones entirely missing and only a rudiment of the occipital bone no cerebrum. The cerebellum was exposed as were also the optic nerves and yet the thing lived and breathed for some minutes. The other child a male was perfectly normal in all respects. The patient was the wife of one of our men Frank Kneipf who also furnished the wagon. The mother is doing as well as could be expected under the circumstances. She is also a daughter of Britten's. Hoping to hear from you soon.

April 20, 1885

Letter from Charles Louis Metz to Frederick Ward Putnam

I have been worrying on Mr. Low to get you an annual pass over the B&O Railroad. I learned from Mr. Frazier that passes were issued to Major Powell and three others of the S.I. I concluded that the representative of the only institution doing *genuine* archaeological and ethnological work should have a pass also. When I first spoke to Mr. Low about it he told me that "passes did not grow on trees." I learned however that Mr. Orland Smith, the president of the C.W.B.R.R. was somewhat interested in archaeology. I called on some of his friends with the photographs and I have since learned that he is very anxious to see the photographs also. My next move was to take the photos to Mr. Low and have him show them to the presidents of the road and bring up the past question; which after taking a drink or two of "Runckels Pasticular" he agreed to do it. I hope you will receive the pass and visit us often.

April 23, 1885
Letter from Charles Louis Metz to Frederick Ward Putnam
Mr. Low informed me that he had sold his collection to the S.I. (Smithsonian Institution) and that Professor Holmes would be on to arrange the packing of the material of the Ferris Woods. He also demanded all of the field notes of the exploration conducted by the L & S Society of this place (Literary & Scientific Society of Madisonville). Now I claim the field notes as my exclusive property since the L &S Society has been dissolved and I refuse to give them up. There is a breeze between Mr. Low and myself. He argued that the S.I. people have done so much for the L &S Society giving Madisonville an international reputation and that they had some reference or other to Madisonville in every one of their publications while you had done nothing as yet. I shall get a written consent from the members to allow me to retain the notes that I have and also the records of the Society. I have them all in my possession and intend to keep them out of the hands of S.I. people. We will get through with the Hahn Field exploration during the next two weeks. I am making preparations to go to Sims [*sic*] and Remington to the stone graves fields. I was over to the grounds yesterday and Mrs. Hahn was anxious for us to get through with our work for the present as she had already delayed with her cropping. She is a widow with two sons 19 and 22 and pays a money rent for the lands she consented to our going to work. She wants compensation because of the delays and has fixed the limit at $15.00 giving us the privilege to return to explore when there are no crops on the grounds

whenever we so desire. I told her I would write you. I have made her no promises. Please write as soon as you can about this.

Very truly yours,

P.S. Do not let Low know that I have written to you about this. Keep this matter quiet until I have full particulars. I think he gets $500.00.

May 21, 1885

Letter from Charles Louis Metz to Frederick Ward Putnam

Your letter of the 7th duly received. We have finished the work on the Hahn Field for the present. I took the men to Symmes Station above here and explored several stone graves of which I will forward a report today. Learning that McLean intended to explore a beautiful mound situated near Loveland I at once left for the locality and prevailed Mr. John Pollack on whose land the mound is to let me explore it for the Peabody Museum. After considerable persuasion and by the help of maps and Fletcher's Indian music and yours 16th and 17th report I got him in a good humor and he went back on McLean. Went to work the next morning with five men and am expecting results tomorrow. Nearby on several of the high hills along the Little Miami River are stone graves and things of interest may be obtained from them. In regard to the young man you spoke of I should be pleased to have him here as soon as I get permanently fixed in some place such as the Sand Fields or Hahns or at some large mound. However, if you think he can be of any use to us now send him on. I am going to cut the S.I. fellows out wherever I can in the region. I have not remained in one place for more than four to six days since I left the Hahn Field. The stuff from the Hahn Field is all packed as is what little material we have from the stone graves and will be shipped to Boston Monday.

May 29, 1885

Letter from Charles Louis Metz to Frederick Ward Putnam

During the past three weeks I have been making explorations along the Little Miami River at Symmes in Loveland and yesterday I looked over the ground at Foster's Crossing between Remington and Ft. Ancient. There

are numerous stone burial places that ought to be examined. The stone grave and cists are judging from the contents of the graves I think them as of the same period as out the mound sand earthworks. The Miami Valley is now all in cultivation and we cannot do any work until in September. Now shall I open some of the mounds about Newtown, go into the Ferris Woods or camp the men out along the Miami and explore the stone graves and such mounds as may be practical? I have examined some very interesting stone graves one mile north of Loveland the details of which I shall send on at once. I have passed two of the graves so that if our young friend comes on he may see them and sketch them also. Oh, how many times I have wished for you, Kimball and the camera. One grave was especially so different from anything that I have ever heard about that after examining it I allowed it to remain as it was for you to see some future time. The proprietor of the ground was also anxious for me to leave it uncovered and notices were put up to visitors not to disturb anything about it. The reason I did not write for the young man to come on was that I had no steady work at any one place longer than a few days at a time. How could he rough it? Sleep in at Hammock, live on ham fat and out in the woods? Such will be our arrangement should we go into camp—we have one satisfaction—we beat McLane and consequently the S.I. Peabody Museum and the Harvard College are well known about Foster's Crossing in Warren County. 16 miles from here and there are two students at Harvard named Bridge, sons of W. H. Bridge. Inquire for them perhaps something may be learned about the archaeology in our home region. Two and a half miles above Foster's is an ancient cemetery on the Newhall Farm and many wonderful tales were told to me about it. They are judging from what I can learn stone graves. I have not yet visited the place. I have not told Low about our friends and will keep him in the dark for the present until he gets over the S.I. fever. I have been working five men this month.
Sincerely yours,

June 2, 1885
Letter from Charles Louis Metz to Frederick Ward Putnam
I have forwarded via the Bee-Line freight eleven creates containing 24

boxes of material from the Hahn Mound and Hahn Field, stone graves. Among the things in the boxes, you will find small packages of relics, which were donated to the museum by individuals whose names and addresses are marked on the label with the package. Will you please acknowledge the same as I promised that you would, and at the same time it will beneficial in other ways. Can you send me more of the Peabody Museum Reports. They are such good things in the way of getting permits to explore, and when will the 18th annual report of the museum be ready? Are you doing anything with the Turner Group? Mr. Low will visit you probably on next Sunday and he is going east on Thursday evening. Hoping to hear from you soon.

June 6, 1885
Letter from Charles Louis Metz to Frederick Ward Putnam
We are now working on the Turpin Farm one-half mile east of the Union Bridge in Anderson Township. The field is proving very rich and we will probably make another hit soon. The results of today were two pipes, the one with an unfinished skeleton. A quantity of shell beads and also a long chisel shaped stone, a vase. All of the things are on the way. I will keep my eye on the S.I. men. I call on every man that has anything of interest to you and arrange for the P.M. to explore exclusively. My next move is the Sand Ridge and we may consider ourselves fixed for the balance of the year and I am now ready to have the young man come on. My youngest brother has removed to Madisonville with his family and is now working with Britten and the excavation. I have him to take notes when I am away.

June 7, 1885
Letter from Charles Louis Metz to Frederick Ward Putnam
Among the things found today was a broken pipe still showing some carving on the sides, a vase, and several skeletons. In the dorsal vertebrae of one of the skeletons was embedded a deer's horn point similar to many we found in the Ferris Woods ash pits. All of what we have found so far was

in a space 50 x 50 feet. By the by, I have taken a number of lessons in photography and am now enabled to make fair pictures. I intend to get a camera and lens as soon as I can afford the money. I will fit me up a dark room and as I intend to use the camera in helping to make my notes more easily understood. The present field we are working is about three-fourths of an acre in area and our results are good. I wish ever so much to see you and would give anything almost to be with you and have a good talk even for an hour or two however Cambridge is so far away it cannot be. Hoping to hear from you soon I am sincerely yours,
C.L. Metz

June 11, 1885
Letter from Charles Louis Metz to Frederick Ward Putnam
Our young friend has arrived. He came here Tuesday night at 11:00 o'clock. I left the young man at Mrs. Sterns for the present but will look up a place near the digging. We were over the excavations yesterday and three of us were kept busy taking notes, making measurements, taking up skeletons and examining pits. The young man was very much interested and surprised at the many different things found. I shall have him to take notes and make diagrams and my brother will assist him when necessary. The ash pits in the new field are similar to the ones in the Hahn Field, some of them having burned sides. We discovered a handle of a small vase on which is a head of a bear very faintly done. (Drawing of a bear.) Apparently we shall get a larger and better lot of material from this place then we have at any time since we made the Turner Field. Mr. Turpin said yesterday that we might dig up the field south of the old homestead. This later place is the richest field in an archaeological way that I know of and when we get in there we may find "elephant pipes" with and without tails. The pottery-crested duck's head that was in my collection is from this field. Now we have the bear's head and lizard ornamentation what is next. The heads I wrote you about a few days ago are similar to numbers 19, 20 and 21 figured in your photograph of altar mound 3. I dare say we will get a number of pipes as this is the region for them. I am going to try what I can in pho-

tographing a mound in the Turpin yard as a friend of mine here has a camera and will loan it to me for the occasion.

June 11, 1885
Letter from Charles Louis Metz to Frederick Ward Putnam
Mr. Low has returned this A.M. and he spent three hours with me relating about his trip East. I think you have converted an S.I. man for here is what he says about the Peabody Museum: "Of all the museums that I have seen the Peabody is the crown jewel of them all." "The S.I. compares with it about as the society of natural history collections of Cincinnati would to the S.I." "The arrangement of the Peabody collection is all that a student could desire and the S.I. is a junk shop in comparison." He also found fault (Low) with an oil painting of the Serpent Mound by Mrs. McLean representing a frog making frantic efforts to escape the open jaws of a serpent. He told Thomas that it didn't. I have failed to get McKerron a fit boarding place near the diggings. Nickerson and myself have packed twelve boxes of material today and have seen many things of interest to him.

June 29, 1885
Letter from Charles Louis Metz to Frederick Ward Putnam
I have shipped today ten crates containing 21 boxes of material from the Turpin Field. We are now exploring a mound on the Johnston Turpin Farm. This mound is just east of the Village of Newtown located on the third terrace of drift gravel formation designated as Mound No. 16, Group C of chart Anderson Township. This will be our second day's work and we have found several fragments of soapstone pottery. Nickerson has been boarding at Mrs. Stern's place but I will charge him to go to Newtown today so as to be near the mound. Have been looking for a letter from you and also some editorial reports but they have not arrived.

August 1, 1885
Letter from Charles Louis Metz to Frederick Ward Putnam

I forward today the bill for July amounting to $292.00 from which please deduct $35.50 and place to credit of my note. On account of the fine weather we were able to put in every day this month and have explored three mound notes of which exploitations and results I will forward soon as I have a good lot of stuff ready for shipment this coming week.

August 1, 1885
Letter from Charles Louis Metz to Frederick Ward Putnam
We are working on a mound near the Turpin homestead and as soon as that is finished we go into the right Turpin Field west of the house. When did you go to Ann Arbor? And can you not be with us on your return? By the way we are working on a mound near the Turpin homestead and as soon as that is finished we go into the right Turpin Field west of the house. And can you not be with us on your return? By the by what are the requirements that are necessary to become a fellow of the AAAS? Am I eligible? If so, I am a candidate. In our friend Nickerson I am extremely disappointed. The why and wherefore I shall tell you when we see all each other again. I have not been enable to go to the mound for over a week but on next Monday I shall go over and see what is going on. I am convalescing from a severe cold.

August, 1885
Note from Charles Louis Metz to Frederick Ward Putnam
Enclosed please find bills for June and July. I was obliged to buy two wheelbarrows as the others were worn out altogether. I shall leave for Buffalo on the evening of the 16th if nothing prevents my going. I am not well and anxious to get away for a rest.

August 17, 1885
Letter from Charles Louis Metz to Frederick Ward Putnam
My health has at times been very bad always the result of losing rest at night. I cannot complain just now. A full account of the exploration of the

mound that contains the bone disks will be forwarded tomorrow. We have explored five mounds since the time we explored Mound 16. The trouble with Nickerson (the young men previously referred to) is with him and the men it seems they cannot get along together at all. At the time Nickerson arrived, my brother had charge of the men that is, taking notes and measurements. I took Nickerson to the ground, showed him how things were done and the next day or two I sent him along with the men. That day he told my brother that he would take the notes himself and the measurements also and then told the men that Professor Putnam had seen him here to take full charge of the work as the work had been heretofore done and he was going to see that it was done right. The next day he made a very unfavorable impression on Britten by telling him that he did not earn five cents, and that he, Nickerson, would write to you about him. Britten has not spoken a word to him since. The men drove up to Mrs. Streans place every morning to take Nickerson on and there was always a delay of 10 to 20 minutes waiting and one morning the men began whistling for him, and he came to the side porch and sat down and told the men he was no dog, they need not whistle for him if they wanted him. One should get off the wagon and come and tell him that they are ready. This they refused to do and after waiting for 20 minutes for him outside and he looking out from the window they drove on and left him behind. I tried to resolve the matter by telling all to be at one point at a given time from which the wagon would start. To make himself still more unpopular with the men he told them that he considered a working man nothing at all and that they were no better than beasts that they knew only enough to eat and sleep. After which the men refused to ride with him in the wagon and refused to let him get in. Many such petty differences cause all the trouble. As for myself I have to say what is best said to you when I shall see you. The young man could make himself very useful in many ways to us. He is anxious to go home. I do not wish to be annoyed by the complaints of both sides. The men are now in the "Peach Orchard" which will finish in a day or two and then begin work near the old homesteads. In regard to Chillicothe I am ready to go anywhere you may wish me to go and the men would be pleased also. I would want that use my six men. We could do as much work in a day as we did last season with all the hands we had. When we get to Chillicothe I should like to hunt up Sullivan and Dyer. Two weeks would about finish the work on the harness mound. We have a good quantity of material obtained from the several mounds and shall ship it on to the museum. Hoping you are well.

August 29, 1885
Letter from Julius Metz to Frederick Ward Putnam
Dear Sir:
By request of my brother, Dr. C. L. Metz I write informing you of his serious illness. The doctor was taken down with an acute attack of dysentery, which has acquired a serious form. Professor McKenzie of Cincinnati is in daily attendance. I will keep you advised as the changes.
Very respectfully,
J. A. Metz

August 30, 1885
Note from Julius Metz to Frederick Ward Putnam
8:00 a.m.
Dear Sir:
The doctor is slowly improving. He rested easy the greater part of the night and has gained a little strength. He is able to converse a little and expects to improve during today.
(Written by Metz's assistant).

August 31, 1885
Letter from Charles Louis Metz to Frederick Ward Putnam
My Dear Professor Putnam:
I have been very sick during the last week or so seriously that some of my kind friends felt greatly alarmed. As about myself I knew very little as I was unconscious most of the time until Friday night. At 4:00 p.m. my family thought I was dying. I regained consciousness at that time and found

the Doctor rubbing my body. I am yet very weak and have no control of my bowels. Today I am being fed ice and limewater and mile every two hours. Oh I would like to hear from you. Dr. McKenzie thinks I will be all right in a week from now. I begged him to let me write to you and he consented. Good-bye dear Professor Putnam. Please write to me. I promise you I will write again when I an able to sit up. Good-bye.
I am, faithfully yours,
C. L. Metz

September 2, 1885
Letter from Julius Metz to Frederick Ward Putnam
Dear Sir:
Yours of the 18th instance at hand and read to my brother who was greatly pleased to hear from you in fact your letter being the best tonic that could have been exhibited at the time. He is feeling very cheerful for hours afterwards. His condition has been one of slow improvement ever since. He not only seems to worry now that he will not be able to do about by the time you arrive here. The doctor is still troubled with circumscribed inflammation at the head of the colon. The fever is about gone and general condition improved. His physician has forbidden him to ride for three weeks. The work is progressing favorably at the excavations.
Very respectfully your servant,
J. A. Metz

September 5, 1885
Letter from Charles Louis Metz to Frederick Ward Putnam
I am pushing the work in the Turpin Field as fast as possible so as to get over the ground before frost sits in. The richest part of our diggings will be reached in about two weeks. In October we proposed to work the "Sun's Fields" for all it's worth. In the present excavations we are finding peculiar trenches from 10 to 20 feet long in the bottom of which are little circular pockets three to four inches apart. The trench is usually filled with

black soil and many of the pockets with ashes. We are finding many shell beads of various patterns, only one perfect stone pipe has been found. Many bone implements of similar pattern to those in the Ferris Mounds. Some of the mounds we have opened will prove of general interest as regards their construction. When you come one we will open up some stone graves near Madisonville that I think will be of interest to you. Suffered all night and the ulcers in my bowels are yet very sore and Dr. McKenzie says it will be some time before I am well. Today I will remain in bed and not get up at all. Hoping you are well.

I am faithfully yours,

October 8, 1885
Letter from Charles Louis Metz to Frederick Ward Putnam
We are now working on the Turpin Ridge. On the first day we secured a good cranium and a perfect vase. The vase is a beautiful one. The mold above the skeleton is from 18 to 20 inches in depth and we may succeed in getting a goodly number of perfect cranium and other things. The stone graves found on the Kendall farm near Madisonville differed greatly from any others that we have found in this vicinity. I would like to have a set of photographs of the Turner figurines.

October 28, 1885
Letter from Charles Louis Metz to Frederick Ward Putnam
Among the interesting finds of this week was a burial four feet and seven inches below the surface of the ground. The skeleton was enclosed by upright stones and rested beneath a large limestone several feet in breadth and width and at the left four copper pins about three inches in length and one-eight inch in thickness were found. I send them by mail together with an implement of flint dug from a depth of eight feet from the surface when the men were digging my cistern. The implement came for a stratum of coarse gravel eight feet from the surface, and two feet above this in the clay a smooth stone was found which was water worn. It may have been

worked into its present shape by human agency. About the flint implement I have not the least doubt but what it has been chipped by human hands. I send these things on with the copper pins and would like to know what you think about them. The plain on which Madisonville is located is probably the ancient river or lake bed and the flint implement may have been lost in the water or the ground above the point where the implement was found and has apparently never been disturbed. Work in the Turpin Field is progressing fast and we are working up towards the best part of the field as rapidly as possible. The copper I send today is the first found in the trip in Cemetery. I may possibly come on during next month provided I can do any good in the way of making connections or explaining some of the first notes of the Turpin group. About what time will you start for Baltimore? I can secure a good photographic outfit for $60.00 including developing trays, printing frames and a good lot of chemicals and I think seriously of buying the lot. It might be that photographs of some of the good finds or excavations would assist in understanding the diagrams.

On October 31, 1885
Letter from Charles Louis Metz to Frederick Ward Putnam
On driving into my place tonight I met the men coming from work. Martin Noon who was in advance cried out "Oh Doctor we have found the baby and it is a darling." The darling baby proved to be a large stone pipe resembling a human figure in a squatting position. It is of compact sandstone almost six inches in height and four inches across the base. It resembles figure 148, page 248 in Squire [*sic*] and Davis in the head, the head and headgear, the most not so prominent however. It is somewhat like figure 149 Squire Davis, but in a more upright position resembling a person squatting in the act of defecation. The arms are thrown backwards and extend at the full length. The hands spread out as if supporting the buttocks and the body is leaning forward and resting on the flexed knees. The specimen is finer than anything figured in Squire and Davis and was found at a depth of four feet in a grave containing a small skeleton. The two pipes make a fitting close for the month of October. The digging is getting

more interesting as we approach the higher ground and we may yet find "the finest relic that was ever found and nicer than anything Professor Putnam has ever seen or anybody else in the world" as Britten says and all the men are anxious to find. Britten, poor fellow, the tears roll down his cheeks when he saw the relic and did not find it himself—Jacob Ruscic being the lucky one. Of course, I had to set up the beer for the men. What a treat it would have been to have you present when the find was made and also our friend Kimball. Of course, I want a photograph of it.
With kind regards to all.

November 1, 1885
Letter from Charles Louis Metz to Frederick Ward Putnam
I have concluded to pack the pipes and forward them by express. I shall insure them for $100.00. I will photograph the large one today so that in case it gets lost we will know at least what it looked like. Mr. Low has seen the pipe this a.m. I let him see it after he promised me that he would not speak of it to anyone even Judge Cox. Britten is so worked up over the find that I am afraid he will get his "feet freezed" as he styled it and have a sore head to go to work tomorrow. On Friday in the *Enquirer* I read as follows: Mr. John Cone Kimball of the Peabody Museum of Cambridge, Massachusetts was the guest of Mrs. Florence Conkling, Saturday and Sunday.

November 3, 1885
Letter from Charles Louis Metz to Frederick Ward Putnam
I still have the carved pipe here and as the moisture is drying out it appears to have a reddish cast probably the material from which it is made is compact red sandstone. The following are the notes of the skeleton found with the pipe. Skeleton No. 7, Block 2, Section 4, skeleton of child, horizontal position. Skull is badly broken. Length of skeleton—2'8". Length of Grave—5'8". Depth surface to bottom of grave—3'. At elbow of right arm a stone pipe representing a blank figurine in a squatting position was found at depth of 3'9" from the surface to the ground. Face of the figure

lay downwards. Grave filled with black soil to near the bottom where the soil was mixed with yellow clay. Found October 31, 1885. We had a slight frost this a.m. It is going to be a very warm day and I shall go to the field as the men reported three skeletons found last evening.

November 4, 1885.
Letter from Charles Louis Metz to Frederick Ward Putnam
Professor Putnam:
Your letter was received. In answer to your questions I will say I am certain that the flint implement came from the gravel at the bottom of the cistern and that it was not pushed down from the surface while digging. Second, I saw it taken out. The colored man was using the pick to loosen the gravel when he pressed out the fluid saying here is a black stone. I told him to toss it up and I then observed that it was worked and I showed it to Mr. Kimball the next a.m. when he came from the City. Third, the men were colored men and knew nothing about relics or flints. Fourth, I am positive it came from the coarse gravel in the bottom of the cistern. I shall write you in more detail of this matter soon.—I called on Nickerson today and showed him the pipe found at Turpin's and the poor fellow was delighted. He has begun the map and chart of Hamilton. Today the men found six skeletons and secured very good cranium.

November 13, 1885
Letter from Charles Louis Metz to Frederick Ward Putnam
Among the contents of a pit explored today, November 13, a fragment of a pipe was found of which I will give a sketch. I'm looking for the photographs that were taken the last day he was here (Kimball) and my little girls are dreadfully anxious. I have not been very well for several days past being overworked. Scarlatina is proceeding epidemically in this region and I have from 16 to 20 calls a day besides a number of confinements which cause me to lose my night's rest but you must harvest when the wheat is ripe and reap when you can. Hoping to hear from you soon.

November 24, 1885
Letter from Charles Louis Metz to Frederick Ward Putnam
Since writing to you my previous letter I have been again housed up and feel troubled with a severe neuralgia in my left side localizing itself in the region of my heart. Sometimes in my neck, arms back and face. Today we have had our first signs of snow. A few flakes are falling yet it is not cold and we have had no freezing weather. My Hermosa rose bush still blossoms in the front yard. The work in the Turpin field goes on. Many skeletons of children are found and with all of them are beads and shell ornaments. Today they found a fragment of a pottery pipe in the general digging. I called on Mr. Michael Turner a few days ago and looked over the old mounds. On leaving the house Mr. Edward Turner presented me with a small stone ax and also the little cone-shaped mass of hematite. You remember that you tried to induce young Turner to let you have the hematite for the museum? While we have it now and I will send it on packed with the shell ornaments and beads. If you can spare any money for the men, please send it on as Martin Noon intends to remove to Indianapolis and I would like to pay him in full when he quits us.
P.S. Have you seen Kimball?

December 1, 1885
Note from Charles Louis Metz to Frederick Ward Putnam
Enclosed please find statement for month of November from which please deduct $35.00 and place to my credit on my note. The clippings are from the *Times Star* and from the Sunday *Commercial* of November 29. If we could only push the work now with additional men the men would not agree to a reduction but have only 20 minutes for a noon spell.

December 5, 1885
Letter from Charles Louis Metz to Frederick Ward Putnam
I am greatly improved as regards my health. I have concluded to do quiet

all night work and attend to office and day calls during the wintertime. Today is the cold snap part of the season. The temperature was two degrees below freezing and now at 10:00 a.m. it is four degrees above with a cold wind blowing. I think I shall put off my visit until after the holidays. Now in regard to our mound work, if we leave the Turpin field now we cannot get into it again before next fall and probably never again as Turpin is a little clearer. As far as the men are concerned they are willing to wait for their pay until you get ready to pay them and again there will not be as many working days during December, January and February. I have divided the $100.00 among the men. I shall advance Nickerson a few dollars and it can be deducted from my note. By the by how do I stand on my note?

January 7, 1886
Letter from Charles Louis Metz to Frederick Ward Putnam
I have to apologize for not acknowledging the receipt of the box sent us before this. It was duly received and the unpacking was the only bright spot in our otherwise dull Christmas. Wilbur, and Beatrise, the baby, were quite ill at the time and we had no Christmas tree in consequence. It made us all feel so good that friends far away had been thinking of us. Many, many thanks. Wilbur wants me to tell "Fesser Putnam that he can build the house and that he will take good care of it." Beatrice says me like Fesser Putnam and Kimball. I took the liberty to send you two mummies by express, which I hope you have received ere this. They were supposed to be edible. I am very busy. Measles prevailing as an epidemic, scarlatina bronchitis and fevers prevailing with numerous other cares thrown in as a variety. I have had a steady run of five days and six nights and it wears a fellow down and gives him the blues. Makes one look glum and soused. I will pick up here and give you a synopsis of what has been my daily and nightly routine during the last week. I leave home at 8:30 a.m. My first family—they have the measles. Then drive one-half miles further and a child is seen with the Quinsey. Next a colored woman with the Varoloid. Next a mile further and a case of pneumonia. Next two miles further a

child with bronchitis. Next I see a patient in the last stage of phthisis. Next two families with measles. My next call is a lady with a ulcer. My next is the most impatient man in Ohio and he is suffering with rheumatism—my next call is on a young lady with St. Vitres, and my next and last call on the route is a lady that has had too much Christmas and may be classified as having a head of *malade imaginaire* but she is a good lady and owns the Ferris ancient cemetery—17 patients daily and every other night or day an obstetric call had for this last week. Now you are probably aware that I get into a tight place. I have no one to consult with. "City doctors" are expensive and cannot be readily called in so you must dare you own responsibility—patients reside far enough apart so as to give you time to think of their cases, the plan of treatment and when the last call is made with a sigh of relief you are home bound and sometimes Mr. Langdon and myself have a song and a smoke. I have the box packed and in it you will find some of the Turpin notes, Ferris notes. I have also the notes of Red Bank mound. Mound No. 6, Group A, Columbia and small mound by the Davis graves. Klotte mound, Hall's mound and Jones's mound—these last are all being copied.

January 19, 1886
Note from Charles Louis Metz to Frederick Ward Putnam
Today I have sent on 11 crates and one box. 21 boxes in all of material obtained from the Turpin field. I have a few shell beads and ornaments, carbonized matting of the basket pleating. It is well preserved. A copper implement was also found four inches in length and over a quarter is about three-fourths dug over. I have written a half dozen letters but have received no answer from you.

February 13, 1886
Letter from Charles Louis Metz to Frederick Ward Putnam
Sometime since I sent you a telegram asking for instructions meaning thereby if I should resume work and the weather permitted us to do so or

discontinue all explorations until further orders from you. The frost is all out of the ground and the work could be pushed successfully now. We have but a moment left before the spring plowing begins and the men are anxious to go to work at once. We should have our own team. One could be purchased for less than $150.00 and the keeping would not exceed $4.00 per week thereby saving considerable in the way of that expense. Four or five men would be a sufficient force. I am keeping the men in corn, oil and wine and they are all fat and jolly. I vowed a short time ago that I would not write to you again until I had first received a few lines from you, but that good resolution has gone where so many good ones go or where it is said to a place where good resolutions are used for planning stones.

February 22, 1886
Letter from Charles Louis Metz to Frederick Ward Putnam
Your letter of the 11th containing a check was duly received and then men were made serenely happy. I did not have the blues very badly myself, but the men were put on account of having nothing to do but loaf about the corners and they are still very anxious to go to work at something. Nickerson returned east last Tuesday looking well and strong. He expects to return again after paying you a visit. I attended the meeting of the State Archaeological and Historical Society last week at Columbus. The meeting was rather a mixed up concern and seemed no one had fully considered what he went there for. The *Marietta Centennial* seemed to be the principal object however. Some suggested that a monumental shaft be erected, others a monumental building, others were for a great blowout generally. In the midst of the hubbub Professor Wright asked for permission to say a few words. This being granted he began speaking of the ancient monuments of Ohio, their neglect, the care that should be taken to preserve them and then reading your letter to the meeting. This turned the attention of the meeting to archaeology and the proceedings were more to my idea. Mr. Douglas Putnam spoke of the vandalism of the Marietta Councilmen, calling the embankments the "scared way." Finally it was resolved to print

circulars and send them about the state appealing to all parties to protect the earth works and to excite an interest in the archaeology of the state and to request the newspapers of the state to publish the circular every three months so as to keep the matter before the people. What will the farmers that plow over high bank, cedar banks or any other earth work care for a circulars or newspaper articles? It is only a matter of dollars and cents that will preserve the earth works of the ancient people. It was finally moved that a committee be appointed to present the matter to the legislature and secure an appropriation for the purpose of purchasing the ancient monuments especially Ft. Ancient, Ft. Hill, the Serpent, Alligator and Forts on the Miami River and at Hamilton. This motion was knocked in the head by the Marietta people who thought it was not a good time to ask for an appropriation as they had already a resolution drawn up to request funds from the legislature for the *Marietta Centennial*. This started the Marietta ball rolling and archaeology was again squelched for this meeting and I do not think that anything will be done to amount to anything until after the Ohio Centennial and Marietta is over with. Professor Wright made a noble appeal but there was no archaeologist to support him in the good work. I was greatly disappointed in the so-called archaeological collection at the State University. Poor arrangement ala Smithsonian.

April 19, 1886
Letter from Charles Louis Metz to Frederick Ward Putnam
I have been so very busy with my professional duties that I could not find time to arrange the stack of field notes of the Turpin Excavations to send on. I shall arrange them soon however. My little daughter Birdie two years old had the misfortune to fall and break her arm about two weeks ago. She is doing nicely however. The rest of the family is very well. I am working Britten and my brother together in opening several small mounds about here and shall send on the notes and material. I should like to work a force of three men camping them out where ever the mound should be located and I have this to propose should you feel enabled to go on with the work. Take three men pay them $1.50 per day per man. They are funding them-

selves. Camping them at work. This would make an expense of $4.50 per day when they worked. There are so many places where mounds are located four to ten in a group and with three men camped around them we could accomplish about as much as four men and a team could by camping. By camping we could save a team's expense. Should you favor such an arrangement to explore the mounds here and about the enjoining counties, I would suggest that the working force be Britten, Tom Ryan and my brother to take the notes and make the diagrams. Has Nickerson arrived at the museum yet?

I am truly yours,

C. L. Metz

May 6, 1886

Letter from Charles Louis Metz to Frederick Ward Putnam

Britten and my brother are camped in the old Marriott house on the riverbank near the Whittlesey work. Hoping that you will be enabled to carry on the work with at least two men this summer and that we shall make some food finds right along. My sister-in-law, Mrs. Risch died and was buried in Brown County, Ohio. She was the wife of Jacob Risch who worked for us at Turpin's and ran the wagon.

May 16, 1885

Letter from Charles Louis Metz to Frederick Ward Putnam

On account of the severe storms during the last week the men did not work but will go into camp tomorrow morning. On most every prominent point along the East Fork the Little Miami River are stone graves and at one place on the Stone Lick Creek are probably about 100. I would like to add one made to the camping force so as to have three for I think we ought to have the first chance at them. The force now is Britten, my brother and I would like to add Tom Ryan which would make the daily expense $4.50 when they worked. It is understood they provisioned themselves. Cannot three men be employed? I shall examine the banks of the

Miami River to see whether the recent freshets have explored anything or not. Did you receive the book *Algoonah* I sent you? What did you think of Professor Wright's letter to me?

June 25, 1886
Letter from Charles Louis Metz to Frederick Ward Putnam
Your letter of the 15th duly received. I am greatly pleased with the photographs. Mrs. Metz is disappointed in not getting the photograph of the two children Wilbur and Bertie under the maple tree in my dooryard. Probably Mr. Kimball overlooked that one. The men are all willing to wait for their pay until you get funds to pay them. They like camp life very well and work like good fellows as four mounds and one lot of stone graves have been explored already. The results have not been of the best, yet the burials are a very ancient. The expenses now are $4.50 per day when the men work. They board themselves, which they can do at $1.50 a week per man. I propose to attend the Buffalo meeting of the AAAS and shall be accompanied by my daughter Annie. I have many relatives living at Buffalo whom I propose to visit. Camp Putnam is indeed a lovely place, 600 feet above the river. The view is grand indeed. The mound on this point is about six and a half feet high. The men will finish up there this week. The little mound at Turners we cannot get at until fall.

July 8, 1886
Letter from Charles Louis Metz to Frederick Ward Putnam
The enclosed precious little squib was cut from the *Clermont Courier* of June 16. The last half is especially bad and if not they have something especially valuable in their mounds and will go to digging themselves. We are in a region now where nothing has as yet been disturbed and which we are sure to make a good hit soon. Do you not think it advisable to sent a communication to the *Courier* stating the object of the exploration; what becomes of the finds, how they are arranged for study and that they are not bartered for in the market. That the work we are doing is paid by money contributed by individuals and this is in the interest of archaeological science.

July 20, 1886
Letter from Charles Louis Metz to Frederick Ward Putnam
We have up to now explored five mounds and are working on the sixth one besides several stone graves. The results so far are very meager and I am discouraged and seriously think of discontinuing the work often. The mound we are working at is completed and the ground is leveled up. We are working in a new country full of mounds that have only lately been cleared of the forest and yet are finds do not amount to anything. The skeletons are badly decayed. Nothing but small fragments can be obtained of them. Should you desire to have the work continue please inform me at once. The next mound may result in a good find such as has been our expectations all along. In the back of Newtown are two mounds that I think we should open before we suspend the work in the valley. I have received the certificate of election as a Fellow several days ago. Thanks. Will try and be at the Buffalo meeting if all goes right here.

July 26, 1886
Letter from Charles Louis Metz to Frederick Ward Putnam
Your letter of the 20th containing a check for $373.54 duly received. This closes up all but some time of Britten's and probably of my brothers that came in after March 8, 1886. The new campus is called Camp Kimball. I should go to work on a mound in the valley having lost faith in the mounds on the "high places." What relics we have obtained are fine of the kind but they are not what I want to find—altars and contents alone will satisfy me. I have a region of stone graves in reserve for you to explore when you come out. I have gotten rid of Noon—he was angry because I put Tom Ryan to work and not him. Hoping you are well with best wishes to your family and Mr. Kimball.

October 23, 1886
Letter from Charles Louis Metz to Frederick Ward Putnam

I do not know what to say about Nickerson coming out here. I candidly think that he is not nor never will be an archaeologist. Adopting archaeology for a profession seems to me a very queer idea. He was out here. He made very little out of the opportunity. He would pay no attention to what suggestions I made. Professor Marsh is probably like a great many other people—ignorant of the great work that you are doing. I agree with Mr. Low in that the time has come for you to blow your blast and stir up the pot not only Marsh but many others also.

October 24, 1886

Letter from Charles Louis Metz to Frederick Ward Putnam

During the delightful weather we have been enabled to push the exploration right along. Discovered a grave containing a skeleton in horizontal position. Deep pit found containing a few fragments of animal bone. On the north side of the barn nothing was discovered expect nine feet from the northwest corner of the barn was a heap of burned human bones among which fragments of flint knives was found. Mr. Turner refuses to allow us to dig in the field west of the road. He says we can go into it all we want next summer.

November 4, 1886

Letter from Charles Louis Metz to Frederick Ward Putnam

The mound at which we are working is proving of great interest. One adult was 5'10" in length. This mound contains an enormous quantity of animal remains, fragments of pottery, shells some with perforations, fragments of burned masses of clay. In fact, the mound seems as far as we have gone to have been made of all kinds of refuse—a veritable kitchen midden. The burial under the mound is truly of great interest. The bones are so well preserved. My professional business is extremely dull owing to the fine weather no doubt. I am at the mound daily between 11:00 a.m. and 4:00 p.m. If you should think it proper to put more men on please telegraph me at once.

On November 6, 1886

Letter from Charles Louis Metz to Frederick Ward Putnam

I have been looking up the Ft. Ancient matter. The first step I took was to get acquainted with a man in the neighborhood that would represent that he wanted to buy land. This I succeeded in doing through Mr. L. Simonton at Blanchester. We are feeling are way slowly and carefully so as to avoid suspicion. It would be best to transfer to me and then to the Museum. I think $6,000.00 will buy the whole Fort from both parties together with enough slope to protect the work. I shall visit Ft. Ancient next Wednesday and would like to hear from you at once.

November 10, 1886

Letter from Charles Louis Metz to Frederick Ward Putnam

Yesterday Mrs. Metz presented me with a little daughter. Both mother and child are doing well. I have called in the camp much to the disgust of Britten who would of preferred to remain out all winter to coming home. I have laid off all hands but Britten and Tom and have them at work in an old cemetery that I have recently discovered situated on a gravel ridge. The weather is now delightful and clear. The thermometer is dropping down to 28 at night and rising to 50 and 60 during the day. We have had no snow and everything is very dry. Both my cisterns have given out and we must have our water hauled to us.

November 15, 1886

Letter from Charles Louis Metz to Frederick Ward Putnam

I have just received word from Mr. Simonton in regard to the Ft. Ancient matter. The Cowden heirs won the land enclosed in the Fort except a few acres at the north end and all of the land forming the slopes of the hill 291 acres in all. This they will sell at $30.00 per acre if taken altogether. Mr. Rich has not yet made a proposition as yet and he may come to terms at about $50.00 to $75.00 per acre. On the slopes are several burial places. I am going up to the Fort soon and note down all that. I am going up to the Turner mound today to take up two more skeletons up to the present time. I have five original and two intrusive. The men feel very comfortable in the camp as old Britten says, "We have not been frostbitten yet." The tent is lined with two feet depth of straw as high up as the square sides. What do you think about Ft. Ancient? Can you not get it now? Is it not more important than the serpent? Will not some moneyed individual immortalize himself or herself by advancing $10,000.00 to save one of the greatest monuments on the American Continent? Had I but the means Peabody should have Ft. Ancient for Thanksgiving present. By the by I have two turkeys that I will sent on Monday morning November 22 by Adams Express. Will you please give me the number and street at which your home is located.

November 28, 1886
Letter from Charles Louis Metz to Frederick Ward Putnam
The Turner Mound No. 1 is completed and we are now working in two places. This grave had its ends lined with upright limestone and the bottom was paved with flat round stones. Now this does to prove that my theory may be probably correct, that wherever we find limestone laying on the surface they mark either a burial or other place that has been used for some purpose or another.

December 18, 1886
Note from Charles Louis Metz to Frederick Ward Putnam
Enclosed please find a note. Could not this be discounted so as to have some money for the men. They want some for Christmas. I have stopped all work on account of the weather. Am convalescing rapidly from my throat trouble. I almost began to think that old Nick's chances for toasting a doctor have come.

January 31, 1887,
Letter from Charles Louis Metz to Frederick Ward Putnam
What about Ft. Ancient? Have you written to Mr. Simonton at Blanchester or what would you think advisable for me to say to him. Has Mr. Luken of this place been elected a member of the AAAS. You will remember I have his $8.00. All of the accounts for the year 1886 have been sent in. We have settled in full up to June 1 to January 1, 1887. I have received $600.00 to date. I trust you and your family are well. Also that Mr. Kimball is yet among the living and getting the photographs ready to send on.
Faithfully yours,
Charles

April 20, 1887
Letter from Charles Louis Metz to Frederick Ward Putnam
Several days ago I sent in a registered package. The two fish hooks belonging to Mr. J. A. Hosbrook's collection from the Ferris Woods Cemetery. I will see the gentlemen and try to induce him to present them to the museum. In yesterday's mail I sent you a copy of Shephard's [sic] *Antiquity's of Ohio* [sic] in which much of the three last Peabody Museum reports is embodied. When will your work of the Turner group be published? I am afraid that the cream of your labors in Ohio will be gathered by others before you are ready. Today I met Dr. Gustav Brühl of Cincinnati who has just returned from Yucatan and the Myan Country. He visited every place mentioned by Stevens and the doctor says that Stevens' measurements were very correct. The doctor thinks that the Myans have been overestimated by many writers. Dr. Brühl is waiting on publishing a book in German. The doctor said that he should have published in English instead of German. I called on Mr. Turner and turned over to him the photographs. He was very please with them indeed. He presented me with a bill in return for $6.00 for the following items. "Hauling stone from field, rebuilding fence from barn." Mr. Turner sold the strip of land 400 feet south of the south ditch of the Whittlesey work and west of the railroad track. The railroad is running gravel and workmen have found three skele-

tons. The Turpin Peach Orchard Ridge is now so built upon that we will never have a chance to dig there again. Oh that we had the wherewithal to finish the places that can only be explored now while they exist. Our men have all sought other employment except old Britten who is waiting to hear when he can go to work again. Dear Professor, cannot you send me one dozen of the photographs of the group on the mound in Brown County?

August 13, 1889
Letter from Charles Louis Metz to Frederick Ward Putnam
It will be necessary to put on a larger force of men as Mr. Turner intends to put the field down in wheat and is only waiting for rain to being plowing. I have found Mr. Saville to be all right and I think he will prove the right man for you. Mr. Turner is confined to his bed and cannot last more than two or three weeks. *We must make haste to get through with the Turner work this fall.* It will be our last chance. Please telegraph whether to put on more men or not.

August 26, 1889
Letter from Charles Louis Metz to Frederick Ward Putnam
Another hit has been made today in the discovery of a small altar containing numerous relics such as perforated shark's teeth, copper beads, copper earrings, oblong copper ornaments, one or two copper buttons, two little cones of meteoric iron, one flat pin of bone finally carved and representing the Central American carved figurines more closely than anything I have yet seen from here, numerous pieces of cylindrical bone carved, and mica.

September 26, 1889
Letter from Frederick Ward Putnam to Charles Louis Metz
Dr. C. L. Metz, Madisonville, Ohio.

Dear Metz:

This morning's mail has brought me your account of expenses up to the last of August, which is all right except that you have not put down for your own time. That you must do on your next bill for I consider that you are still under the old arrangement of $25. for every month you look after the work of the Museum; and the Museum wants all the time you can give it and all the specimens you can obtain. I sent you a check the other day for 400 dollars on your new account, and I now enclose a check for 500 dollars for you to pay note that comes due on October 4, in Cincinnati. Don't forget the note for I would not have it protested on any account. I hope this rainy weather we are having has not extended to Ohio, to interfere with our work at the Turner group, which I should judge was panning out well, from all that you and Saville write. Push the work there as fast as it can be done in a thorough manner. How do you find Saville, and how does he take hold now that he is left by himself so much? I hope to make a good archaeologist of him, and trust that you are doing your part in putting him through in the right way. In your former letter you stated that you had sent an estimate of expenses, but there was no such thing in the letter. I have been very much driven since my return, trying to pick up the loose threads of work, and arranging for a place to live in this winter. I think it would be advisable for you to send on everything you have in hand as fast as they can be packed; and I am very anxious to see the results of the late work at Turner's. So the poor old man has gone at last. With the horrible disease that he had, we can only be thankful for him. Please give my sympathy to his son. With kind regards to Saville and the men in camp, I remain,

Yours faithfully, F. W. Putnam

P.S. That I may have my vouchers all right, please sign the enclosed receipts and return to me as soon as you can.

October 2, 1889

Note from Charles Louis Metz to Frederick Ward Putnam

I have been suffering from a carbuncle on my neck and in consequence I have not been at the camp since the 21st but shall go up tomorrow and after that daily.

Note from Charles Louis Metz to the members of the LSSM
March 17, 1891
In the death of C. F. Low we recognize the loss of one of the most active and efficient members of this Society. He was one of its founders and has contributed much to make it celebrated throughout civilized World. For several years he was Secretary of this Society and edited several passages in the archaeological explorative. He also contributed many papers of high scientific value. We lose in him a worthy member and a something companion. Our heartfelt sympathy is extended to his family in their loss.

July 3, 1891
Letter from Frederick Ward Putnam to Charles Louis Metz
World's Columbian Exposition, Chicago, 1893
Department of Ethnology and Archaeology
Peabody Museum of Archaeology, Cambridge, Massachusetts
Dr. C. L. Metz, Madisonville, Ohio.
Dear Metz:
The enclosed is a formal letter in relation to World's Fair matters, copies of which have to be kept for file. I am seeing how I can manage about exploration at New Boston. If I cannot manage to have it done for the Museum, it will have to be done for the World's Fair. I will let you know in about a week.
Sincerely yours,
F. W. Putnam

July 3, 1891
Letter from Frederick Ward Putnam to Charles Louis Metz
Dr. C. L. Metz
Madisonville, Ohio.

Dear Sir:

Enclosed please find check for $25, your salary for the month of June. I enclose voucher for your signature, which please return as soon as possible. I am having letterheads printed for your special use, which will be forwarded to you within a week. I shall also write to you very soon in relation to some special work in Ohio.

Respectfully yours,

F. W. Putnam

July 27, 1891

Letter from Frederick Ward Putnam to Charles Louis Metz

Dr. C. L. Metz

Madisonville, Ohio

Dear Dr. Metz:

Enclosed please find check for $25 in payment of your salary for July for which please send me voucher in regular form and receipted the same as for June. Now in relation to work in the field, it is my wish to have you conduct an exploration for the World's Fair and I think it will be well for you to go on exploring the stone graves that you mention near New Boston. I am having a survey made of Fort Hill in order to prepare a model of the Fort, and Mr. Cowen writes me that he has finished that work. I am about to send Mr. Saville to make an exploration at Fort Hill; he will have a young man, a Mr. Cook a student at the Museum who has been with him there. Now I have another student here, Mr. Harlan I. Smith whom you had at Turner's last summer, and he was with us also at Foster's. This young man is able to do good photographic work, as well as conscientious and thorough work in the field, and I think he would be a good man to work under your direction. Another matter comes up just at this point, Mr. Moorehead who finished his work at Fort Ancient last month has been here working over his collection that he obtained and getting his notes and descriptions ready. He will be through with this in about ten days. He has told me of a very interesting place on Caesar's Creek, which he has the privilege of exploring for the World's Fair. The man in fact is holding his field out of wheat that we may do it. So I propose sending Mr. Moorehead to that place in about ten days and as he will need a photographer I propose sending Mr. Smith with him. The question is if it would not be better for you to go up there with Mr. Moorehead and Mr. Smith and sort of get that place started, then leave them to work it up, you visiting them from time to time until they are through with it. Then take Mr. Smith to your New Boston locality. In this way you put Martin and George and three or four others to work on Caesar's Creek and then take them as needed for your New Boston work. Mr. Moorehead will call upon you at Madisonville on his way out so as to have everything perfectly harmonious and satisfactory between you. Moorehead is working fully in the interest of the Museum and the World's Fair, and I want everything to be smooth and harmonious between you. He is ready to work under your general guidance. Were it not that I leave for Washington on the 9th of August for the Association meeting I should ask you to come on here at once to talk matters over; but you would hardly get here before I should have to leave; and I am so driven that it would be really unsatisfactory, as when you do come I want you to spend some time with me. I shall therefore trust to calling on you in connection with World's Fair matters later in the season, any October or November. As soon as the Association meeting is over which will be about the first of September, I shall start West and shall stop to see you on my way and see what is going on in the field. We will then talk over matters and arrange for all the work and what I expect you to do in connection with the World's Fair. In the meantime write me what you think about the plans proposed in this letter.

Believe me sincerely yours, F. W. Putnam

August 7, 1891
Letter from Frederick Ward Putnam to Charles Louis Metz
Dr. C. L. Metz
Madisonville, Ohio.
Dear Dr. Metz:
Yours of the 4th at hand and I suppose Mr. Saville and Mr. Smith have

reached you by this time. Mr. Moorehead telegraphed me that he only had two tents one of which was small and that he could not stow his party away in them. He asked permission to purchase another. I did not understand what had become of all our tents but supposed some misfortune had befallen them and authorized him to purchase another one as low as possible. I see now that you still have two good tents on hand, and if you can stop Mr. Moorehead's purchase and send him one of these it will be a good thing, as I do not like to get such a stock of canvas stored away to rot. The trouble is they are put up damp and so tear and decay. I have telegraphed Moorehead now to stop the purchase and get the tent from you, but it may be too late, unless you know where he was buying one. I send enclosed several letters for the men in Ohio; please forward them to such an address as will reach them. Sent me a bill of storage made out to the Peabody Museum. All the cameras we have are now in the field, four in number. But as Mr. Smith will be with you a good part of the time he can take such photographs as you require or you can use his camera when he does not require it. When Mr. Smith returns he can leave his camera with you. Mr. Cowen has finished his survey at Fort Hill and wants another job. I suppose he would be as good as any one to make the model of the Turner Group under your direction. As we already have Hasbrook's survey it would only be necessary for Mr. Cowen to take a few elevations and measurements in the field. I should say a week's work in the field added to Holbrook's survey would give us all the data needed for the model. Please look into this matter and confer with him about it and see what it can be done for in two ways; first for him to make the additional survey added to Hasbrook's; and second to make the model ready for casting, the same as he did for the Serpent Park, and as he is doing for Fort Hill. The plan mentioned in a previous letter relating to an archaeological map of the Little Miami Valley is a good idea and I should like to have you carry it out. I think all that is necessary is to get the largest State map you can and make an enlarged copy of the whole valley and then locate the various work upon it, so as to show the full archaeology from the implements in the gravel to the old fire-places in the river bottom and the earth-works, mounds, village sites, burial-places, etc. We could then have a careful drawing made of the whole map. You would probably do your work on sec-

tional maps so as to have it as large as possible.
Sincerely yours,
F. W. Putnam

September 2, 1891
Copied letter to Charles Louis Metz from Warren King Moorehead to Frederick Ward Putnam
Dear Prof. Putnam:
When I came to you Monday morning, I did not have time to say before you a number of imperative questions would arise for solution. If you will read carefully Squire and Davis' Report on this earthwork and the twenty-six mounds enclosed, you will note that some of their finest objects were found here, that evidence of burning were in the embankments (as at Fosters), that calcined human bones were found in the mound, that numerous surface finds led to the belief of the existence of a village site, that the three great connected central mounds were in their estimation too large to be explored, that nearly all the remains were of sacrificial (altar) nature, etc. I have carefully gone over all in Hopewell's work on account. I see the imperative need of a map. Why? Decay on the embankments have greatly changed since Squire & Davis' survey and because the circle and a square are nearly obliterated, and because the gentlemen did not accurately locate any of the mounds, and last but not least, because of the indication of a rich harvest when we shall begin to excavate in earnest. You would be surprised at the magnitude of these works. They cover nearly three miles (in length) of ground. No survey since the days of S. & D. has ever examined them. I am aware that Dr. Thomas spent several days here with Fowke and Middleton, two Government Surveyors; but Fowke himself admits that their stay was too brief for them to gain a comprehensive idea of either the interments or the wonderful earthwork itself. My present force is amply competent and sufficient to carry out excavations properly. But we have no surveyor. I cannot survey sufficiently well myself to locate accurately each feature of the place, nor could any of us make an intelligent map of it. I would therefore most urgently request that when you shall deem it good

time, you send same surveyor (if you cannot get any one else send Mr. Cowen, but I would prefer another one) to make a large map and give the old embankments the examination which they surely both need and deserve. We got provisions cheap. My Mom for the most part works for $5,00 per week and board, some of the men at $1.00 per day and board, and my right-hand man gets $1.50. I shall use every endeavor to keep expenses within the bounds of reason. Please consider this request and let me hear from you at your earliest convenience.

Very sincerely yours,

Warren Moorehead

Send vouchers, envelopes, and monthly statement blanks.

August 5, 1896

Letter from Charles Louis Metz to Frederick Ward Putnam

I am just working day and night to save my home and family. I am trying to earn every dollar that I can and fortunately I have been very much in demand—if collectors were in proportion to the amount that I am obliged to charge—all would be well, but you know there is no money in the West among the people. I am going to fight it out until better times come.

January 27, 1897

Letter from Frederick Ward Putnam to Charles Louis Metz

My Dear Metz:

Here I am for my week in New York. Your letter and the sketch of the Ferris land came alright. I had a copy made of the part of your letter relating to the bequest (the Ferris bequest). I sent all to President Elliott but just too late for the last meeting of the Corporation. He will bring it up at the next meeting and then action will be taken. Now that the museum is part of the university the Corporation will act in all property matters. In the meantime, I know you will have a fatherly eye on the place and keep off all vandals. There is no doubt but that your suggestions will be followed when the Corporation acts in the Spring. I shall probably go out to see the place and I hope to raise money to carry on the exploration. How I shall like to be at work again in Ohio. It is a longtime since I've been there. How about yourself—yes we all lose our chances—I was away when Mrs. Ferris called and you did not let her know your troubles. It is too bad for us both but my dear fellow what you write about you having to go to your creditors. I will order a raise of $200.00 on February 1st. It has made me very unhappy and I have tried to get hold of money that I have let others have in their time of need so as to help you, but nary a cent can I get and I am all our of funds myself at present. I started housekeeping October 1 after seven years of boarding and of course my expenses were pretty big in getting started and are pretty big keeping things up. Then one of my daughters went to Europe and the other in college to keep two young ladies sufficient. I wish I had the cash in hand that I could send it to you but I haven't so I enclose a note for $200.00. If you can get this cashed I should think you could at 6% discount (will not Mr. Clark our old friend do it if no one else). I will look after it when it comes due if you are not able to meet it. From what you want I take it that if you just meet this payment on the first of February you will probably save the house and then before the note is due you can do something or another as by that time things will evidently be better. If you just can't buy, I know what a little help means when one is in distress. I would gladly send you $200.00 in cash if I had it. I hope this note will get you out of your troubles with my blessings.

Always faithfully and sincerely yours,

Your Friend, Fredrick Putnam

P.S. I have added 6% interest to the note so that if you get it discounted at 6% (the present rate in Boston) you will get the full $200.00 on the note.

August 4, 1897

Note from Charles Louis Metz to Frederick Ward Putnam

The ash pits and skeletons take up considerable time—about 28 of the latter have been found. We want to do as much as we can before a possible injunction might be served on us—we want to carry this trench 40 feet wide clear away cross the level to the foot of the bluff.

February 22, 1898
Note from Charles Louis Metz to Frederick Ward Putnam
I am just recovering from an attack of La Grippe, which was so as to confine me to my bed for 8 days. Things are getting better with me soon. I have received the appointment of District Physician, which will pay me $475.00 per annum and also the appointment of Health Officer—the salary to be fixed at the next meeting of the Board. My practice has also increased wonderfully. I will make you a remittance or account now very soon in the coming months.

October 26, 1898
Letter from Charles Louis Metz to Frederick Ward Putnam
I do wish Dear Prof that you would send me a statement of what is still due you and figure the interest to Nov. 1st. About the Ferris lawsuit, which has been going on since the 19th of this month and will probably run for a week or two yet, this daily attendance at Court takes much of my time and a great loss financially to me. Yesterday the depositions taken at Boston were read and the comments made by the Plaintiff's attorneys were not of the pleasantness they might have been. They tried to make me out of a very bad man—Ex-Judge Harmon of our side of the case vindicated me however and our side of the case is still on top. The Plaintiff's witnesses have all been coached as to what they were to say—but under Judge Harmon and Mr. Coffy's cross-examination they fell to pieces. I enclosed newspaper articles about the trial. My little daughter—Ethel is very ill. Mrs. Metz and the rest of the family are well.

November 30, 1898
Letter from Charles Louis Metz to Frederick Ward Putnam
I thought it is proper for me to let you know how I have done in arranging matters in regard to my affairs. I am indebted to the Madison Building and Loan Association in the sum of $10,250 and other individuals in the sum

of $3,140. I am worrying until I lay awake at night and could not sleep. I sold part of my property for $2,750, keeping my horse and barn. My life insurance and taxes total $14,000 and must be paid. As regards my being too often in beer saloons I will say this in defense—I seldom, very seldom drink beer at all—none of our saloons keep good wine—I do not think I would drink any of the whiskey dispersed therein and if the saloon keepers were first put under oath the one in the East End would say the Metz doctor has been in my place twice in six months and then I called him in—another would say I have been in business 4 years and the doctor has been in my place not over 4 times, twice to see my wife professionally and when he came to get the money. Another would say the doctor has been attending my wife and daughter and has been in my place about 12 or 15 times within the last year and a half. Once in a while he would stop at the bar take a cigar, a glass of cider or lemonade. I have not seen him take more than one or two glasses of beer at my place—Dear Prof I do not spend my time in the saloons for I should not find anything congenial there. I might at my own house take a glass of wine. In regard to the will case it has not yet come up but I think in the January term of Court we will hear from it. I think the result will be favorable for us. I do hope dear Prof that you will come out next spring.
Yours faithfully,
C. L. Metz

May 8, 1905
Letter from Charles Louis Metz to Frederick Ward Putnam
On last Friday I visited the Turner Group, which I had not seen for four years. I cannot express the regret and astonishment at the railroad excavations, the Cincinnati and Eastern Railroad. Our old man Britten is dead at an age of 81 years. About the picture, I know it is valuable. Cincinnati has no market for such things. I would take however anything that will cover any debt to you and if possible something over.
Yours faithfully,
C. L. Metz

May 24, 1905

Letter from Charles Louis Metz to Frederick Ward Putnam

At the Turner site the railroad has made great inroads into the tower terrace—about one third of it is removed. Mr. Turner is willing to allow us to excavate the circle if he is paid for the corn. Of the beautiful circle and mound in the Stites Grove it has vanished. It is sad to see these interesting monuments and landmarks disappearing rapidly. Dr. Dabney the new dean of the University of Cincinnati is agitating to create a department of Anthropology but they are so slow and all the while so many interesting sites and places are being lost or destroyed forever. Just a few months ago the site of Cornwall's Station one of the pioneer settlements on the Little Miami River was graded down for a roadway and which passed through the burial place of those hardy pioneers—their bones were torn apart and dumped in a fill in the valley and this work was done by the very descendants of the brave settlers. I have been agitating the propriety of erecting a monument at each one of the early sites, but the people are too slow. Perhaps, in a few years from now when all traces of the early settlements are abolished they will make up. So it is with the mounds and burial places. Every lecturer that has anything to say about the prehistoric mounds of this region is in Eastern Colleges and Universities. They have carried off carloads of objects that rightfully belong to Cincinnati and CC—Yes, it is a fact that you could not raise $100 to carry on an exploration or marl a site of historic interest in or about Cincinnati for the life of you. I do wish you could find time to come here. Perhaps we arrange a lecture.

August 7, 1905

Letter from Charles Louis Metz to Frederick Ward Putnam

Dear Prof:

The following is a list of what I have furnished to camp to date:

1 tent	22.50
2 frying pans	$0.55
¼ doz. knives and forks	$0.25

½ doz. Tin-plates	$0.20
1 small bucket	$0.20
1 hatchet	$0.50
[Other provisions]	———
This amount I have paid out	43.39
Please credit to my account.	

September 25, 1905

Letter from Charles Louis Metz to Frederick Ward Putnam

Mr. Turner is being extremely reasonable. We should do more work at the Ferris site because the men in plowing found many stone graves. Our prehistoric cemetery is being torn up by parties of vandals who are hunting for relics. They should be stopped. Would advise you to place someone in charge of the grounds, or hasten the exploration of the grounds. This place ought to be explored. The crops are now being gathered and now is our chance.

Appendix C

Madisonville History

CHARLES TOOK HIS TURN ENTERTAINING MEMBERS of the Madisonville Literary and Scientific Society. He especially enjoyed talking about the history of Madisonville. Charles kept his lecture notes on handwritten stationary, which are transcribed below.

The History of Madisonville

In most of the states and territories west of Allegheny Mountains the United States owned the soil of the country after obtaining the aboriginal Indian titles and was known as congress lands and were subsequently sold to purchasers by the officers of the general government. These lands were regularly surveyed into townships of six miles square each, under the authority of the national government. The townships were again subdivided into sections of one miles square each containing 640 acres and numbering 36 sections to each township and were numbered in the congressional land beginning at the northeast corner of the township from one to six extending westward and the next from 7 to 12 from west.

Section No. 16 of every township was reserved for the use of schools and leased or subsequently sold for the benefit of schools and Sections No. 29 was appropriated for the support of religious or ministerial institutions. An act of the national Congress was passed on April 18th, 1802 authorizing the calling of a convention to form a state constitution. This convention assembled at Chillicothe on November 1, 1802, and on November 29th of that year the Constitution of state government was ratified and signed by members of the Convention. By this act of the convention Ohio became one of the states of the Federal Union. The act of Congress providing for the admission of the new state into the Union also offered certain propositions to the people. The most important was that Section No. 16 of each township, or where that section had been disposed of, other contiguous and equivalent land should be granted to the inhabitants for the use of schools. The ordinance of 1785 had already provided for the appropriation of Section 16 to the support of the schools in every township sold by the United States; and this appropriation thus became a condition on the sale and settlement of the western country. The Convention of Chillicothe, November 1802, determined to accept a proposition of Congress and thus began the public school system in Ohio.

The platting of the town of Madisonville

On the 27th day of January 1809 by an act of the state legislature authorizing a survey and platting of all Sections No. 16 and also appointing a commission consisting of three trustees to dispose of the land by lease or sale was passed. In pursuance of this act John Hones, Felix Grossman and William Armstrong were appointed for Section 16 of Columbia Township with Moses Morris as Clerk and Ezekial Lanard, Joseph Reeder and Joseph Clark were appointed to fix the value of the land.

The trustees lost no time in proceeding to act and decided to lie out a town site in the north part of the section. Abraham Stepps made a survey and plat in March of 1809 with Oliver Jones and William Darling. The town was named Madisonville in honor of James Madison who had just been inaugurated the President of the United States. Soon after the platting of the town the following notice was posted:

> NOTICE
> The condition on which lots will be let or
> leased are as follows. Lot No. 1 of the
> first block of lots will be first offered and
> so on in rotation at the appraisements, and
> the highest bidder shall be the lessee. Six
> percent on what they bid will be the sum they
> pay annually, paying the first payment on the
> first day of April next. There will be

required of the lessee a bond and security
for the building of a house at least 18 feet
by 20 feet of good hewed logs, frame, stone,
or brick at least one and a half stories high
with a stone or brick chimney, and a good
shingle roof within two years from the date
of this lease; any person bidding off two
lots will be excused by building one house of
the above description, the four corner lots
accepted, any person not complying with the
terms of the Articles of Sale shall forfeit
and pay to the trustees the sum of $5.00, the
lessees will pay in proportion the expenses
of laying out and blazing.
Moses Morrison, Clerk
By order of the Trustees April 24, 1809 N.B. The Trustees will meet
at the house of Willis Pierson on the first day of May next in order
to execute leases.

A settlement of squatters who had already gathered in and about the proposed town site lost no time in proceeding to act thereon, the same day of the date of the above notice April 24, 1809, entries of leases were made as follows:

Block No. 1, Lot 1, William Coppes $10.00.
Block No. 1, Lot 2, William Armstrong $21.00
Block No. 1, Lot 3, John Armstrong $31.00
Block No. 1, Lot 3, Thomas Skinner $20.00
Block No. 1, Lot 5, Thomas Skinner $18.00

On these lots, minimum values had been fixed by the values as follows:

Lots No. 1, $10.00
Lots Nos. 2 & 3, $5.00
Lots Nos. 4 & 5, $3.50

Lot No. 1 was forfeited and was leased on the 13th day of October 1810 as follows "We or either of us promise and agree with the Trustees for section No. 16 that we will build a house of at least 10 x 18 feet one and a half stories high with a good shingle roof brick or stone chimney on

Lot No. 1, first block of lots in the town of Madisonville within two years under penalty of $100.00 given under our hands and seals this 13th day of October, Moses Richards and William Richards."

The expense of a first sale and to May 1, 1809 was $14.70 and the amount of interest on the sale of lots for the first year was $15.34. The accruing rents from sale by lease of the property in Section 16 were to be applied to school purposes. The leases were drawn for a period of ten years, renewable for 99 years. The last of these leases was canceled and surrendered to the state and deeds exchanged in the year 1871. The usual form of a lease was as follows:

> Known all men by these presents that Phillip
> Richfield and Clement Dowden of Hamilton
> County, State of Ohio are held and jointly
> and firmly bound unto John James, James
> Baxter and William Armstrong of the County
> and state aforesaid or their successors in
> office as trustees for Section No. 16.

Pioneers

Among the names of some of the first pioneers settlers of Madisonville in the year 1809 and 1810 are many of the ancestors of prominent families of this day. They are the following:

> 1809—William Morrison, Moses Morrison, John Jones,
> Felix Grossman, Meyer Ward, Samuel McKee, Wilbur Harris, Samuel Muchmore, William Armstrong, Peter Fleak, Henry Starsel.
> 1810—Joseph Ross, Jeramia McKee, Thomas Thomas,
> Phillip Crichfield, William Harvey, Clermont Dawden, John Whitcomb, John Whitcomb, Jr.
> 1815—William H. Moore.

First built houses

Some of the first built houses are still standing. The Maple family has owned one on Lot No. 1 in the Seventh Square and first block built in the year 1810 for many years. It is located on the west side of what is now called Whetsel and north of Grimes Drug store. Another building still standing is a log building that was built in the year 1812 by Patrick McCullum who had built the first one of frame on a stone foundation, on this lot and which was the wonder of the community and the pride of the owner;

this was in 1810. The great earthquake of the year 1811 so rocked the stone foundation as to cause a collapse the building while those constructed of logs remained in tact. Poddy, as he was familiarly called, was so ridiculed that he immediately rebuilt on the same lot of Queen logs and this house occupying the rear of the lot is yet a comfortable home to this day. In this log house the first method of society assembled and services were presided over by the late James Langdon or Jimmie Langdon as he is best known who came over Lemrick for that purpose.

Brick buildings

In the early days of the village and township it was customary to dispose of the indigent or paupers at auction. It was also incumbent on the constable to notify strangers to depart from the township who were in indigent circumstances. The authorities would not be responsible for the support of strangers. The following is a copy of one of these notifications.

> Madisonville, June 14, 1811 to John Jones
> Constable. You are to order and warn J.W. and his family to at once depart from the tow
> and township and you are to comply with this order with no delay.
> Joseph Reeder. Wyley Pearson.
> Overseers Of The Poor.

The young and abled bodied poor people under age were bound out to farmers and others requiring help. The older people were sold outright at auction to the lowest bidder for a term to anyone who was charitably inclined to care for them. School kids were as low as $1.00 a week. The following is a true copy of an original indenture in my possession.

> This indenture made this third day of May in the year of our Lord one thousand eight hundred and nineteen witnessed that Wilson Griffin and Andrew Harrell overseers of the poor for the township of Columbia, Hamilton County, State of Ohio by and with consent of John Jones, a Justice of the Peace of said county and township having put and placed by these presents do put and place Mary Bowers, a poor girl of said township aged 15 years, and five days, apprentice to William Gerrard with him to dwell from the day of the date of

these presents and until the said apprentice shall arrive at the age of 18 years according provided during all of which term the said apprentice her said master faithfully shall serve on all lawful business according to her wit and ability and shall honestly, orderly and obediently in all things demean and behave herself towards her said master and all his during the said term.

The poor were sold for a term of one year always to the lowest bidder. The following is a copy of a report of such sale.

To the Commissioners for the County of Hamilton. The overseers of the poor of Columbia Township certified that on the fourth day of May 1811 sold Thomas McCormick one of the poor of Columbia Township for one year for $51.09 George Galsby being the lowest bidder. Likewise, on the 16th of May we sold Sarah Fiers one of the poor for $59.00 until first Monday and May next. The lowest bidder being price sold by us. Joseph Reeder and Pearson, overseers of the poor. In the next year Thomas McCormick was again sold for $52.00 to Robert Fleck.

Distinguished men

Madisonville was the home of several men who became distinguished. Among them was Dr. Alexander Duncan who was a member of the state legislature for several terms and a member of the national Congress two terms. He acquired great notoriety by making his famous "Coon speech" in Congress and subsequently greatly disappointed his Democratic friends by becoming a free "soiler." He finally settled down on his farm southwest of the village on the Red Bank Road conducting a gristmill. The old Duncan house is still standing on the bank of the Duck Creek. The doctor had two children a son and a daughter. Dr. Duncan also owned a beautiful home and grounds at the west of the village. The grounds were beautifully laid out. There was a springhouse and a reservoir containing numerous goldfish. Of this once beautiful place is now covered by our Ice Plant and other buildings. A few years later Dr. Duncan met his untimely death. He had been out with his team of horses and wagon hauling rails and posts for fencing. He failed to return in the evening but that caused no uneasiness as he often worked until dusk. After dark however, search was made and all during the night. At dawn the team was found standing in the Duck Creek. The body of the doctor was lying in the water. The driving line was wound around his shoulders and neck. It was evident that the team had wandered up and down the creek dragging the body of the doctor behind them.

James Whitcomb

James Whitcomb was a distinguished citizen of Madisonville. He later removed to the state of Indiana and became a Governor of Indiana. Later he became a United States Senator from that state. In his youth while he had great love and devotion to piscatorial pursuits. This love was so strong as to render him oblivious to the conditions of his clothing. He was often subjected to ridicule and laughter of many of our other citizens. James made money enough to buy books, attend school. This he did in between there was some report about him in the United States Senate. "Oh yes" they said "the fellow who would climb out of Duck Creek with mud from his nose to his feet."

Imprisonment from debts

Imprisonment for debt is also a painful reminder of the early days of Madisonville. A document before me dated 22 days of April 1817 is as follows:

> John Jones constable is notified to collect a judgment of $2.74 together with costs and to levy on the goods and chattels of the defendants but for want of such property the latter defendants man and wife shall be conveyed to the jail of the county and attained until the said debts and costs that may accrue be paid or otherwise legally discharged. Attested William McEllwain. Judgement was rendered against the defendant in the amount for which the suit was brought 70 and ¾ cents the costs and all amounted to $2.00.

Town amusements

Election days and Saturday afternoon were considered generally as holidays. Each community or town had what they called "their best man" or champion fighter. Madisonville had the distinction of Larry. Bare fist fighting was a frequent occurrence. Two or three of his friends accompanied the challengers. The challenger would go up to the man he wanted to meet and would tell his something like "John they tell me you are a pretty good man. I am a good man in our town, and I have come to whoop you or be whooped. Just to see who is the best man of us to." Then they would go at each other hammer and tong until one or the other was defeated. The vanquished one would pay for a pint of whiskey, which the parties would drink. They would shake hands and depart seemingly the best of friends. I witnessed the last bouts of this character 52 years ago. The first was believed to be between B. K. champion of Mount Carmel and J. W. who was at work in a shop engaged in showing a horse. B. K. went up and said to J. W., "I come to whoop you for they tell me you are a better man than I, and I want you to prove it." J. W. told his to wait until he got the horse shod and "will settle that when I get through". He then laid aside his leather togs. B. K. required the stipulation that the defeated man must crawl between a double row of chains and barrels to the bar, in addition to paying for the drinks. This was acceded by J. W., J. W. however, was the victor. The last bout of its kind was between a man by the name of Kellogg from the town of Columbia and Mr. S. The men fought up and down the street on what is now Whetsel Avenue from Madisonville Road to Seina Street to and fro for over an hour with the victory going to the Madisonville champion.

Horse racing was another favorite diversion. The course extended from Prentice Street north to the foot of the Indian Hill on Whetsel Avenue. Wrestling was a common feature also. In addition jumping, hop, step and jumping, shooting with rifles at targets, and another great day was the military training day when every able bodied citizen between the ages of 12 and 50 years was required to drill in the military tactics. The men and boys would march up and down Madisonville Road with rifles on their shoulders until they got thirsty and then they would retire to a shady place to resolve their thirst.

Madisonville's early industries

Madisonville in the earlier days was a thriving business center and the voting place for the entire township of Columbia. From the years 1818 to

1845 the town contained several manufacturing enterprises, which were of considerable magnitude for the times. Among these was the Mann factory, which made wooden bowls. Horsepower operated the machinery of this factory. There was also a pottery plant, which produced crude crockery and earthenware that was used by the early settlers. There was a mill where homespun clothes were made. This was located where Dr. Davis's drug store is now located.

A large cooperage shop was located in Madisonville where barrels were made for the several distillery plants and gristmills in the vicinity. This cooperage occupied a large lot. The southeast corner of what is now Madisonville Road and Whetsel was where the gristmill was erected in 1823. Another gristmill was built in 1825 east of the town in what was then called "Dutch Hollows." This mill stood just north of the Gano residence on the now Camargo Road. The power was derived by an overshoot wheel supplied by the water that was conducted from the creek nearby. There was also a hat shop where the present Odd Fellows building is located. There were also in Madisonville a number of stores and several cabinet-makers, one of which was owned by Adam Maffet who employed several men. There were two wagon shops where wagons were made.

Tavern

The first tavern or "house of entertainment for man and beast" was built of logs and had a veranda along its entire front. Its site was on the lots just west of Dr. Ames Drug Store. Another tavern was on the corner opposite on the east side. The brick building on the east side of Deerfield Road now Whetsel was added to and extended to a frontage on what is now Madisonville Road. It was owned and managed by the late Mr. Timothy Maffet. The old signpost of this tavern was in the recent possession of the lately deceased Mr. Timothy Maffet. In later times this old tavern was occupied by a grocery business for many years.

Summary

In 1811 the town of Madisonville contained 20 houses. In 1841, there were 100 houses and a population numbering 400. Madison Road began as a turnpike leading to Cincinnati begun in 1836 and completed in 1840. However the road had been opened in 1830 from the completion of the turnpike. In 1865 the Marietta and Cincinnati railroad was completed. Heretofore the progress of the village was slow. An old story told in Madisonville to especially young audience was called a snake story.

Snake story

One summer evening Mr. H was sitting on the veranda of the corner tavern. Several of us boys driving several cows from the pasture, as was the custom in those days to our village homes were passing the tavern. We dragged with us a large black snake, which we had found and killed. On seeing it Mr. H said "Boys that is a fierce size snake. But if you will hurry home with the cows and come back here I will tell you of a snake I once killed." The boys soon returned and gathered around H. and the following tale was told to us.

> Sometime ago I found that my tan pits or vats in the tan yard were often broken into and hides taken from them. This usually was done during the night time. Myself and hired help kept watch on the pits at night but it was in vain. The pits were found broken open each morning and some hides missing. The mystery was unsolved until one morning after a heavy fall of snow I went to the pits and as usual we found one pit with an opening freshly made and form this hole in the pit a broad trace leading across the ridge following this trail it continued on to the top and across a piece of bottom land ending in a large opening in the roots of a large Sycamore tree growing on the bank of the stream west of the town. Calling some of my men to bring picks and shovels we followed the opening which had a tunnel which went down for 40 feet into the ground. At the end of the 40 foot tunnel there was a good size den in which we found curled up a snake of a very large size. After we killed it, and boys I tell you it was a tough fight, we dragged it out and laid it along the ground and it measured 32 feet in length and was four feet wide at the biggest part of its body. On cutting open the body boys what do you think we found? Well you cannot guess so I will tell you. We found 17 of my stolen hides in its belly. Good night boys I am going to roost.

The bee story

Boys, when I was keeping the tavern there was a heavy snowstorm one night. I was aroused from a deep sleep by a strange buzzing and humming sounds. It being a cold night I had a large gown over my underclothes. I went out to see and learn what was causing such awful and weird noises. I was astonished to find it was caused by a large swarm of bees and as I stepped from the door the Queen Bee settled on my nose and in a few moments the entire swarm had followed the queen and covered my nose and head. I turned up my outer gown over the bees and went into the house. My wife who had learned of the cause of the noise and seeing me with the bees came to my aid bringing an empty hive in which we hived the bees. During the following summer we took 67 pounds of the finest and sweetest honey from the hive that you may have tasted or laid your eyes on. And that boy's is how you go about getting honey the easy way.

Notes

Preface

1. Gordon R. Willey and Jeremy A. Sabloff, *A History of American Archaeology*, 3rd ed. (New York: Freeman and Co., 1993). D. H. Hymes, "On Studying the History of Anthropology," *Kroeber Anthropological Society Papers* 26 (1962): 81–86.
2. Hymes, "On Studying the History of Anthropology"; C. William Clewlow, Jr., "Some Thoughts on the Background of Early Man, Hrdlicka, and Folsom," *Kroeber Anthropological Society Papers* 42 (1970): 26–46.
3. Hymes, "On Studying the History of Anthropology"; Clewlow, "Some Thoughts on the Background of Early Man, Hrdlicka, and Folsom,"
4. *Annual Report of The Cincinnati Historical Society*, January 1969–June 1970, Robert M. Galbraith, president.

Introduction

No Endnotes.

Chapter 1
The Early Life and Times of Charles Louis Metz

1. H. Glenn Penny, "The German Love Affair with American Indians," *Common Place* 11, no. 4 (2011).

2. Charles Metz, Charles Louis Metz Papers, 1969, Cincinnati Museum Center, Cincinnati, Ohio.
3. Ibid.
4. Ibid.
5. Kate A. Berry and Melissa A. Rinehart, "A Legacy of Forced Migration: The Removal of the Miami Tribe in 1846," *International Journal of Population Geography* 9 (2003), 104.
6. John Forster, *The Life of Charles Dickens: Third Book*, 1872–1874; Charles Dickens, Maeline House, Graham Storey, Kathleen Tillotson, and Nina Burgis, *Letters of Charles Dickens, Pilgrim Edition* (Oxford, Ohio: Clarendon, 1988).
7. Stewart Rafert, *The Miami Indians of Indiana: A Persistent People, 1654–1994* (Indianapolis: Indiana Historical Society Press, 1996).
8. Metz, Charles Louis Metz Papers.
9. *Lafayette* (IN) *Courier*, December 8, 1848.
10. Metz, Charles Louis Metz Papers.
11. Ibid.
12. Ibid.
13. Ibid.
14. Ibid.
15. Ibid.
16. Ibid.
17. Murray Morgan, *Puget's Sound: A Narrative of Early Tacoma and the Southern Sound* (Seattle: University of Washington Press. 1979).
18. Metz, Charles Louis Metz Papers.
19. Ibid.; Claire E. Nolte, "The German Turnverein," *Encyclopedia of 1848 Revolutions* (2011); Henry Metzner and Theodore Stempfel, Jr., *A Brief History of the American Turnerbund* (Pittsburgh, Pa.: National Executive Committee of the American Turnerbund, 1924).
20. Metz, Charles Louis Metz Papers; Lester V. Horwitz, *The Longest Raid of the Civil War* (Cincinnati: Farmcourt Publishing Inc., 2001).
21. Horwitz, *Longest Raid*.; Gary Hicks, "The Invalid Corps," in *History of Camp Dennison, Ohio: Third Edition* by Mary Rahn Sloan. (n.p.: Queen City Printing, 2003).
22. Hicks, "Invalid Corps"; National Park Service, Soldiers and Sailors Database (http://www.nps.gov/civilwar/soldiers-and-sailors-database.htm).
23. Hicks, "Invalid Corps"; Constantin Grebner, *We Were The Ninth: A History of the Ninth Regiment, Ohio Volunteer Infantry, April 17, 1861, to June 7, 1864* (Kent, Ohio: Kent State University Press. 1987).

24. Metz, Charles Louis Metz Papers; National Park Service, Soldiers and Sailors Database; Grebner, *We Were the Ninth*; Jacob Dolson Cox, *Military Reminiscences of the Civil War V1*, (n.p., 2007).
25. Hicks, "Invalid Corps."
26. Ibid.; Judith Metz, "The Sisters of Charity in Cincinnati: 1829–1852," *Vincentian Heritage Journal* 17 no. 3, art. 4, (1996).
27. Hicks, "Invalid Corps"; Metz, "The Sisters of Charity in Cincinnati."
28. Metz, Charles Louis Metz Papers; Anita J. Ellis, Susan L. Meyn, George P. Horse Capture, *Rookwood and the American Indian: Masterpieces of American Art Pottery from the James J. Gardner Collection* (Cincinnati: Cincinnati Art Museum; Athens, Ohio: Ohio University Press, cop. 2007).
29. Horwitz, *Longest Raid*; Hicks, "Invalid Corps"; "Morgan's Great Raid: His Movements in Ohio, Camp Dennison, Near Cincinnati, Threatened," *New York Times*, July 15, 1963.
30. Horwitz, *Longest Raid*; Hicks, "Invalid Corps"; "Morgan's Great Raid," *New York Times*, July 15, 1963.
31. Horwitz, *Longest Raid*; Hicks, "Invalid Corps"; "Morgan's Great Raid," *New York Times*, July 15, 1963.
32. Horwitz, *Longest Raid*; Hicks, "Invalid Corps"; "Morgan's Great Raid," *New York Times*, July 15, 1963.
33. Horwitz, *Longest Raid*; Hicks, "Invalid Corps"; "Morgan's Great Raid," *New York Times*, July 15, 1963.
34. Metz, Charles Louis Metz Papers; Horwitz, *Longest Raid*; Hicks, "Invalid Corps"; "Morgan's Great Raid," *New York Times*, July 15, 1963.
35. "Morgan's Great Raid," *New York Times*, July 15, 1963.
36. Metz, Charles Louis Metz Papers; John Carroll Power. "Abraham Lincoln: His Great Funeral Corte?ge, from Washington City to Springfield, Illinois with a History and Description of the National Lincoln Monument," *Report of Messrs. Brough and Garrett to Secretary Stanton*, April 18, 1865.
37. Power, "Abraham Lincoln."
38. Metz, Charles Louis Metz Papers.
39. Ibid.
40. Ibid.
41. Ibid.
42. Ibid.
43. Ibid.
44. Ibid.
45. Ibid.

46. Ibid.
47. Willey and Sabloff, *History of American Archaeology*.
48. Robert Silverberg, *Mound Builders of Ancient America: The Archaeology of a Myth* (Greenwich, Conn.: New York Graphic Society, 1968).; Albert E. Castel, *The Presidency of Andrew Johnson* (Lawrence: The Regents Press of Kansas, 1979).
49. Castel, *Presidency of Andrew Johnson*.
50. Metz, Charles Louis Metz Papers.
51. Henri D. Grissino-Mayer, "An Introduction to Dendrochronology in the Southeastern United States," *Tree Ring Research* 65, no. 1, (2009).
52. Metz, Charles Louis Metz Papers.
53. Ibid.

Chapter 2: The Literary and Scientific Society of Madisonville

1. Metz, Charles Louis Metz Papers.
2. G. Terrence McConville and Fred L. Rutherford, *Pioneers of the Lower Little Miami River*, (Mariemont, Ohio: Mariemont Preservation Foundation, 2005).
3. Ibid.
4. "Will Attacked—Phebe Ferris Estate in Litigation," *Cincinnati* (OH) *Post*, October 18, 1898.
5. McConville and Rutherford, *Pioneers*.
6. Metz, Charles Louis Metz Papers; "Will Attacked," *Cincinnati Post*.
7. Metz, Charles Louis Metz Papers.
8. Cincinnati Art Museum, *Art of the First Americans: From the Collection of the Cincinnati Art Museum* (Cincinnati: The Museum, 1976); Ellis, et al., *Rookwood and the American Indian*.
9. Metz, Charles Louis Metz Papers.
10. Ellis, et al., *Rookwood and the American Indian*.
11. Papers of Carlos Montezuma, Newberry Library, Chicago, Illinois.
12. Metz, Charles Louis Metz Papers.
13. Ibid.
14. Cincinnati Art Museum, *Art of the First Americans*.
15. Ellis, et al., *Rookwood and the American Indian*.
16. Elisabeth Tooker, "Lewis Henry Morgan: The Myth and the Man," *University of Rochester Library Bulletin* 37 (1984).
17. Tooker, "Lewis Henry Morgan"; Edward G. Longacre, *General Ulysses S. Grant: The Soldier and The Man*, (Cambridge: Da Capo Press, 2006).

18. Metz, Charles Louis Metz Papers.

19. Ibid.

20. "Great Depression of 1873–1896" in David Glasner and Thomas F. Cooley, *Business Cycles and Depressions: An Encyclopedia* (New York: Garland Publishing, 1997), 148–49.

21. Metz, Charles Louis Metz Papers.

22. Ibid.

23. Ibid.

24. Ibid.

25. Proceedings of the Society, *The Journal of the Cincinnati Society of Natural History* 1, no. 3 (1978): 109–110.

26. Ibid.

27. Ibid.

28. E. G. Squier and E. H. Davis, *Ancient Monuments of the Mississippi Valley: Comprising the Results of Extensive Original Surveys and Explorations* (Washington: Smithsonian Institution, 1848).

29. Metz, Charles Louis Metz Papers.

30. Tooker, "Lewis Henry Morgan."

31. Ibid.

32. Metz, Charles Louis Metz Papers.

33. Ibid.

34. Longacre, *General Ulysses S. Grant*.

35. Tooker, "Lewis Henry Morgan."

36. Tooker, "Lewis Henry Morgan"; Longacre, *General Ulysses S. Grant*.

37. Longacre, *General Ulysses S. Grant*.

38. Ibid.

39. E. A. Hooton, E. A. and C. C. Willoughby, "Indian Village Site and Cemetery near Madisonville, Ohio," *Papers of the Peabody Museum of American Archaeology and Ethnology*, 8, no. 1 (Cambridge: Harvard University, 1920); S. Frederick Starr, "The Archaeology of Hamilton County, Ohio," *Journal of the Cincinnati Museum of Natural History* 23, no. 1 (1960).

40. Metz, Charles Louis Metz Papers.

Chapter 3: Frederick Ward Putnam and the Peabody Museum

1. Willey and Sabloff, *History of American Archaeology*; Metz, Charles Louis Metz Papers.

2. David Rains Wallace, *The Bonehunters' Revenge: Dinosaurs, Greed, and the Greatest Scientific Feud of the Gilded Age* (Houghton Mifflin Books, 1999).
3. Ibid.
4. Ralph W. Dexter, "Contributions of Frederic Ward Putnam to Ohio Archaeology," *The Ohio Journal of Science* 65, no 3 (1965): 110–17.
5. Ibid.
6. Ibid.
7. Ibid.
8. Ibid.
9. Ibid.
10. Willey and Sabloff, *History of American Archaeology.*
11. Alfred M. Tozzier, Biographical Memoir of Frederick Ward Putnam 1839–1915, *Biographical Memoirs, National Academy of Sciences (U.S.) Biographical Memoirs, 4th Memoir.* Presented to the Academy at the Annual Meeting, 1933, vol. 16 (Washington: The National Academy of Sciences, 1935).
12. Willey and Sabloff, *History of American Archaeology.*
13. Metz, Charles Louis Metz Papers.
14. Hooton and Willoughby, "Indian Village Site and Cemetery."
15. Christopher S. Peebles, "Moundville and Surrounding Sites: Some Structural Considerations of Mortuary Practices II," in *Approaches to the Social Dimensions of Mortuary Practices,* James A. Brown, ed. Memoirs of the Society for American Archaeology, no. 25 (1971): 68–91.
16. Metz, Charles Louis Metz Papers.
17. *New York Times*, 21 Feb 1883.
18. Wayne Orchiston, "C/1881 K1: A Forgotten 'Great Comet' of the Nineteenth Century," *Irish Astronomical Journal* 26 no. 1 (January 1999): 33.
19. Penelope B. Drooker, "The View from Madisonville: Protohistoric Western Fort Ancient Interaction Patterns," *Memoirs of the Museum of Anthropology, University of Michigan,* no. 31 (1997).
20. Metz, Charles Louis Metz Papers.
21. Hooton and Willoughby, "Indian Village Site and Cemetery"; Drooker, "The View From Madisonville."
22. K. B. Tankersley, "Archaeological Geology of the Turner Site Complex, Hamilton County, Ohio," *North American Archaeologist* 28 (2007): 271–94.
23. Ibid.
24. Ibid.
25. Orchiston, "Great Comet."

26. Tankersley, "Archaeological Geology of the Turner Site Complex."
27. Ibid.
28. Ibid.
29. Ibid.
30. C. C. Willoughby and Earnest A. Hooton, "The Turner Group of Earthworks Hamilton County Ohio," Papers of the Peabody Museum of American Archaeology and Ethnology, Harvard University 8, no. 3 (1922).
31. Metz, Charles Louis Metz Papers.

Chapter 4: The Cost of Archaeology

1. Metz, Charles Louis Metz Papers.
2. Ellis, et al., *Rookwood and the American Indian*.
3. Ibid.
4. Ibid.
5. Metz, Charles Louis Metz Papers.
6. "The Great Floods," *Harpers Weekly, Journal of Civilization*, New York, Saturday, February 23, 1884.
7. Rendigs Fels, "The American Business Cycle of 1879–85," *Journal of Political Economy* 60 no 1 (1952) :60–75.
8. W. Laird Kleine, "Anatomy of a Riot," *Bulletin of the Historical and Philosophical Society of Ohio* 20 no. 4 (1962) :234–44.
9. Ibid.
10. Willey and Sabloff, *History of American Archaeology*.
11. Kleine, "Anatomy of a Riot."

Chapter 5: AAAS and Beyond

1. Metz, Charles Louis Metz Papers.
2. Donald Worster, *A River Running West: The Life of John Wesley Powell* (New York: Oxford University Press, 2001); Frederick Ward Putnam, ed., *Proceedings of the American Association for the Advancement of Science 33rd Meeting held at Philadelphia, Penn.* (Salem, Mass.: Printed by Salem Press, 1885).
3. Putnam, *Proceedings of the American Association for the Advancement of Science*; A. Edward Evenson, *The Telephone Patent Conspiracy of 1876: The Elisha Gray—Alexander Bell Controversy and its many players* (Jefferson, N.C.: McFarland, 2000).
4. Carl Schurz, *The Reminiscences of Carl Schurz* (three volumes), New York, 2001.
5. Ibid.

6. Stephen D. Bodayla, "Can An Indian Vote?: Elk v Wilkins, A Setback for Indian Citizenship," *Nebraska History* 67 (1986): 372–80.
7. Stephen Dando-Collins, *Standing Bear Is A Person* (New York: Da Capo Press, 2005).
8. Bodayla, "Can An Indian Vote?"
9. Ibid.
10. Ibid.
11. Schurz, *The Reminiscences of Carl Schurz*.
12. William K. Beatty, "When Cholera Scourged Chicago," *Chicago History* 11 (Spring 1982).
13. *Annual Report of the Trustees of the Peabody Museum: Peabody Museum of American Archaeology and Ethnology* (1884).
14. Ibid.
15. Ibid.
16. Ibid.
17. Ibid.
18. Ibid.
19. Ibid.
20. Ibid.
21. Ibid.
22. Ibid.
23. Ibid.
24. Ibid.
25. Ibid.
26. *Railway World* 34, (December 12, 1890).
27. "Obituary," *New York Times*, October 4, 1903.
28. Register to the Papers of Alice Cunningham Fletcher and Francis La Flesche, National Anthropological Archives, Smithsonian Institution.
29. *The Daily* (Fort Wayne, Ind.) *Gazette*, (May 22, 1885).

Chapter 6: Turning Back the Hands of Time

1. Charles M. Oehler and Cincinnati Museum of Natural History, *Turpin Indians: A Revised Report of the Findings of the Cincinnati Museum of Natural History's Archaeological Exploration of the Turpin Site, Hamilton County, Ohio, 1946 to 1949* (Cincinnati: Cincinnati Museum of Natural History, 1973).
2. Metz, Charles Louis Metz Papers.

3. K. B. Tankersley, *In Search of Ice Age Americans* (Salt Lake City: Gibbs Smith Publishers, 2002).
4. Ibid.
5. K. B. Tankersley, "The Mariemont Earthwork: A Fort Ancient Serpentine Hydraulic Structure," *North American Archaeologist* 29 (2008): 123–43.
6. Ibid.
7. Ibid.
8. *Annual Report of the Trustees of the Peabody Museum: Peabody Museum of American Archaeology and Ethnology* 3 (1887): 14–20.
9. Dr. Callaghan, "Account of the Epidemic Scarlatina Anginosa," *Boston Medical Surgeons Journal* 4 (1831).

Chapter 7: Revisiting the Turner Site

1. Charles L. Metz and Frederick Ward Putnam, *Explorations in Ohio: Conducted for the Peabody Museum of American Archaeology and Ethnology, In Connection with Harvard University Volume 1, The Marriott Mound, No. 1. The Eighteenth Report of the Peabody Museum, 1884* (Cambridge, John Wilson and Son, University Press, 1886).
2. Ibid.
3. Metz, Charles Louis Metz Papers.
4. Metz and Putnam, *Explorations in Ohio*.
5. Frederick Ward Putnam, "On Methods of Archaeological Research in America," *Johns Hopkins University Circular* 5, no. 49 (1886).
6. Ibid.
7. Ibid.
8. Ibid.
9. Ibid.
10. Ibid.
11. Harry Barnard, *Rutherford Hayes and his America* (Newtown, Conn.: American Political Biography Press, 2005).
12. George Frederick Wright, *Representative Citizens of Ohio: Memorial-Biographical*, (Cleveland, Ohio: The Memorial Pub. Co., 1918).
13. Ibid.
14. Tankersley, "Archaeological Geology of the Turner Site Complex."
15. Ibid.
16. Nancy Ann Sahli, *Elizabeth Blackwell, M.D., (1871–1910): A Biography* (New York: Arno Press, 1982).

17. Henry Howe, *Historical Collections of Ohio, Volumes 1 and 2* (Cincinnati, Ohio: C.J. Krehbiel & Co., 1888).
18. S. M. Barrett, *Geronimo, His Own Story* (New York: Ballantine Books, 1971).
19. Willoughby and Hooton, *The Turner Group of Earthworks.*
20. Ibid.
21. *Twentieth Annual Report of the Trustees of the Peabody Museum of American Archaeology and Ethnology* 3, (1887).
22. Ibid.
23. Tankersley, "Archaeological Geology of the Turner Site Complex."
24. Ibid.
25. *Twentieth Annual Report of the Trustees of the Peabody Museum of American Archaeology and Ethnology* 3, (1887).
26. Barrett, *Geronimo*
27. Willey and Sabloff, *History of American Archaeology.*
28. Ibid.
29. Frederick Wright, *Man and the Glacial Period* (Akron, Ohio: Werner Company, 1892).
30. Stanley Appelbaum, *The Chicago World's Fair of 1893* (New York: Dover Publications, Inc., 1980).

Chapter 8: The World's Columbian Exposition

1. Metz, Charles Louis Metz Papers.
2. Ibid.
3. Ibid.
4. Ibid.
5. Reid Badger, *The Great American Fair: The World's Columbian Exposition and American Culture* (Chicago: N. Hall, 1979).
6. Ibid.
7. Ibid.
8. Neil Harris, Wim de Wit, James Gilbert and Robert Rydell, *Grand Illusions: Chicago's World's Fair of 1893* ([Chicago]: Chicago Historical Society, 1993)
9. Ibid.
10. Ibid.
11. Charles W. Allen, *From Fort Laramie to Wounded Knee: In the West That Was* (Lincoln: University of Nebraska Press, 2001).

12. Allen, *From Fort Laramie to Wounded Knee;* Karen A. Bearor, "The *Illustrated American* and the Lakota Ghost Dance," *American Periodicals: A Journal of History and Criticism, and Bibliography* 21 no. 2 (2011).
13. Allen, *From Fort Laramie to Wounded Knee;* Bearor, "The *Illustrated American.*"
14. Bearor, "The *Illustrated American*"; Ellis, et al., *Rookwood and the American Indian.*
15. Bearor, "The *Illustrated American*"; Ellis, et al., *Rookwood and the American Indian.*
16. Bearor, "The *Illustrated American*"; Ellis, et al., *Rookwood and the American Indian.*
17. Norm Bolotin and Christine Laing, *The World's Columbian Exposition: the Chicago World's Fair of 1893* (Urbana: University of Illinois Press, 2002).
18. Bearor, "The *Illustrated American.*"
19. Ibid.
20. Ibid.
21. Ibid.
22. Ibid.
23. Bearor, "The *Illustrated American*"; Bolotin and Laing, *The World's Columbian Exposition.*
24. Ellis, et al., *Rookwood and the American Indian.*
25. Metz, Charles Louis Metz Papers.
26. Ellis, et al., *Rookwood and the American Indian.*
27. Ibid.
28. Metz, Charles Louis Metz Papers.
29. Metz, Charles Louis Metz Papers; Badger, *The Great American Fair;* Harris, et al., *Grand Illusions.*
30. Ellis, et al., *Rookwood and the American Indian.*
31. Ibid.
32. Badger, *The Great American Fair;* Harris, et al., *Grand Illusions.*
33. Badger, *The Great American Fair;* Harris, et al., *Grand Illusions.*
34. Metz, Charles Louis Metz Papers.
35. Bolotin and Laing, *The World's Columbian Exposition.*
36. Ibid.
37. Ibid.
38. Ibid.
39. Ibid.
40. Ibid.
41. Ellis, et al., *Rookwood and the American Indian.*

42. Ellis, et al., *Rookwood and the American Indian*; Bolotin and Laing, *The World's Columbian Exposition*.

43. Ellis, et al., *Rookwood and the American Indian*.

44. Ellis, et al., *Rookwood and the American Indian*; Melissa Rinehart, "To Hell with the Wigs! Native American Representation and Resistance at the World's Columbian Exposition," *American Indian Quarterly*, 36, no. 4 (2012): 403–42.

45. Ellis, et al., *Rookwood and the American Indian*; Bolotin and Laing, *The World's Columbian Exposition*; Rinehart, "To Hell with the Exposition."

46. Ellis, et al., *Rookwood and the American Indian*; Bolotin and Laing, *The World's Columbian Exposition*; Rinehart, "To Hell with the Exposition"; K. B. Tankersley and Robert Pickering, *Sitting Bull's Pipe: Separating Myth from History; Rediscovering the Man, Correcting the Myth* (Braunschweig, Germany: Tatanka Press, 2006).

47. Rinehart, "To Hell with the Exposition."

48. Ibid.

49. Ibid.

50. Richard White, Patricia Nelson Limerick, James R. Grossman, ed., *The Frontier in American Culture* (Chicago: The Library; Berkeley: University of California Press, c1994).

51. Ibid.

52. Ibid.

53. Ibid.

54. Richard H. Timberlake, Jr., "Panic of 1893." in *Business Cycles and Depressions: An Encyclopedia*, David Glasner and Thomas F. Cooley, eds. (New York: Garland Publishing, 1997) 516–18.

55. Bolotin and Laing, *The World's Columbian Exposition*; David Franke, *The Torture Doctor* (New York: Hawthorne Books, 1975).

56. Franke, *The Torture Doctor*.

57. Harris, et al., *Grand Illusions*.

58. Ibid.

59. Ibid.

60. Ibid.

61. Ibid.

62. Ibid., Bolotin and Laing, *The World's Columbian Exposition*.

63. Appropriations, World's Columbian Exposition (PL 203, August 5, 1892) 52d Cong. 1st Sess, chap. 381, 27:205–206.

64. Metz, Charles Louis Metz Papers.

Chapter 9: The Phebe Ferris Will

1. Ellis, et al., *Rookwood and the American Indian*.
2. Ibid.
3. Ibid.
4. Ibid.; Metz, Charles Louis Metz Papers.
5. Metz, Charles Louis Metz Papers.
6. Ibid.
7. Ibid.
8. Ibid.
9. "Will Attacked—Phebe Ferris Estate in Litigation," *Cincinnati* (OH) *Post*, October 18, 1898.
10. Ibid.
11. Metz, Charles Louis Metz Papers.
12. Ibid.
13. "Drank Milk After Which Pioneer Woman Died," *Cincinnati* (OH) *Post*, October 20, 1898.
14. "Will Attacked—Phebe Ferris Estate in Litigation."
15. "Land of Archaeological Value," *Cincinnati* (OH) *Enquirer*, October 21, 1898; The Last Will and Testament of Phebe Ferris, Deceased, December 29, 1896.
16. *The Library Journal* 22, no. 1 (January 1897).
17. "Will Attacked—Phebe Ferris Estate in Litigation,"
18. Record of the Meeting of the President and Fellows of Harvard College in Boston (May 10, 1897).
19. Metz, Charles Louis Metz Papers.
20. Ibid.
21. Last Will and Testament of Phebe Ferris; "Scientists Will Testify in Phoebe [*sic*] Ferris Case," *Cincinnati* (OH) *Post*, October 21, 1898.
22. "State of Mind of Phoebe [*sic*] Ferris Now Under Discussion," *Cincinnati* (OH) *Enquirer*, October 20, 1898.
23. "Drank Milk After Which Pioneer Woman Died."
24. Ibid.; "Land of Archaeological Value."
25. "Drank Milk After Which Pioneer Woman Died"; "Land of Archaeological Value."
26. "Drank Milk After Which Pioneer Woman Died"; "Land of Archaeological Value."

27. "Consanguity Figures in the Ferris Will Contest," *Cincinnati* (OH) *Enquirer*, October 26, 1898.
28. "Drank Milk After Which Pioneer Woman Died"; "Consanguity Figures in the Ferris Will Contest."
29. "Consanguity Figures in the Ferris Will Contest."
30. Ibid.
31. Ibid.
32. Court of Common Pleas, Hamilton County, Ohio, *Action to set aside will and other relief*, No. 111031; "Scientists Will Testify in Phoebe [*sic*] Ferris Case."
33. *Action to set aside will and other relief*; "Scientists Will Testify in Phoebe [*sic*] Ferris Case."
34. *Action to set aside will and other relief*.
35. Metz, Charles Louis Metz Papers.
36. Ibid.; "Scientists Will Testify in Phoebe [*sic*] Ferris Case."
37. "Consanguity Figures in the Ferris Will Contest"; Map of Ferris Property, current owners, and values, 1908.

Chapter 10: The Twentieth Century

1. Willoughby and Hooton, *The Turner Group of Earthworks*.
2. Ibid.
3. Ibid.
4. Ibid.
5. Ibid.
6. Ibid.
7. Ibid.
8. Ibid.
9. Ibid.
10. Ibid.
11. Ibid.
12. Tankersley, "Archaeological Geology of the Turner Site Complex."
13. Ibid.
14. Metz, Charles Louis Metz Papers.
15. Hooton and Willoughby, "Indian Village Site and Cemetery."
16. Metz, Charles Louis Metz Papers.
17. Ibid.
18. Ibid.

19. Ibid.
20. Hooton and Willoughby, "Indian Village Site and Cemetery."
21. Carl Wittke, *German-Americans and the World War (with Special Emphasis on Ohio's German-Language Press)* (Columbus, Ohio: The Ohio State Archaeological & Historical Society, 1936).
22. Ibid.
23. David Kahn, *The Codebreakers: The Story of Secret Writing* (New York: MacMillan Co., 1967).
24. Ibid.
25. Wittke, *German-Americans and the World War.*
26. Ibid.
27. Metz, Charles Louis Metz Papers.
28. Ibid.
29. Ibid.
30. Ibid.
31. Ibid.
32. Ibid.
33. Ibid.
34. Ibid.
35. Ibid.
36. Ibid.
37. Ibid.
38. Ibid.
39. Ibid.
40. Ibid.
41. George J. Stein, "Biological Science and the Roots of Nazism: The Promotion of Racist Doctrines in the Name of Science," *American Scientist* 76 (January–February 1988): 50–58.
42. Ibid.
43. Daniel S. Lamb, "The Story of The Anthropological Society Of Washington," *American Anthropologist* 8 (1906): 564–79, 1906.
44. Ibid.
45. Barry Isaac, *Central States Anthropological Society (CSAS) History: The Early Years*, AAANet.org, 2011; "Anthropology Notes: Organization of the Central Section of the American Anthropological Association," *American Anthropologist* 24 (1922): 247–49.

46. "Proceedings of the Central Section of the AAA." *American Anthropologist* 25 (1923): 284–86.
47. President and Fellows of Harvard College v Jewett, 11 F.2d 119, Circuit Court of Appeals, Sixth Circuit, 1925.
48. Ibid.
49. Ibid.
50. Ibid.
51. Ibid.
52. Ibid.
53. Kenneth, B. Tankersley, *In Search of Ice Age Americans* (Salt Lake City: Gibbs Smith Publishers Press, 2002).

Chapter 11: And In the End

1. Metz, Charles Louis Metz Papers.
2. Tankersley, *In Search of Ice Age Americans*.
3. Metz, Charles Louis Metz Papers.
4. Ibid.
5. Ibid.
6. Ibid.

Epilogue
The Legacy of Charles Louis Metz

1. *Archaeology Laws and Ethics*, National Park Service, 2010.
2. Bernard K. Means, *Shovel Ready: Archaeology and Roosevelt's New Deal for America* (Tuscaloosa: University of Alabama Press, 2013).
3. Ibid.
4. Ibid.
5. Ibid.
6. Tankersley, *In Search of Ice Age Americans*.
7. Ibid.
8. Ibid.
9. Bradley Thomas Lepper, *Ohio Archaeology: An Illustrated Chronicle of Ohio's Ancient American Indian Cultures* (Wilmington, Ohio: Orange Frazier Press, 2005).
10. Ibid.
11. S. Frederick Starr, "The Archaeology of Hamilton County, Ohio," *Journal of the Cincinnati Museum of Natural History* (1960).

12. Oehler, *Turpin Indians*.
13. Starr, "The Archaeology of Hamilton County, Ohio."
14. Ibid.
15. Ibid.
16. Ibid.
17. Compton Allyn, "Twenty Years of What to Do With This Old House: A Chronical of the Miami Purchase Association for Historic Preservation." *Journal of the Cincinnati Historical Society* 46 no. 3 (1988): 3–18.
18. Ibid.
19. Ibid.
20. *Archaeology Laws and Ethics*
21. Ibid.
22. Allyn, "Twenty Years of What to Do With This Old House."
23. *Archaeology Laws and Ethics*
24. Ibid.
25. Ibid.
26. Allyn, "Twenty Years of What to Do With This Old House."
27. Ibid.
28. Christopher Vacsey, *Handbook of American Indian Religious Freedom*, (New York: Crossroad Press, 1991).
29. Ibid.
30. *Archaeology Laws and Ethics*
31. Ibid.
32. Ibid.
33. Ibid.; Vacsey, *Handbook of American Indian Religious Freedom*.
34. *Archaeology Laws and Ethics*; Vacsey, *Handbook of American Indian Religious Freedom*.
35. *Archaeology Laws and Ethics*; Vacsey, *Handbook of American Indian Religious Freedom*.
36. *Archaeology Laws and Ethics*; Vacsey, *Handbook of American Indian Religious Freedom*.
37. *Archaeology Laws and Ethics*.
38. Ibid.
39. Joseph Shaffer, "Protohistoric Fort Ancient Social and Climatic Adaptation at the Wynema Site (33Ha837)" (master's thesis, University of Cincinnati, 2014).
40. James H. Kellar, *An Introduction to the Prehistory of Indiana* (Indianapolis, Ind.: Indiana Historical Society, 1983).
41. Ibid.

Index

A

A Brief Description of the Turner Group of Prehistoric Earthworks in Anderson Township, Hamilton County, Ohio (Metz) 170
Abbott, Dr. Charles Conrad 99
"Account of Continued Explorations of Mounds in Ohio" 88
Acton Camp Meeting Grounds 238
Adams Express 269
Adams, James 198
Advisory Council on Historic Preservation 199
Africa 125
African American 42
Albright House 67
Alden, John M. 34
Allegheny Mountains 285
American Anthropological Association (AAA) 179, 180
American Anthropologist 179
American Antiquity
  "The Chronological Position and Ethnological Relationships of the Fort Ancient Aspect" (Griffin) 194
American Association (baseball team) 64
American Association for the Advancement of Science (AAAS) 5, 75–78, 95, 96, 111, 112, 113, 237, 251, 265, 270
American Civil War 2, 3, 18, 21, 33, 98, 109, 114, 118, 124, 173
  end 21
  military hospital 19
American Indian Religious Freedom Act 200–201
American Indian School 136
American Indians 1, 11, 17, 25, 26, 27, 50, 64, 65, 72, 79, 81, 82, 85, 107, 108, 120, 126, 127, 135, 137, 138, 147, 150, 179, 188, 193, 196, 206
  Albert Billy 172
  Algonquian 8, 9, 36, 67, 101, 149, 167–168, 194, 205
  Apache 34, 114, 132
  Arapaho 36
  artifacts 33, 34, 39, 124
  Ben Carterby 172
  Ben Hampton 172
  books about 20
  Calvin Wilson 172
  Carlos Montezuma 137
  cemetery 43
  Charles Eastman 137

Cherokee 12, 51, 137
  stories 101
Cheyenne 36
Chickasaw 12, 101
Chief Cocuyevah 34
Chief Geronimo 114, 116, 125
Chief Macunajin (Standing Bear) 135
Chief Manchú-Nanzhí 80
Chief Mapíya Lúta (Red Cloud) 126
Chief Onwanonsyshon 77
Chief Red Cloud 126
Chief Sealth (Seattle) 16
Chief Standing Bear 135
Chief Summunduwat 13
Chippewa 135
Chiricahua Apache 114, 132, 135
Choctaw 12, 51, 101, 135, 172
Coahuila 135
Cochise 132
code talkers 172
Crazy Horse 36
Cree 135, 147
Creek 12, 51, 101
crematories and mortuaries 43, 44, 49, 50, 52, 60, 63, 68, 69, 76, 83, 84, 87, 88, 100, 106, 112, 114, 118, 131, 166, 169, 170
Crow 136
culture 148
Dakota 90, 137
Delaware 12, 67, 149
Dine' 135
Donehogawa 37
Duwamish 16
Elias Boudinot 137
Five Civilized Tribes 12
genocide discussions 3, 25
George Davenport 172
Ghost Dance 126, 127
Hasaneanda 37
Haudenosaunee 135, 136
Hunkpapa 127
Húŋkpapha 148
Hupa 137
Huron 150
in Ohio Valley 13
in World War I 172
Inuit 135
Iroquois 51, 101, 135, 150
James Edwards 172
Jeff Nelson 172
John Rollin Ridge 137

Joseph Davenport 172
Joseph Oklahombi 172
Kickapoo 12
Kicking Bear 136
Kiowa 137
Kutchin 137
Kwakiutl 135, 136
Kwakwaka'wakw 136
Lakota 36, 65, 90, 126, 127, 128, 135, 136, 137, 148, 149
Lenape 12
Little Turtle 36
Menominee 135
Miami 1, 12, 13, 149
Mitchell Bobb 172
Modoc 135
Mohawk 77
Moqui 135
Muskogees 87
Navajo 135, 137
No Neck 136
Noel Johnson 172
Oglala 126
Oglala Lakota 136
Ojibwa 14, 101, 149
Omaha 137
Otis Leader 172
Papago 135
Passamaquoddy 135
Pawnee 65
Penobscot 135
Peter Maytubby 172
Pima 34
Pine Ridge Indian Reservation 126
Plains 65
Ponca 135
Potawatomi 135
Quick Bear (photo) 161
Rain-in-the-Face 136
Red Cloud 136
removal of 13, 16
reservations 79, 128
  Pine Ridge 126
  Rosebud 148
Robert Taylor 172
Rocky Bear 136
Rosebud Reservation 148
Schlicht Billy 172
Seminole 12
Seneca 37
Shawnee 1, 7, 8, 9, 12, 32, 51, 67, 100, 101, 149, 150, 194

Chaouanons 150
Ouchaouanag 150
Sicangu Lakota 148
Sitting Bull 127, 136
Solomon Louis 172
Standing Bear 80, 90
stereotypes 37
stories 2, 168
Suquamish 16
Susette Bright Eyes LaFlesche 137
Thilgeya 34
Tobias Frazier 172
Two Strike 136
Victor Brown 172
Walter Veach 172
Wampanoag Caleb
    Cheeshahteaumuck 137
Wassaja 34
Western Hemisphere 100
Winnebago 79, 135
Wyandot 12, 13
Yaqui 135
Yavapai 137
Yavapai Apache 34
Young Bull 136
Young Man Afraid of His Horses 136
Zuni 135, 137
American Journal of Science 103
American Museum of Natural History 188
American Paleolithic 99
American Red Cross 176
American Revolution 18, 32
Ames Drug Store 293
Amherst College 113
Amherst University 203
Ancient Monuments of the Mississippi Valley: Comprising the Results of Extensive Original Surveys and Explorations 2, 5, 14, 58, 100, 131, 194
Ancient Society (Morgan) 37
Anderson, Levi 131
Andes Mountains 167
Andres, Professor 211
Annual Reports of the Trustees of the Peabody Museum of America and Ethnology 88
Anthony, Rev. 27
Anthropological Society of Washington (ASW) 179
Antiquities Act 193
The Antiquities of the Miami Valley (Day) 59
The Antiquities of the State of Ohio (Shepherd) 270

Antonio 132
Appalachian Mountains 110
Archaeological and Historic Preservation Act 1974 200
"Archaeological Explorations by the Peabody Museum of American Archaeology and Ethnology Communicated by the Trustees of the Museum" 77
Archaeological Resource Protection Act 201
The Archaeology of Hamilton County, Ohio 198
Archer, William 57
Argentina 167
Arizona 132
    Fort Bowie 114
    Skeleton Canyon 114
Armleder Park 149
Armstrong, John 287
Armstrong, William 286, 287, 288
Art Academy of Cincinnati 197
Asia 125
Atwater, Caleb 26
Australia 55
Austria 171, 172

B

B&O Railroad 244
Baird, Professor 235
Baird, Spencer Fullerton 71
Baltimore and Ohio Railroad 88
Bank Street Grounds 64, 65, 81
Barber, Charles E. 141
Bartlett, George 126, 127
baseball
    American Association 64
    Cincinnati Baseball Grounds 81
    Cincinnati Red Stockings 64
Bates, Joshua 18
battle at Camp Dennison 21
battle of Greasy Grass 36
battle of Little Big Horn 128, 148
battle of Seattle 16
battle of Shiloh 19, 20, 77
battle of the Little Big Horn 136
battle of Wounded Knee 128
battle with the Lakota 128
Baxter, James 288
Beadle and Company 20
Belgium 171, 174
Bell, Alexander Graham 5, 77
Bell, Mr. 236

Benziger Brothers' Press 119
Berger, Amelia (Molly). *See also,* Metz, Amelia 23–24
Berger, Andrew 24
Berger, Caroline 37
Berger, Ethel Helen Carolina (née Metz) 183
Berger, Frederick Joseph 175, 183
Berger, Frederick Wilbur 183
Berger, Julia 24
Bering Strait 188
Berlin Society for Anthropology, Ethnology and Prehistory 42
Berner, William 70
Big Bone Lick Creek
 Gum Branch 82
Billy, Albert 172
Billy, Schlict 172
Black Robes 7
Black, Glenn A. 195
Blackwell, Elizabeth 113
Blasie, Ferdinand 53
Boas, Franz Uri 125, 180
Bobb, Mitchell 172
Bolivia 167
The Book of Algoonah 242, 265
Book of Mormon 85
Booth, John Wilkes 21
Boston Society of Natural History 49, 100
Boston University 77
Boudinot, Elias 137
Bowditch, Ingersoll 154
Bowers, Mary 289
Brennans 212
Bridge, sons of W. H. 247
Bridge, W. H. 247
Brinkerhoff, Roeliff 109
British Columbia
 Tsaxis 136
British Museum 190
British Royal Society 42
Britten, Matthias 43, 50, 52, 78, 87, 94, 102, 111, 114, 210, 211, 233, 234, 235, 241, 242, 243, 244, 248, 252, 257, 263, 264, 266, 268, 269, 271, 281
Brockhaven 213
Brooke, General 128
Brooke, John Rutter 128
Brown University 109
Brown, Victor 172
Brown's Hotel 54

Brühl, Dr. Gustav 42, 47, 119, 172, 173, 216, 217, 270
Brühl, Theodore A. 42, 216, 217
Brush Creek 131
Brushy Fork 111
Buckingham, Dr. Alfred 19
Buffalo Bill. *See under* Code, William Frederick
Buffalo Bill's Wild West Show 64–65, 127, 137–138, 139
Bulgaria 172
Buntline, Ned 34
Bureau of American Ethnology 99
Bureau of Ethnology 81
Bureau of Indian Affairs 109, 148
Burnet House 17, 75, 237
Burnet, Jacob 26
Burrows Brother Publishing Co. 150
Bush, George H. W. 202
Busycon whelks 54
Butterfield, A. S., Jr. 216
Byland, James 17, 18, 23
Byrnes, Dr. R. M. 47, 216

C

Caesar's Creek 274, 275
California 154
Calle Ocho 153
Camp Dennison 2, 18–22, 29, 98
Camp Kimball 266
Camp Shady 21
Camp Sherman 176
Canada 113
 Manitoba 110
 Ontario 110
 Quebec 110
Capra, Frank 190
Carlisle, John G. 7, 133
Carlson, Eric 197
Carlson, Gustav "Gus" 197–199
Carmichael, Porter James 18
Carr, Lucien 56, 99
Carter, James Earl (Jimmy), Jr. 200, 201
Carterby, Ben 172
Carver, Dr. William Frank 65
Casou, Louis W. C. 38
Catholic Order of Foresters 188
Catholics 7, 16, 66, 130, 176, 188
Central America 120
Central States Anthropological Association 180
Charlemagne 51

Cheeshahteaumuck, Wampanoag Caleb 137
Cherokee Phoenix 137
Chicago Fire Department 140
Chicago Medical College 35
Chicago Symphony Orchestra 133
Chicago Tribune 126
Chillicothe Fairground Mound 91
Chillicothe Greys 89
China, Kumming 197
Choctaw land (German Coast) 12
Christian Advocate 238
Church of the Holy Ghost 24, 189
Cincinnati and Eastern Railroad 165, 281
Cincinnati Art Museum 57, 183, 197
Cincinnati Baseball Grounds 81
Cincinnati Board of Health 169, 174
Cincinnati Centennial Exposition of 1888 125
Cincinnati College of Music 133
Cincinnati Enquirer 155
Cincinnati Exposition of 1878 40
Cincinnati Exposition of 1879 210, 211, 212
Cincinnati Industrial Exposition 3, 34, 67
Cincinnati Industrial Exposition of 1879 50
Cincinnati May Festival 133
Cincinnati May Music Festival 38
Cincinnati Medical College 169
Cincinnati Museum Association 197
Cincinnati Museum of Natural History 8, 57, 170, 197
Cincinnati Natural History Society 96
Cincinnati Orchestra 34
Cincinnati Post 155
Cincinnati Preservation Association 8
Cincinnati Public Schools 177
Cincinnati Red Stockings 64
Cincinnati Sängerfest 38
Cincinnati Society of Natural History 39, 40, 53, 54
Cincinnati Zoo 149
Cincinnati Zoological Society 147
Cincinnati, Washington, and Baltimore Railroad (CWBRR) 88
Citizenship Clause 79, 80
Civil Rights Act of 1866 80
Civilian Conservation Corps (CCC) 8, 194
Clark, Joseph 286
Clark, Mr. 279
Clasgens, Joseph 24, 27

Clendenin, Dr. 22
Clermont Courier 112, 265
Cleveland, Grover 7, 133, 134, 138
Cleveland-Columbus-Cincinnati Railroad 22
Clovis artifacts 6
Cody, William Frederick "Buffalo Bill" 34, 64–65, 81, 137
Coffy, Mr. 158, 280
Collis, R. O. 40, 215
Colorado River 77
Colston, Edward 151, 152
Columbia University 195
Columbian Exposition. *See under* World's Fair
Columbian March and Hymn 133
Columbus and Cincinnati Midland Railroad (CCMRR) 88
Columbus, Christopher 7, 13, 132, 133, 134, 136, 141
Commercial 259
Commissioner of Indian Affairs 37
Confederate army
    Morgan's cavalry 20, 21
    prisoners of war 19
Confederate States of America 17
Congressional Medal of Honor 128
Conkling 213
Conkling, E. A. 40, 56, 85
Conkling, Florence 102, 257
Connecticut 32
    Greenwich 31
    Waterbury 141
Convention of Chillicothe 286
Conyers, John 99
Cook, Harold J. 183, 188
Cook, Mr. 274
Coolidge, Calvin 172
Cooper, James Fenimore 11
Cooperative Collecting: An Opportunity to Add to Your Collection (Moorehead) 180
Cope, Edward Drinker 126
Coppes, William 287
Cornwall's Station 282
Couden, James 229
Court Archaeological Research Facility (CARF) 203
Court Family Foundation 203, 204
Court, Georgia 204
Court, John C. 203–204, 205
Courthouse Riot of 1884 70
Couthoui, Jessie 133, 134

Covington, S. F. 40, 215
Cowden estate 66, 117, 268
Cowden, Alfred 118
Cowden, Clinton 118
Cowen 276, 278
Cowen, Mr. 274, 276
Cox, Jacob D. 19, 20
Cox, Joseph 3, 33, 36, 40, 41, 52, 71, 102, 211, 215, 235, 238, 257
Cox, Joseph, Jr. 215
Cox, Mrs. 41
Crania Americana (Morton) 26
Cregier, DeWitt C. 124
Crichfield, Phillip 288
Croffut, William Augustus 133
Crook, George R. 80, 132
cultural periods
  Archaic 196
  Early Woodland 204
  Fort Ancient 9, 196, 204
  Late Woodland (Newtown) 9, 196
  Mesoamerica 120
  Middle Woodland (Hopewell) 9, 196, 204
  Paleo-Indian 196
  Woodland 196
Culture of the Americas 119
Cumberland River valley 87
Cushing, Frank H. 179
Custer, George Armstrong 36, 37, 127, 136
Custer, Tom 136
Cutler, Rev. Manasseh 27

D

Dabney, Dr. 282
Dakotan 126
Danaddelp's 209
Darling, William 286
Darwinism 110, 178
Davenport, George 172
Davenport, Joseph 172
Davis, Dr. 293
Davis, Dr. Edwin. *See also,* Squier & Davis 13, 14, 59, 194
Davis, George R. 124, 133, 134, 142
Dawden, Clermont 288
Day, T. C. 59
de Soto, Hernando 7
Deadwood Dick Jr. in Cincinnati 20
Deadwood stagecoach 65
Declaration of Independence 36

Deerslayer: or The First Warpath (Cooper) 11
Democrats 42, 50, 290
Denison University 118
Dennison, William 18
Denver Museum of Natural History 188
Department of Defense 203
Department of the Interior 80
depression of 1884 70
"Description of Human Remains in the Intrusive Pit in the Large Mound of the Turner Group, Little Miami River Valley, Ohio During the Explorations of Messrs Metz and Putnam" 77
Descriptions of Ancient Works at Cincinnati (Whittlesey) 26
Descriptions of Ancient Works in Ohio (Whittlesey) 59
Descriptions of Antiquities Discovered in Ohio and other Western States (Atwater) 26
Dickens, Charles 13
Dickinson, Jno. T. 142
Die Culturvolker Alt-Amerika's (Brühl) 119, 172
Die Neuner 2, 18
"The Diversity of the Mounds and Earthworks in the United States" 113
Dixon, R. B. 154
Dogwood Park 183
Douglas, Mr.
  (photo) 91
Dowden, Clement 288
Dr. Ames Drug Store 293
Drake, Dr. Daniel 25, 198
Drury College 109
Duck Creek 149, 290, 291
Duke of Veragua XVI (Cristobal Colon de la Cerda) 133
Duke, Basil 20, 21
Duncan, Dr. Alexander 290, 291
Dundy, Elmer S. 80
Dunham family 118
Durham, Mr. 82, 240, 241
Dury, Ralph E. 197
Dutch Hollows 293
Duval Hotel 54
Dyer 253
Dyer, Frank B. 177

E

earthworks 2
  Alligator 109, 263
  Anderson Twp. 250

Index   321

Anderson Twp., Hamilton Co., Ohio 60
Anderson Twp., Hamilton County, Ohio 230
Arkansas Mound 83
Benham Mound 200
Broadwell Mound 82, 240
Burchenal Mound 200
Cincinnati, Ohio 198, 203
Clark's Earthworks 141
Clermont County, Ohio 59, 227
Clough Creek site 200
Clovis, N.Mex. 100
Conrad Mound 200
Dunlap site 200
Edwards' mounds 232
Europe 32
Ferris Cemetery 3, 43, 44, 52, 53, 54, 55, 56, 57, 58, 61, 64, 65, 66, 83, 86, 88, 93, 94, 101, 117, 149, 150, 151, 152, 153, 154, 157, 159, 169–171, 178, 179, 181, 182, 183, 187, 196, 216, 228, 229, 230, 243, 244, 248, 270
Flint Ridge 118
Folsom, N. Mex. 183
Fort Ancient 8, 14, 66, 109, 117–119, 128, 131, 195, 263, 274
    Wynema site 205
Fort Hill 8, 15, 109, 131, 141, 195, 263, 274, 276
Foster's Crossing 237, 246, 247, 277
Gulf of Mexico 51
Hahn Field 4, 5, 6, 9, 64, 72, 82, 86, 87, 88, 90, 91, 93, 94, 103, 194, 196, 200, 225, 236, 241, 242, 243, 244, 245, 246, 248, 249
Hall's Mound 261
Hamilton, Ohio 109, 263
Harness Mound 96
Hopewell 14, 60, 64, 66, 131, 141, 277
Incan sites 167
Jones's Mound 261
Kendall farm 98
Klotte Mound 261
Little Miami River valley 36, 39
London gravel pit 99
Loveland 6, 91, 104, 246
Madisonville site 1, 3–4, 6, 7, 9, 56, 151, 157, 194, 196, 200, 205
    Mississippian vessel (photo) 61
Mariemont Earthwork 4, 200, 205
Marietta Mound 109

Marriott Mound 87, 105, 106, 242
Mathew Mound 200
Mexico 32, 42, 81
Miami Fort 198
Miami River 109, 263
Milford 5, 64, 71, 221, 226, 227
Missouri Mound 83
Mound City 14, 131
New Mexico 187
Newark, Ohio 14, 48
Norwood Mound 51, 200
Odd Fellow's Cemetery Mound 200
Perin Village site 200
Plum Run Mound 15
Pottery Field 3, 32–33, 43
Red Bank Mound 261
Rennert Mound 200
Rocky Fork Mound Group 15
Sand Ridge site 4, 5, 6, 9, 65, 66, 71, 72, 82, 90, 93, 194, 196, 200, 229, 230, 232, 235, 236, 241, 242, 246, 248
Scioto River 131
Seip 14
Serpent Mound 8, 14, 15, 94, 109, 129, 131, 194, 250, 263
    (photo) 122
Shawnee Lookout 198, 200
Shawnee Snake Town cemetery 101
Spice Bush 43, 44
Stateline site 200
Stites Grove 4, 36, 58, 67, 71, 165, 166, 230, 236, 282
Sun's Fields 254
Sycamore Twp.
    Millcreek Valley 236
Trenton, N.J. 99
Turner site 4, 5, 6, 8, 9, 58–61, 63, 64, 66, 67–69, 71, 76, 82, 87, 91, 105, 106, 110, 111, 114, 115, 116, 117, 118, 120, 121, 129, 153, 165, 166, 167, 168, 169, 170, 178, 179, 196, 217, 218, 219, 221, 225, 226, 227, 231, 233, 235, 236, 240, 241, 242, 243, 248, 249, 255, 265, 269, 270, 272, 276, 281, 282
    (map) 184
    (photos) 73
Turpin Farm site 4, 6, 9, 71, 93–98, 103, 194, 196, 197, 200, 242, 243, 248, 250, 251, 254, 256, 258, 259, 260, 261, 263, 271

United States 32
Wesley Butler site 200
Whittlesey mound 60, 61, 87, 111, 221, 222, 264, 270
Workman 15
Wynema site 205
East Asia 188
Eastman, Charles 137
Easton, Rev. 228
École des Beaux-Arts 132
economic depression 55
Eddy, K. E. 176
Edison, Thomas Alva 90, 134, 140
Edwards 223
Edwards, James 172
Edwards, Samuel 222
"Egypt and the Pyramids" 41
Eiffel Tower 124, 135
1876 Centennial Exposition in Philadelphia 3, 34, 36–37, 124, 125
Eleventh Cincinnati Industrial Exposition 67
Eliot, Charles William 153, 169, 278
Elk, John 79, 80
Emery, Mary Hopkins 181
Emmitt House. *See also,* Warner House 79
Endicott Hotel 152
England
    London 12, 190
Environmental Assessment 199
Environmental Impact Statement 199
epidemics 82, 102, 103, 108, 258
Essex Institute of Salem 48, 49
Europe
    affects from Krakatoa 69
European 8, 14, 196
    Paleolithic 99
"Explorations in Ohio: Conducted for the Peabody Museum of American Archaeology and Ethnology, In Connection with Harvard University" 105
Exposition Universelle of 1889 124, 125, 132

F

Farny, Henry François 148
Ferris estate 278
Ferris family 47
Ferris, A. J. 216
Ferris, C. K. 216
Ferris, Eliphalet 31

Ferris, Howard 152
Ferris, James 156, 157
Ferris, Joseph 31, 32, 151, 216
Ferris, Phebe 3, 31–33, 44, 58, 108, 147, 151, 152, 153, 154, 155, 156, 157, 158, 159, 165, 169, 170, 175, 181, 182, 183, 279
Field Museum 190
Fiers, Sarah 290
Figgins, Frank 187
Figgins, Jesse 187
Fillmore, Millard 113
Finch, Mr. 244
fire of 1871 124
First Regiment Infirmary 176
Fisher, Frederick W. 198
Fleak, Peter 288
Fleck, Dr. 15, 16
Fleck, Robert 290
Fletcher, Alice Cunningham 90
flood of 1883 63, 69
flood of 1884 69
Florida 52, 53–54, 114, 116, 150
    Jacksonville 54
    Pensacola Bay 116
    St. Augustine 116
Force, M. F. 51, 52
Forsyth, James W. 128
Fort Ancient 229, 237, 246, 268, 269, 270
The Fort Ancient Aspect: Its Cultural and Chronological Position in Mississippi Valley Archaeology 194
Fort Benjamin Harrison 174
Fort Marion 116
Fort Monroe 132
Fort Pickens 116
Fort Sumter 17
Fortschritt 23
Fourteenth Amendment 80
Fourteenth Annual Meeting of the Society for American Archaeology 195
Fowke, Gerard 118, 277
France 171, 174, 176
    Paris 124, 171
Francis, Professor 236
Frank Leslie's Illustrated Newspaper 126
Franklin, Benjamin 136
Franz Ferdinand (archduke of Austria) 171
Frazier, Mr. 244
Frazier, Tobias 172
French 7, 150
French colonies 125

Furber family 12

G

Gage, Lyman 124
Galsby, George 290
Gano residence 293
Gentile, Carlos 34
Georgia 110
   Macon 52
Georgia, Macon 54
German Americans. *See under* Germans
German Anthropological Association 42
German Coast (Choctaw land) 12
German Turner Society 2, 17, 18, 19, 21, 22, 79
Germans 1, 2, 11, 17, 18, 24, 34, 42, 64, 65, 79, 119, 125, 139, 148, 172, 235, 270
   Catholic 11, 12
      rivalry with Scots-Irish Protestants 130
   during WWI 171, 172, 173, 176
   in New Orleans 12
   newspaper 23
   Over-the-Rhine 13
Germany 42, 172, 174, 217
   Bavaria 165
   Berlin 190
   Jockgrim, Bavaria 11
   Metz 12
   Rheinland-Pfalz 12
Gerrard, William 289
Ghost Dance by the Ogallala Sioux at Pine Ridge Agency, Dakota (Remington) 127
Gibbs, George 26
The Glacial Boundary in Ohio, Indiana, and Kentucky (Wright) 110
Goldsmith 151
Goode, George Brown 125, 137
Goshorn, Alfred Trabor 34
Gould farm 236
Grand Canyon 77
Grant, Ulysses S. 37
Grave-mounds and their contents: a manual of archaeology, as exemplified in the burials of the Celtic, the Romano-British, and the Anglo-Saxon periods 50
Gray, Asa 48, 83
Great Britain 34, 171, 172
Great Comet of 1881 55
Great Depression 194
Great Lakes 7, 110

Great Miami River 51, 67, 69
Great Miami Valley 228
Great Parks of Hamilton County 198
Green River 77
Gresham, Walter 7, 133
Griffin, Isaac 149
Griffin, James Bennett 194
Griffin, Wilson 289
Grimes Drug Store 288
Grossman, Felix 286, 288
Gulf Coast 54
Gulf of Mexico 54

H

Hahn, Mr. 240, 242
Hahn, Mrs. 245
Hamilton, George 242, 275
Hampton, Ben 172
Handel, George Frederic 136
Harmon, Colston, Goldsmith, and Hoadly 151
Harmon, Judge 156, 158, 280
Harper's Weekly 127
Harrell, Andrew 289
Harris, Wilbur 288
Harrison, Benjamin 127, 138, 140
Harrison, Carter, Sr. 140
Harrison, William Henry 26, 120, 128, 198
Harvard College 153, 157, 181, 182, 247
Harvard University 125, 137
   Peabody Museum of Archaeology and Ethnology 4, 5, 9, 47–48, 49, 51, 56, 57, 78, 94, 105, 111, 129, 132, 153, 154, 169, 170, 171, 178, 179, 181, 182, 183, 187, 190, 206
Harvard University Corporation 170
Harvest Home Magazine
   "The Mound Builders" (Metz) 3, 36
Harvey, William 288
Hasbrook 276
Hawes, A. A. 215
Hayden, Irwin 169
Hayes, Rutherford B. 79, 109, 114
Haymarket Square Riot 124
Heck, William S. 147, 148
Heller, Mary 198
Henderson, Alice Palmer 141
Herbert, Hilary A. 7, 133
Hill, Dr. Howard H. 47, 216
Hitler, Adolf 178
Ho Chi Minh 197
Hoadly, George 109

Hobson, Elizabeth 198, 205
Hogans, Lewis Zachariah 54
Holbrook 276
Holmes, Dr. Henry Howard 139
Holmes, William Henry 5, 80, 81, 89, 99, 239, 245
Holocaust 178
Holy Ghost Parish Cemetery 189
Hones, John 286
Hooton, Earnest Albert 178, 179
Hosbrook, D. S. 215
Hosbrook, J. A. 215, 270
Hosbrook, Mr. 60
Hotel Lafayette 77
Hrdlička, Aleš 188
Hungary 171, 172
Hunt, Samuel F. 41, 46
Huxley, Thomas Henry 42
Hyde, Professor 157

I

Ice Age 2, 6, 26, 50, 82, 98, 100, 103, 110, 111, 120, 135, 183, 187, 188
Idaho 110
Illinois 51
   Chicago 6, 121, 124, 132, 133, 139, 143, 190
   Springfield 22
Illustrated American 126, 128
immigration
   European 12
Independent Order of Odd Fellows (IOOF) 40, 50, 211, 293
Indian Citizenship Act 80, 172
Indian Removal Act 1, 12
Indian Village Site and Cemetery near Madisonville, Ohio 179
Indian Wars 114, 125, 136, 148
Indiana 51, 138, 174, 291
   Crawford County 168
   Indianapolis 259
   Peru 13
Indiana University 195, 199
Ingalls, John 140
Instructions for Archaeological Investigations in the United States (Gibbs) 26
Invalid Corps 21
Israel 85
It's a Wonderful Life 190
Italy 172

J

Jackson Park 132
Jackson, Andrew 12
James, John 288
Jealous Wife (painting) 24, 28
Jesuit Relations 150
Jesuits 7, 150
Jewett, Col. 236
Jewett, John Brown 158, 159
Jewett, John Ferris 154, 155, 156, 157, 159
Jewett, Uri 155
Joe Phenix's Double Deal 20
John C. Court Memorial Scholarship 204
Johns Hopkins University 106
Johns Hopkins University Circular
   "On Methods of Archaeological Research in America" (Putnam) 106
Johnson, Andrew 3, 25
Johnson, George Henry Martin 77
Johnson, Lyndon Baines 198
Johnson, Noel 172
Johnston Turpin farm 250
Johnston, Dr. Alex M. 215
Jones, John 288, 289, 291
Jones, Oliver 286
Joseph Ferris Memorial Library 152, 159, 165, 181, 183, 187
Journal of Ethnology 42
Journal of the Cincinnati Museum of Natural History 198
Journal of the Cincinnati Society of Natural History 39
   "Archaeological Explorations near Madisonville, Ohio" 4, 52
   "The Madisonville Pre-Historic Cemetery Anthropological Notes" 4, 56
   "The Prehistoric Monuments of Anderson Township, Hamilton County, Ohio" (Metz) 4, 57
   "The Prehistoric Monuments of the Little Miami Valley" (Metz) 3
Jovial Fishing Club 38

K

Kansas 1
Kellar, James H. 199
Kellogg, Elizabeth R. 197, 205
Kellogg, Mr. 292
Kendall farm 98, 255
Kentucky
   Bellevue 147

Big Bone Lick 82
Lexington 47
Newport 17
Kentucky Geological Survey 47
Kimball, John Cone 102, 111, 114, 119, 247, 257, 258, 259, 260, 265, 266, 270
King, Joseph Warren 118
King's Powder Mills 118, 126
Kirsch 213
Kissinger, Dr. Henry 203
Kneiff. *See also*, Kneipf 242
Kneipf, Frank 244
Knight, Dr. Arthur Levy 123, 175, 176, 183
Knights of Labor 118
Krakatoa (volcano) 69
Kratsack 213
Kropp, Tracy 198

L

La Flesche, Francis 90
La Flesche, Susette Bright Eyes 90, 137
Lac des Allemands 12
Lafayette Hotel 77
Lake Michigan 132
Lake of the Germans 12
Lake Superior 101
Lanard, Ezekial 286
Lane, P. P. 56, 85, 216
Langdon, Dr. Frank Warren 3, 33, 36, 40, 41, 52, 56, 57, 83, 215, 261
Langdon, James 289
Lasher, Dr. G. N. 41
Lasher, Dr. G. W. 215
Last of the Mohicans: A Narrative of 1757 (Cooper) 11
Lawrence, Elias D. 20
Leader, Otis 172
Lebowitz, Rev. Bartholomew 24
Lee, Robert E. 21
Lexington Hotel 133
Libby, Willard Frank 195
The Life and Adventures of Joaquin Murieta, the Celebrated California Bandit 137
Lilly, Eli 195
Lincoln, Abraham 2, 17, 21, 22, 79, 136
assassination 21
Lincoln, William "Willie" 22
Lincoln-Douglas debates 79
Lingardner, George 212
Linton, Ralph 180

Literary & Scientific Society of Madisonville (LSSM) 245
Literary and Scientific Society of Madisonville (LSSM) 3, 4, 37–38, 40, 41, 43, 46, 47, 50, 51, 52, 53, 54, 55, 57, 71, 72, 89, 96, 119, 129, 172, 176, 177, 273
Little Big Horn 36
Little Miami River 4, 20, 27, 31, 32, 51, 54, 58, 64, 67, 69, 72, 76, 86, 99, 111, 114, 117, 120, 149, 150, 167, 168, 203, 221, 223, 225, 237, 246, 282
confluence 72
East Fork 236, 264
train 21
Little Miami River valley 1, 4, 5, 7, 8, 9, 24, 33, 34, 40, 41, 42, 50, 51, 52, 57, 61, 63, 64, 67, 69, 78, 80, 86, 87, 93, 101, 107, 111, 112, 118, 119, 120, 128, 135, 151, 165, 166, 167, 171, 178, 179, 193, 195, 196, 197, 198, 199, 200, 201, 205
map of archaeological sites 142
Little Miami Valley 236, 276
Locke, John 14
locomotive
Kilgore 21
The Lone Indian 16
lost white race of giants 25
Louis, Solomon 172
Louisiana
New Orleans 11, 12, 32
Low, Charles Frank 3, 33, 36, 40, 41, 43, 44, 50, 52, 54, 55, 56, 57, 58, 60, 67, 77, 83, 85, 89, 94, 101, 114, 128, 129, 209, 215, 217, 218, 224, 225, 229, 235, 244, 245, 246, 247, 248, 250, 257, 267, 273
(photo) 91
Lowe, Mr. 210, 211, 212
Luken, Mr. 270
Lunken Airport 31
Luxembourg 171
Lyell, Charles 27, 42
Lytle, William Henry 14, 58, 59

M

Madison Building and Loan Association 280
Madison, James 286
Madisonville Hook and Ladder Co. 90

Madisonville Literary and Scientific
    Society 285
Madisonville Monday Club 178
Madisonville News 225
Madisonville Public Library 183
Madisonville Public School 174, 190
Madisonville Round Table 176, 178
Madisonville-Obanion-Cambridge Turnpike
    Bridge 20
Maffet, Adam 293
Maffet, Timothy 293
Magoffin, Beriah 17
Maine
    Lewiston 88
Manhattan Project 195
Manitou Lake 101
Mann factory 293
Maple family 288
Marais des Cygnes River 13
Marbach, Chris 242
Mariemont Company 181, 182, 183
Mariemont Gardens 152, 205
Marietta and Cincinnati Railroad 293
Marietta Centennial 262, 263
marine life
    bivalve shells 54
    Busycon whelks 54
    gastropod shells 54
Marlow 224
Marquette, Jacques 150
Marriott family 105
Marriott house 111, 264
Marriott, Benjamin 105
Marsh, Mary (née Peabody) 48
Marsh, Othniel Charles 48
Marsh, Professor 267
Maryland 110
    Baltimore 256
Mason, Dr. Otis Tufton 137
Masonic Hall 15
Massachusetts
    Boston 158, 246, 280
    Cambridge 183, 238
    Rockport 121
    Salem 49
massacre at Wounded Knee 136
May Music Festival 50
Mayan 119, 270
Maytubby, Peter 172
McBride, James 14
McCafferty, John 174
McCafferty, Robert 115

McCall 241
McConn, Frances 27
McCormick, Thomas 290
McCullum, Patrick "Poddy" 288, 289
McEllwain, William 291
McGuffey Reader 2, 16
McJunkin, George 183
McKee, Jeramia 288
McKee, Samuel 288
McKenzie, Professor 97, 253, 254, 255
McKerron 94, 250
McKinley Club 148
McKinley, William 148
McLane (also McLean) 247
McLean 246
McLean House 21
McLean, Mrs. 94, 250
McMicken College of Arts and Science 157
McNally, Andrew 124
McNamara, Robert 203
Medical Officers' Training Corps 174
Mein Kampf (Hitler) 178
Merwin, B. W. 170
Merwin, R. E. 169, 170
Mesopotamia 85
Metz family 1, 169
    Civil War 18
    home (photo) 45, 145
    in Cincinnati 12–15
    in Highland County, Ohio 15–16
    in Plainville, Ohio 16–17, 22
Metz, Amelia "Molly" (née Berger) 3, 27,
    28, 34, 35, 36, 37, 38, 40, 52, 53, 54,
    55, 67, 69, 77, 78, 79, 94, 95, 113,
    117, 123, 132, 138, 139, 147, 159,
    176, 177, 188, 189
    (photo) 184
Metz, Anna Teresa 27, 69, 111, 112, 113,
    123, 147, 160, 175, 208, 209, 210,
    211, 212, 213, 265
Metz, Beatrice Amelia 69, 108, 123, 147,
    160, 260, 263, 265
Metz, Charles Wilbur 53, 69, 108, 120,
    123, 138, 139, 147, 160, 169, 174,
    176, 260, 265
    (photo) 186
Metz, Clara Isabel 37, 69, 123, 138, 139,
    147, 160, 175, 183, 210, 211, 212,
    213
Metz, Dr. Charles Louis
    (photo) 10, 91
    and archaeology 25–27

and Molly Berger 23–24
and Phebe Ferris 31–33
background 1–9
begins association with Putnam 49–50
childhood 15–17
Ferris site publication 83–85
letters 216–283
medical school 22–23
microscope 30
obituary 189
Metz, Dr. Franz (Francis) Michael 2, 11, 12, 13, 15, 16, 19, 24, 35, 81
Metz, E. A. 215
Metz, Ethel Helen Caroline 117, 123, 147, 169, 170, 175, 185, 280
Metz, Florence 36, 69
Metz, Franklin 35, 37
Metz, George Francis 132, 174, 175, 176
Metz, Johannes Michael 2, 12, 24
Metz, Julia Marie 120, 123, 147, 175, 183
Metz, Julius Alphonse 94, 96, 97, 98, 253, 254
Metz, Margaret Elizabeth 147, 175, 183, 189
Metz, Maria Anna 17, 23, 35, 78, 207
Metz, Maria Barbara "Babette" (née Reichert) 11, 12, 13, 16, 71
Miami Fort Generating Station 198
Miami Medical College 22, 33, 37, 42
Miami Powder Company 21
Miami Purchase 67
Miami Purchase Association for Historic Preservation (MPAHP) 198
Miami River 247, 265
Miami Valley 247
Miamiville Bridge 21
Michigan 110
  Ann Arbor 95, 251
Middleton 277
Midwest 7
Milburn, Rev. W. H. 133
Miles, Nelson 114
Miller Brothers 149
Mills, William 198
Milton, Maurice M. 126, 127
Minnesota 110
Mississippi River 12
Mississippi River valley 101
Mississippian vessel (photo) 61
Missouri
  Saint Louis 121
  Westport 13

Moliére 108
Montana
  Havre 147
  Little Bighorn Valley 36
Montezuma, Carlos 34, 35, 137
Moore, William H. 288
Moorehead, Warren King 99, 118, 125–135, 180, 181, 274, 275, 276, 277, 278
Moravians 150
Morgan, J. P. 134
Morgan, John Hunt 20, 21, 29, 118
  raiders 2
Morgan, Lewis Henry 37, 107
Morgan, Thomas John, Jr. 136
Morrison, Moses 286, 287, 288
Morrison, William 288
Morton, Julius Sterling 7, 133
Morton, Professor 157
Morton, Samuel 26
Mound Builders 3, 25, 51, 67, 171
mounds. *See under* earthworks
Muchmore, Samuel 288
Mudgett, Dr. Herman Webster 139
Museum East Indian Marine Society 49
Museum of the Peabody Academy of Sciences 49
Music Hall 50, 67
Mussey, Dr. 22
"My Country Tis of Thee" 134
"My Prayer" 23

N

Napoleonic war 2, 12, 24
Nashville 22
National Environmental Policy Act 199
National Geographic 187
National Guard Medical Corps 174
National Historic Landmark District 205
National Historic Preservation Act (NHPA) 198
National Museum 190
National Park Service 194
National Register of Historic Places 9, 199
National Security Council 203
National Youth Administration (NYA) 8, 194
Native American Graves Protection and Repatriation Act 9, 202
Natural and Statistical View or Picture of Cincinnati and the Miami County (Drake) 25

Natural History Society of Cincinnati 225
Nazism 178
Nebraska
   Omaha 80
Neff, George W. 20, 21
Nelson brothers 149, 150
Nelson family 150
Nelson Station 149
Nelson, Jeff 172
New Deal
   archaeology 194–195
New Jersey
   Trenton 50, 99
New Mexico 6
   Clovis 100
   Folsom 183
New Orleans Exposition 81, 239
New York 48, 78, 96, 113, 126, 278
   Buffalo 5, 96, 111, 112, 113, 251, 265, 266
   New York 23, 24, 35, 121, 153
New York Republican 23
New York Times 127
   Metz obituary 189
Newhall farm 247
Nickerson, William Baker 111, 115, 116, 250, 251, 252, 258, 260, 262, 264, 267
Ninth District School 17
Ninth Ohio Volunteer Infantry 2
Nixon, Richard M. 199, 200, 203
Noon, Martin 234, 242, 243, 256, 259, 275
The North Americans of Antiquity (Short) 43
North Carolina 110
Northwestern University
   Chicago Medical College 35

O

O'Connell, Sister Anthony 19
Oakley, Annie 127, 138
Oberlin Theological Seminar 109
Oehler, Charles 197
Office of Indian Affairs 80, 136
Ohio 128
   Adams County 2, 8, 15, 122, 131, 194
   Allensburg 15
   Anderson Twp. 248
   Bainbridge 67
   Blanchester 268, 270

Brown County 2, 24, 115, 208, 209, 264, 271
Camden 228
Camp Dennison 150
Camp Sherman 176
Chillicothe 14, 67, 79, 88, 96, 102, 131, 252, 253, 286
Cincinnati 1, 2, 4, 12, 12–15, 16, 17, 18, 19, 20, 21, 22, 23, 27, 33, 34, 36, 39, 42, 47, 50, 55, 56, 63, 64, 67, 72, 75, 76, 81, 90, 98, 113, 116, 119, 127, 147, 148, 165, 166, 172, 181, 188, 189, 190, 203, 204, 206, 216, 238, 250, 253, 270, 272, 281, 282, 293
   affects from Krakatoa 69
   economic downturn of 1884 70
   flood of 1883 69
   Walnut Hills 32
Clermont County 2
Cleveland 150
Columbia 261, 292
Columbus 211, 262
Danville 15, 16, 37
Dayton 114
Hamilton County 2, 29, 30, 104, 197
   Anderson Township 204
   Columbia Twp. 289
Highland County 2, 8, 15, 37, 195
Hillsboro 15, 37, 66, 230
Hopetown 67
Indian Hill 150, 198, 292
Loveland 104
Madisonville 3, 27, 31, 38, 40, 41, 68, 69, 70, 75, 76, 87, 94, 98, 104, 119, 123, 130, 132, 141, 149, 150, 171, 176, 187, 211, 215, 216, 238, 242, 245, 248, 255, 256, 271, 273, 275, 292
   history of 285–295
   Kendall farm 255
   Metz family home (photo) 45, 145
   schools 177, 190
Mariemont 31, 181–183, 204, 205
Marietta 262
Miamiville 20, 21
New Boston 153, 273, 274, 275
New Germany 18
New Richmond 27, 212
Newark 48
Newtown 59, 204, 247, 250, 266
Oxford 22

Peebles 122
Plainville 16, 17, 22, 24, 30, 94
Portsmouth 51
Remington 87, 234, 241, 245, 246
Ross County 91, 131
Russell Station 15
Sandusky 169
Scioto County 153
Springfield 70, 94, 235
Symmes Station 245, 246
Upper Sandusky 13
Vera Cruz 24, 35, 40, 53, 55, 94, 95, 115, 159, 189, 211, 213
Village of Mariemont. *See under* Ohio, Mariemont
Warren County 8, 117, 195, 247
Worthington 51
Xenia 21, 126
Zanesville 171
Ohio Department of Transportation 205
Ohio Mechanics Institute 67
Ohio Militia
  Chillicothe Greys 89
Ohio National Guard 70, 148, 169, 174
Ohio River 32, 51, 54, 69, 111, 131
  confluence 58, 72
Ohio River valley 2, 7, 13, 14, 25, 26, 31, 108, 110, 118, 130, 150, 181, 193
  archaeological sites 25, 27
Ohio State Archaeological and Historical Society (OSAHS) 109
Ohio State Memorials 8
Ohio State Society for the Prevention of Cruelty to Children and Animals 119
Ohio Valley 1, 8, 50, 95, 107, 179, 180
Ohio Valley Historical Series 25
Oklahombi, Joseph 172
Oliver, A. S. 216
Omaha Daily Bee 127
On the Origin of Species by Means of Natural Selection, or the Preservation of Favored Races in the Struggle for Life 178
148th Infantry 174
107th Congress 202
Ording, Mrs. 139
Orpheus Club 38
Ottoman Empire 172

P

Paine, Professor 133
Panic of 1873 35, 38, 55, 69
Panic of 1884 70
Panic of 1893 138, 148
Parker, Ely 37
The Pathfinder (Cooper) 11
Peabody Museum. *See under* Harvard University
Peabody, George 48
Peabody, W. N. 216
Pearson, Wyley 289, 290
Pennsylvania
  Philadelphia 3, 5, 34, 76, 77, 238
Pennsylvania Geological Survey 110
Peter Claver Society 42
Philadelphia Athletics 65
Pierson, Willis 287
Pike, Samuel N. 34
Pike's Opera House 34
Pillar of the Constitution in the Senate Chamber of Wyandotte Cave 168
Pine Ridge 128
The Pioneers (Cooper) 11
Polk, James K. 15
Pollack, John 246
Popular History of the State of Ohio (Shepherd) 66
Powell, John Wesley 5, 77, 81, 89, 110, 244
Powontonamo 16
"The Prehistoric Monuments of Anderson Township, Hamilton County, Ohio" 60
"The Prehistoric Monuments of the Little Miami Valley" 39, 60
Prendergast, Patrick Eugene 140
Presidential Proclamation 127
Primitive Man in Ohio (Moorehead) 135, 181
Princip, Gavrilo 171
Principles of Geology: Being an Attempt to Explain the Former Changes of the Earth's Surface, by Reference to Causes Now in Operation (Lyell) 27
Proceedings of the Boston Society of Natural History
  "On an Indian grave on Winter Island, Salem, Massachusetts" (Putnam) 49
"The Prophecy" 133
Prussia 172
Prussian Academy of Sciences 42
public school system 286
Puget Sound 16
Pullman, George 124
Putnam family 169
Putnam, Douglas 67, 262

Putnam, Ebenezer 47
Putnam, Frederick Ward 4, 5, 6, 47, 48–
  50, 55, 56, 57, 58, 60, 61, 63, 64, 65,
  66, 67, 68, 69, 70, 71, 72, 75, 76, 77,
  78, 79, 81, 82, 83, 84, 85, 87, 88, 89,
  90, 91, 93, 94, 95, 96, 97, 98, 99,
  100, 101, 102, 103, 105, 106, 107,
  108, 109, 110, 111, 112, 113, 114,
  115, 116, 117, 118, 119, 120, 121,
  148, 152, 153, 154, 156, 157, 158,
  159, 165, 166, 169, 170, 171, 178
  (photo) 91
  family (photo) 122
  letters 216–283
  World's Fair 123–125, 128–142

Q

Quick, Mr. 211

R

race or tribes
  Danes 25
  Hindis 25
  Israel 25
  Toltecs 25
  Vikings 25
radiocarbon dating 195–196
Rafinesque, Constantine 14
railroads 55
  and economic depression 138
  Northern Railroad Freight Depot 63
  shutdown 63
Rainbow Steam Dye Works 94
recession 5
Reeder, Joseph 286, 289, 290
Reichert, Maria Barbara "Babette." *See also,*
  Metz, Maria Barbara 11
"Relic Hunting" 179
Remington, Frederic 127
Republicans 50, 79, 109, 153, 202
  McKinley Club 148
reservations
  Pine Ridge 148
  Rosebud 148
Rhode Island
  Newport 181
Rich family 118
Rich, Mr. 268
Richards, Moses 288
Richards, William 288
Richfield, Phillip 288
Ridge, John Rollin 137

Rienzi 134
Risch, Jacob 264
Risch, Mrs. 264
Robbie 211
Rocky Mountains 77
Rogers, M. L. 215
Rogers, W. 41
Romania 172
Roosevelt, Franklin Delano 194
Roosevelt, Theodore 172, 193
Ross, Joseph 288
Roth, Mezzina 88
Roush, Nat 15
Rowe, Martha 198, 205
Royal Swedish Academy of Sciences 42
Ruscic, Jacob 257
Russia 171
Russians 172
Ryan, Thomas 114, 242, 243, 250, 264,
  266, 268

S

Sacred Lands Act 202–203
Saint Anthony Church 176
Saint Anthony School 174, 176, 177
St. Clair, Arthur 36
Saint John the Baptist Catholic Church 14
Saint Mary's Hospital 42
Saint Michael Church 27
Saint-Gaudens, Augustus 141
Salsbury, Nate 138
Sarajevo 171
Saville, Marshall Howard 153, 271, 272,
  274, 275
Scheldt River 174
Schlotman, Anna Berger 53
Schlotman, Casper H. 37, 207, 210, 213
Schoolcraft, Henry 85
Schurz, Carl 78–79, 109
Schwab, Charles 124
Science 187, 195, 238
  "Definite Evidence of Human Artifacts
    in the American Pleistocene" 183
Scientific American 187
  "The Antiquity of Man in America: Who
    Were the Ice Age Americans? Whence
    Came They?" (Cook) 188
  "The Race and Antiquity of the
    American Indian: There is No Valid
    Evidence That the Indian Has Long
    Been in the New World"
    (Hrdlička) 188

scientific methods 106–130, 135
Scioto River valley 51, 67, 78, 89
Scots-Irish Protestant 130
The Scouts on the Prairie 34
Scoville, Dr. S. S. 194
Second Regiment Heavy Artillery 18
Serbia 171
Serpent Park 276
settlements
 Columbia 31
 European 16
Seventh Cavalry 127, 128, 148
Shaler, Nathaniel 99
Sharp, Joseph Henry 148
Shawnee. *See under* American Indians
Shelton, Mr. 211
"Shepards Popular History of Ohio" 230
Shepherd, Henry A. 66, 67
Short, J. T. 43
Siegbahn, A. W. 94
signal mounds 51
"The Significance of the Frontier in American History" 138
Simonton, L. 268, 270
Sisters of Charity 2, 19, 177
Sites Act 194
Sixteenth and Seventeenth Annual Reports of the Trustees of the Peabody Museum of America and Ethnology 90
Skinner, Thomas 287
slavery 2
smallpox 139, 140
Smith, Harlan I. 274, 275, 276
Smith, M. Hoke 7, 133
Smith, Mr. 275
Smith, Orlando 88, 89, 245
Smith, Thomas 148
Smithsonian Institution 5, 14, 26, 39, 51, 57, 70–72, 75, 81, 89, 94, 99, 109, 118, 125, 137, 179, 189, 190, 235, 236, 244, 245, 246, 247, 250, 263
 Bureau of Ethnology 77
Smithsonian National Museum
 Aboriginal Ceramics 5
Snyder, Homer P. 172
Socialist Party 136
Society of Natural History 225
Society of Natural History of Cincinnati 71, 235
Soldiers and Sailors Home 114, 169

Some Early Notices of the Indians of Ohio: To What Race Did The Mound Builders Belong? (Force) 51
South 80 Park 205
South America 42
South Carolina 110
 Fort Sumter 17
South Dakota
 Pine Ridge Indian Reservation 126
 Wounded Knee 128
Southeast 87
Spanish 7, 150
Spencer, Herbert 178
Squier & Davis 2, 5, 13, 14, 26, 39, 58, 64, 71, 100, 102, 131, 198, 221, 256, 277
Squier, Ephraim. *See also,* Squier & Davis 13, 14, 194
Squier, Ephraim. Squier & Davis 59
Stanton, Dr. R. 41
Starr, S. Frederick "Fred" 197, 198
Starsel, Henry 288
State Historic Preservation Offices (SHPO) 199
steamboats 1, 13
 Colorado 13
Stepps, Abraham 286
Stern, Mrs. 250
Sterns, Mrs. 249
Stevens 270
Stevenson, Adlai 7, 133
Stites family 44, 47
Stites, Benjamin 67
Stites, C. F. 216
Stone Lick Creek 111, 264
Streans, Mrs. 252
Strietmann, Albert 197
Studley, Cordelia A. 111
Sullivan 253
Sullivan, John 90
Sullivan's Printing Co. 90
Swanton, J. R. 154
Swing, Cushing, and Morse 154
Symmes, John Cleves 32, 67

T

Taft-Tytus, Margo 198, 205
Tankersley, Dr. Kenneth Barnett 203
Taylor, Buck 65
Taylor, Robert 172
Tebbutt, John 55
Teniers, David (the younger) 12, 28
Tennessee 110

Confederate state of 18
   Piedmont 18
Terry, W. F. 141
Tesla, Nikola 134
Thacher, John Boyd 142
The Book of Algoonah: Being a Concise Account of the History of the Early People of the Continent of America Known as Mound Builders 87
Thirty-sixth Division 172
Thomas, Cyrus 5, 72, 75, 76, 85
Thomas, Dr. 277
Thomas, Professor 237, 238
Thomas, Theodore 133
Thomas, Thomas 288
Tibbles, Thomas 90
Times Recorder 171
Times Star 259
Transactions of the American Antiquarian Society, Volume 1 68
Transactions of the Historical and Philosophical Society of Ohio (Burnet, et al.) 26
Turkey Bottom 149
Turner 272
Turner family farm 58
The Turner Group of Earthworks, Hamilton County, Ohio 179
Turner, Edward 259
Turner, Frederick Jackson 138
Turner, John 234, 238
Turner, Michael 60, 105, 259
Turner, Mr. 166, 225, 267, 270, 274, 282, 283
Turpin farmhouse 93
Turpin homestead 96, 251
Turpin, Mr. 236, 242, 249

U

U.S. Army Base Hospital 176
U.S. Army Medical Corps 174
U.S. Department of the Interior 194
U.S. Environmental Protection Agency 203
U.S. Geological Survey 5, 77, 110
U.S. Mint 141
U.S. Supreme Court 79
U.S. troops
   XI Corps 89
Union army 17, 21
   1st Tennessee Cavalry 18
   43rd Co., 2nd Battalion 20
   73rd OVI 89
   9th OVI 2, 18, 19
   at Cincinnati 19
   Confederate state of Tennessee 18
   Corps of Invalids 20
   guards 20
   Invalid Corps 20
   Kentucky infantry 18
   Tennessee cavalry 18
Union Association 81
Union Bridge 248
Union Passenger Depot (Macon, Ga.) 54
Union secession 17
unionization 118
United Labor Party 136
United States
   affects from Krakatoa 69
University Corporation 169
University Foundation 116
University of Cincinnati 8, 157, 197, 203, 282
University of Michigan Medical School 139
University of Pennsylvania 125
"Upon the evolution of a race of deaf mutes in America" 77

V

Valley House. *See also,* Warner House 79
Van Doehm, Capt. 20
Vanderburgh 212
Veach, Walter 172
Vickery, Kent D. 199
Virchow, Dr. Rudolf Ludwig Carl 42, 217
Virginia 110
   Appomattox Court House 21
   Hampton 132
Volk, Ernest 166, 168

W

Wagner, Richard 134
Walden Methodist Church 34
Waldschmidt, Christian 18, 150
Walker, Timothy 26
Wanneta: The Sioux (Moorehead) 126
Ward, Meyer 288
Warner House 79
Warner, Jake 79
Washington D.C. 15, 121, 179, 190, 235, 275
Washington Post 127
Washington territory 16
Washington, George 136, 151
Weber 213

Wert, W. M. 216
Western Hemisphere 2, 100, 121, 132, 188
Westinghouse, George 134
Whetsel, H. B. 40, 65, 215, 224, 228
Whetstone, Mrs. 211
Whiskey Run Creek 32, 33
Whitcomb, James 291
Whitcomb, John 288
Whitcomb, John, Jr. 288
White House 21, 79, 203
White, Jason H. 41
Whitney, J. D. 99
Whittlesey 111, 242
Whittlesey, Charles 14, 26, 59, 60
Wild West, Rocky Mountain, and Prairie Exhibition 64–65, 81
Wilhelm, Rev. 14
Wilkins, Charles 80
Williams, Dr. Elkannon 22
Willoughby, Charles C. 178, 179
Willoughby, Charles E. 187
Wilson 289
Wilson, Calvin 172
Wilson, Thomas 118
Wilson, Woodrow 172
Wisconsin 79, 110
Women's Centennial Committee 36
Work Projects Administration (WPA) 8, 194
Works Progress Administration 194
World War I 171–176

World War II 151, 195, 196–197
World's Fair: Columbian Exposition 6, 7, 123, 128, 129, 133, 134, 136, 137, 142, 147, 148, 149, 157, 273, 274, 275
   Anthropology Building (photo) 143
   bronze medal (photo) 144
   Fire Department 140
   souvenir half-dollar 141
   ticket (photo) 143
Wounded Knee massacre 148
Wright, George Frederick 109, 110, 111, 262, 265
Wright, Judge 155, 157, 158
Wright, Professor 263
Wyandotte Cave 168
Wyman, Jeffries 48, 49, 83
Wyoming 110

Y

Yankton Press 127
Yorston, J. C. and Company 67
Yost, Mrs. 209
Yucatan 270

Z

Zeisberger, David 150
Zeitschrift für Ethnologie (Journal of Ethnology) 42

About the Authors

Kenneth Barnett Tankersley is an enrolled member of the Piqua Shawnee. He received his B.S. and M.A. degrees from the University of Cincinnati and a Ph.D. from Indiana University in 1989. He did post-doctorate work at the Quaternary Studies Program of the Illinois State Museum. With funding from the National Science Foundation, the National Academy of Sciences, the L.S.B. Leakey Foundation, Earthwatch, the International Research and Exchange Program, the Court Family Foundation, the Charles Phelps Taft Foundation, and the University of Cincinnati Research Council, he has conducted archaeological investigations across the Western Hemisphere and Eastern Siberia. This research resulted in more than 120 professional publications and has been featured on the *National Geographic Channel,* the *Discovery Channel,* the *History Channel,* the *Animal Planet,* *BBC Nature, NOVA, PBS,* in *Science, National Geographic News, Geo,* the *Wall Street Journal,* the *New Yorker* magazine, *Scientific American, Archaeology* magazine, and on *All Things Considered.* He has served as a Foreign Delegate for the National Academy of Science, a Delegate of the International Geology Congress, a Carnegie Mellon Scholar and Emmons Lecturer, guest editor of *Scientific American* magazine, and a Gubernatorial appointed member of the Native American Heritage Commission.

Robert Brand Newman received his undergraduate degree from the University of North Carolina in 1964. He graduated from Emory Law School in 1967. In 1968 Bob was a Reginald Heber Smith fellow at the University of Michigan Law School. Bob has worked for the Legal Aid Society in Atlanta as well as Cincinnati. He has been in private practice since 1982. He is a member of the Georgia, Ohio, and Kentucky bars. Bob has been admitted to practice in the United States Court of Appeals, Fifth and Sixth Circuits, the Supreme Court of Ohio, and the United States Supreme Court.